The Shame of the Nation

Also by Jonathan Kozol

DEATH AT AN EARLY AGE

FREE SCHOOLS

THE NIGHT IS DARK AND I AM FAR FROM HOME

CHILDREN OF THE REVOLUTION

ON BEING A TEACHER

ILLITERATE AMERICA

RACHEL AND HER CHILDREN

SAVAGE INEQUALITIES

AMAZING GRACE

ORDINARY RESURRECTIONS

The Shame of the Nation

THE RESTORATION OF APARTHEID SCHOOLING IN AMERICA

Jonathan Kozol

CROWN PUBLISHERS
NEW YORK

Published in the United States by Crown Publishers, an imprint of the Crown Publishing Group, a division of Random House, Inc., New York.

Crown is a trademark and the Crown colophon is a registered trademark of Random House, Inc.

ISBN-10: 0-7394-6552-X
ISBN-13: 978-0-7394-6552-3

Printed in the United States of America

Design by Barbara Sturman

For Louis Bedrock:

a good teacher who
has stayed the course

TO THE READER

In writing this book, I have visited approximately 60 schools in 30 districts, situated in 11 different states. Most of these visits took place in the years from 2000 to 2005, although several of the narratives, as will be noted in the text, go back considerably earlier. The names of most of the children and some principals and teachers are disguised. Certain of the schools described have not been named, in order to protect the privacy of those within these schools who have confided in me. Most schools are identified by name, however, either in the text or in the notes, and no school names are disguised.

Quoted dialogue is drawn from notes, teachers' and children's recollections, and my own, and now and then, although not often, tape recordings of our conversations. Discussions of related topics are sometimes combined, and children's writings and extended conversations are at times resequenced or condensed for narrative economy. Updated information on certain of the schools that are described and documentation for all matters that rely upon the public record are provided in the notes, which begin on page 339.

CONTENTS

The Shame of the Nation

Introduction

I began to work among schoolchildren more than 40 years ago, in 1964, when I became a fourth grade teacher in the public schools of Boston, Massachusetts. I had never intended to become a teacher. I had attended Harvard College, where I studied English literature, then spent some years in France and England before coming back to Cambridge, where I planned to study for a graduate degree. In June of that year, three young activists for civil rights, the first contingent of a group of several hundred who had volunteered to venture into Mississippi to run summer freedom schools and organize adults to register to vote, disappeared in a rural area outside a town called Philadelphia. Their bodies were later discovered, buried in the mud beneath a dam beside a cattle pond. As we ultimately learned, they had been killed by law enforcement officers and members of the Ku Klux Klan.

In retrospect, it seems unlikely that it was this one event alone that could have led me all at once to reconsider or postpone the academic plans that I had made. I had been aware already of the rising fervor of the civil rights campaigns, the sit-ins and the freedom rides that had been taking place in several southern states, the growing protest movement in some northern cities also, and the dramatic March on Washington nearly a year before. But, perhaps because I'd been in Europe, I had been detached to a degree from the intensity of passions stirred by these developments among young people of my age. With the murder of these volunteers, that feeling of detachment dissipated quickly. I got in my car one day and drove to Roxbury, the center of the black community of Boston, and signed up to be a reading teacher in a freedom school for children taking place within a local church.

Although I felt very shy and hesitant at first about my role as a white person who had never been in a black neighborhood before, I rapidly made friends among the parents who were active in this program and in others like it taking place at other churches and some storefront centers in the neighborhood. More to the point perhaps, I simply got to *like* that group of eight- and nine-year-olds I was assigned to teach and, like any other very insecure young teacher, I was probably flattered that they seemed to like me in return.

The six-week program ended all too soon; so, with the permission of their parents and the pastor, I extended classes with my students for two extra weeks after the summer program ran its course. It was during those more informal final weeks that I first saw my amateurish efforts bearing fruit in some of those small ways that a beginning teacher prays for. Even to see those 15 children showing up each day in torrid end-of-August weather in a steamy attic classroom in a musty-smelling church, and struggling hard to write a little essay I'd assigned, seemed like a minor triumph, and it made me wish that I could have a lot more time to be with them. As Labor Day arrived, I suddenly made up my mind to see if I could get a job as a *real* teacher.

It proved much easier to get a teaching job in Boston's schools than I had expected. I had no credentials as a teacher, but I quickly learned this did not matter much so long as I was willing to accept a class within one of the schools that served the city's segregated neighborhoods and did not object to being paid the wages of a temporary teacher even after having been assigned a permanent position.

I remember vividly the sense of shock I felt when I first walked into the elementary school in which I was to spend most of a year: a gloomy-looking, overcrowded building that could not provide my students with a classroom of their own. We shared an undivided auditorium with 35 other children in another fourth grade class, and with a choral group, and with a group rehearsing for a play that somehow never was produced, and with a class of fifth grade girls, all black, who were released from educational instruction to be given sewing lessons several hours every day on old machines like those my grandmothers had used.

One windy afternoon that fall, an entire frame of windows in our make-shift class collapsed. I was standing close enough to catch the rotted frame before the glass could shatter on the children sitting just beneath it.

Some of the children seemed to have accepted these conditions or, at least, did not appear to feel they had the right to question them. Others did not suffer these indignities so passively but seemed to simmer with hostility toward many of the teachers and the principal. The anger of these students, which erupted typically when they were not in class but in the corridors or stairways, going to the bathroom for example, was efficiently suppressed. Children who misbehaved were taken to the basement of the school where whippings were administered by an older teacher who employed a rattan whip which he first dipped in vinegar in order to intensify the pain that it inflicted on a child's outstretched hands. One of my students landed in the hospital in the preceding year after he'd received a whipping. His forefinger was permanently disfigured.

In the spring, the principal assigned me to another fourth grade class that had a classroom of its own but was in a state of chaos because it had had a string of substitute teachers almost the entire year. Many children in the class, according to their parents, had not had a permanent instructor since their kindergarten year. That year, I was their thirteenth teacher.

On the day I came into their class, most were reading at a second grade level. Their math abilities were at the first grade level. I have never forgotten one of the brightest students in that class, a very tall girl who sat in the back row and for days on end refused to speak to me. She had a look of stony and implacable resistance in her eyes. I tried my best to bring her out of her silence or at least to make her smile now and then, but I could not. I had the sense that she alone, of all those children, seemed to understand what had been done to them.

Sometimes in the afternoons, when I got out of school, I used to drop by at the office of a minister named James Breeden who had come to be a friend during the summer and who filled a very special role within the black community of Boston at the time, both as a leading figure in the fight for civil rights and as a scholarly and gentle mentor to impatient younger activists, or would-be activists, and to beginning teachers like myself. Breeden was only one of several strong and seasoned leaders in the neighborhood to whom I turned for reassurance and for steadying composure in that difficult first year. Over the next two years, after I rented an apartment in the area and made more friendships there, I grew increasingly attached to several of the older parent leaders, women for the most part, some of whom had been to two-year colleges, some to four-year colleges in Massachusetts, others to traditional black institutions in the South, where they had been immersed in the first stages of the civil rights campaigns and had been shaped by this politically.

These were eloquent and straight-talking people who did not equivocate in speaking of the damage done to children by their racial isolation in the poorly staffed and physically offensive schools that served the neighborhood. Many were deeply religious people and they used a Biblical language—"evil," "sin," "abomination"—to encompass the realities their children and the children of their neighbors underwent. Denunciation and excoriation and politically expensive confrontation were the morally demanding social gospel that these leaders preached. Even when, as in the case of Reverend Breeden, they spoke softly and with meditative self-restraint, the message that they gave their youthful followers—many, like myself, were white and were the graduates of local universities and colleges—was luminous and clear in the explicit challenge that it posed to structural arrangements from which some of us had benefited greatly and, in many cases, up to now, with equanimity.

There was a high level of political sophistication among those in leadership positions in the black community; and, in the course of framing goals and analyzing structures, they recognized the multitude of different forces that diminished opportunity for children in the neighborhood. So the struggle they set out before us was not *only* about ending racial segregation in these schools; and yet that struggle was, for them, for all of us, the moral starting-point of all the rest. The goal was not to find a more efficient way of governing a segregated school. The goal was not to find a more ingenious way of teaching vowel sounds and consonant blends to segregated children. The goal was not to find a more inventive way of introducing pieces of "essential knowledge"—

dates of wars, or names of kings, or multiples of nine—into the minds of segregated children. The goal was not to figure out a way to run a more severe and strictly regimented school for segregated children or, at the opposite extreme, a more progressive and more "innovative" school for segregated children. Nor, as welcome as this might have been, was it to build a smaller school or physically more pleasing school for segregated children. The goal was to unlock the chains that held these children within caste-and-color sequestration and divorced them from the mainstream of American society.

I spent, in all, about a decade working with black schoolchildren in Boston, first in the public schools themselves (I also taught for two years in an integrated public school in Newton, a suburban town that pioneered a voluntary integration program that continues to the present day), then in grassroots programs taking place in storefronts and black churches. By the later 1970s and then increasingly during the early 1980s, I began to visit schools in other sections of the nation. I was writing books during this time, and principals and teachers who were reading them would frequently invite me to their schools. Teachers would sometimes let me teach a lesson to their class and, in the upper elementary grades (fourth and fifth, the grades that I had taught), would sometimes organize a class discussion in which I would be invited to take part.

There was a more optimistic mood in many of the urban schools I visited during these years. Some had been desegregated by court order in the aftermath of the Supreme Court's ruling in *Brown v. Board of Education;* other schools had been desegregated voluntarily. Physical conditions in these newly integrated schools were generally more cheerful, the state of mind among the teachers and the children more high-spirited, the atmosphere less desultory, more enlivening, than in the school in which I'd started out in Boston. Other schools I visited, admittedly, were not so fortunate. Disrepair and overcrowding were familiar still in many districts; and most of the black children I was meeting lived in very poor communities where residential segregation was a permanent reality. As serious cuts in social services and federal assistance for low-income housing took effect during the years when Ronald Reagan was in office, physical conditions in these neighborhoods became appreciably worse.

By the end of the 1980s, the high hopes that I had briefly sensed a decade earlier were hard to find. Many of the schools I visited during this period seemed every bit as grim as those I'd seen in Boston in the 1960s, sometimes a good deal worse. I visited a high school in East St. Louis, Illinois, where the lab stations in the science rooms had empty holes where pipes were once attached. A history teacher who befriended me told me of rooms that were so cold in winter that the students had to wear their coats to class while kids in other classes sweltered in a suffocating heat that could not be turned down. A foul odor filled much of the building because of an overflow of sewage that had forced the city to shut down the school the year before.

I visited, too, the bleak, unhappy schools of Paterson and Camden in New Jersey and similar schools in Washington, D.C., Chicago, San Antonio, and Cincinnati. Back in New England, I spent time with teachers, parents, and their teenage kids in Bridgeport, where the poverty levels, overcrowded public schools, and health conditions of the children, many of whom had been lead-poisoned in the city's public housing, had created a sense of quiet desperation in the all-black and Hispanic neighborhoods I visited. Wherever I could, I started in the schools. Where I could not, I started in the streets. Everywhere I went, I did my best to spend my evenings with schoolteachers.

At the start of the 1990s I began to visit schools in New York City, where I'd come to know a group of children living in a section of the South Bronx called Mott Haven, in which I would end up spending long-extended periods of time in the next 15 years. Yet even in this period in which I grew entangled in my friendships with these children and their parents and with priests and ministers and doctors in the neighborhood (HIV infection ripped its way across the South Bronx in those years, and pediatric and maternal AIDS were added to the routine sorrows many children had to bear), I continued to spend time in schools in other cities too.

And almost everywhere I went from this point on, no matter what the hopes that had been stirred in many cities only a short time before, no matter what the progress that had frequently been made in districts where court-ordered integration programs had been in effect or where a civic leadership had found the moral will to act without court orders in a principled attempt to integrate their neighborhoods and schools, a clear reality was now in place: Virtually all the children of black and Hispanic people in the cities that I visited, both large and small, were now attending schools in which their isolation was as absolute as it had been for children in the school in which I'd started out so many years before.

In Chicago, by the academic year 2000–2001, 87 percent of public school enrollment was black or Hispanic; less than 10 percent of children in the schools were white. In Washington, D.C., 94 percent of children were black or Hispanic; less than 5 percent were white. In St. Louis, 82 percent of the student population was black or Hispanic by this point, in Philadelphia and Cleveland 78 percent, in Los Angeles 84 percent, in Detroit 95 percent, in Baltimore 88 percent. In New York City, nearly three quarters of the students were black or Hispanic in 2001.

Even these statistics, though, could not convey how isolated children in the poorest sections of these cities had become. In the typically colossal high schools of the Bronx, for instance, more than 90 percent of students (in most cases, more than 95 percent) were black or Hispanic. At John F. Kennedy High School, 91 percent of the enrollment of more than 4,000 students was black or Hispanic; only 4.8 percent of students at the school were white. At Harry S. Truman High School, black and Hispanic students represented 96 percent of the enrollment of 2,500 students; less than 2 percent were white. At Adlai Stevenson High School, where enrollment numbers were about the same as those at Truman, blacks and Hispanics made up 97 percent of the student population; a mere five tenths of 1 percent were white.

A teacher at P.S. 65, one of the South Bronx elementary schools I've visited repeatedly, once pointed out to me one of the two white children I had ever seen there. His presence in her class was something of a wonderment to her and to the other pupils. I asked how many white kids she had taught in the South Bronx in her career. "I've been at this school for 18 years," she said. "This is the first white student I have ever taught."

In the district that included P.S. 65, there were 11,000 children in the elementary schools and middle schools in 1997. Of these 11,000, only 26 were white, a segregation rate of 99.8 percent. Two tenths of one percentage point now marked the difference between legally enforced apartheid in the South of 1954 and socially and economically enforced apartheid in this New York City neighborhood.

You go into these deeply segregated schools and do your best—in order to enjoy the kids you meet and to appreciate what's taking place within the classroom here and now—to disconnect the present from the past. Try as I do, however, as the years go by, I find that act of disconnection very, very hard. I walk into a class of 25 or 30 students and I look around me at the faces of the children, some of whom in New York City I have known since they were born, and look into their eyes, and often see them also searching into mine, and I cannot discern the slightest hint that any vestige of the legal victory embodied in *Brown v. Board of Education* or the moral mandate that a generation of unselfish activists and young idealists lived and sometimes died for has survived within these schools and neighborhoods. I simply never see white children.

"We owe a definite homage to the reality around us," Thomas Merton wrote, "and we are obliged, at certain times, to say what things are and to give them their right names." No matter how complex the reasons that have brought us to the point at which we stand, we have, it seems, been traveling a long way to a place of ultimate surrender that does not look very different from the place where some of us began.

There are those, of course, who see no reason to regret this pattern of reversion to an older order of accepted isolation of the children of minorities and even find it possible to ridicule the notion that apartheid schooling might have any damaging effects upon a child's intellectual development or any other aspect of a child's heart or mind. The supposition that "black students suffer an unspecified psychological harm from segregation . . . ," as Justice Clarence Thomas wrote in an opinion on a case the high court heard in 1995, is not merely incorrect, relying upon "questionable social science research," in his words, but also represents a form of prejudice, reflecting "an assumption of black inferiority." This is not dissimilar to the idea, expressed sometimes by white conservatives as well, that arguments for racial integration of our schools insultingly imply that children of minorities will somehow "become smarter" if they're sitting with white children—an idea, which is indeed insulting, that no advocate for integrated education I have known has ever entertained. But arguments like these and the debates surrounding them, in any case, have only the most indirect connection with the thoughts that come into my mind when I am sitting with a group of children in a kindergarten class in the South Bronx.

What saddens me the most during these times is simply that these children have no knowledge of the other world in which I've lived most of my life and that the children in that other world have not the slightest notion as to who these children are and will not likely *ever* know them later on, not at least on anything like equal terms, unless a couple of these kids get into college. Even if they meet each other then, it may not be the same, because the sweetness of too many of these inner-city children will have been somewhat corroded by that time. Some of it may be replaced by hardness, some by caution, some by calculation rooted in unspoken fear. I have believed for 40 years, and still believe today, that we would be an infinitely better nation if they knew each other now.

Whether or not it seems to realistic-minded people to be beyond the limits of all plausibility or practicality even to contemplate a serious reversal of the present pattern of intensifying segregation and resegregation is a question that will be examined in the later sections of this book. Certainly, what reasonable people may regard as possible, or even worth consideration in the present political climate of the nation, needs to be addressed; but what is obvious and plain and truthful needs to be addressed as well. If we have agreed to live with this reality essentially unaltered for another generation or for several generations yet to come, I think we need at least to have the honesty to say so. I also think we need to recognize that our acceptance of a dual education system will have consequences that may be no less destructive than those we have seen in the past century.

I don't think you can discern these consequences solely by examination of statistics or the words of education analysts or highly placed officials in school systems. I think you need to go into the schools in which the isolation of our children is the most extreme, do so repeatedly but, where it's possible, informally and not obtrusively, and try to make sure that you are allowed the time to listen carefully to children. I have been criticized throughout the course of my career for placing too much faith in the reliability of children's narratives; but I have almost always found that children are a great deal more reliable in telling us what actually goes on in public school than many of the adult experts who develop policies that shape their destinies. Unlike these powerful grown-ups, children have no ideologies to reinforce, no superstructure of political opinion to promote, no civic equanimity or image to defend, no personal reputation to secure. They may err sometimes about the minuscule particulars but on the big things children rarely have much reason to mislead us. They are, in this respect, pure witnesses, and we will hear their testimony in these pages.

CHAPTER 1

Dishonoring the Dead

One sunny day in April, I was sitting with my friend Pineapple at a picnic table in St. Mary's Park in the South Bronx. I had met Pineapple six years earlier, in 1994, when I had visited her kindergarten class at P.S. 65. She was a plump and bright-eyed child who had captured my attention when I leaned over her desk and noticed that she wrote her letters in reverse. I met her again a few weeks later at an afterschool program based at St. Ann's Church, which was close to P.S. 65, where Pineapple and a number of her friends came for tutorial instruction and for safety from the dangers of the neighborhood during the afternoons.

The next time I visited her school, it was the spring of 1997. She was in third grade now and she was having a bad year. The school was in a state of chaos because there had been a massive turnover of teachers. Of 50 members of the faculty in the preceding year, 28 had never taught before;

and half of them were fired or did not return the following September. Very little teaching took place in Pineapple's class during the time that I was there. For some reason, children in her class and other classes on her floor had to spend an awful lot of time in forming lines outside the doorways of their rooms, then waiting as long as 30 minutes for their turn to file downstairs to the cafeteria for lunch, then waiting in lines again to get their meals, then to go to recess, then to the bathroom, then return to class. Nearly two hours had elapsed between the time Pineapple's classmates formed their line to go to lunch and finally returned.

On another day when I was visiting, before the children were allowed to have their lunch they were brought into an auditorium where old cartoons like Felix the Cat and Donald Duck and other flickering movies from the past were shown to keep them occupied before their class was called to file down into the cafeteria. The film in the film projector, which must have been very old, kept slipping from its frames. The lights would go on and kids would start to hoot and scream. I sat beside Pineapple and her classmates for three quarters of an hour while a very angry woman with a megaphone stood on a stage and tried to get the room under control by threatening the kids with dire punishments if they did not sit in perfect silence while they waited for the next cartoon.

In the following year, when she was in fourth grade, Pineapple had four different teachers in a row. One of them was apparently a maladjusted person who, Pineapple said, "used swear words" to subdue the children. ("A-S-S-E-S!" Pineapple said politely, since she did not want to speak the word itself.) One was fired for smoking in the building. Another was "only a helper-teacher," Pineapple reported, which, a member of the faculty explained, might have been a reference to an unprepared young teacher who was not yet certified. Pineapple, who had always been a lively and resilient little girl, grew quite depressed that year.

When Pineapple used to talk to me about her school she rarely, if ever, spoke in racial terms. Going to a school in which all of her classmates were black or Hispanic must have seemed quite natural to her—"the way things are," perhaps the way that they had always been. Since she had only the slightest knowledge of what schools were like outside her neighborhood, there would have been no reason why she would remark upon the fact that there were no white children in her class. This, at least, is how I had interpreted her silence on the matter in the past.

So it surprised me, on that pleasant day in April as the two of us were sitting in St. Mary's Park, while Pineapple's little sister, who is named Briana, wandered off at a slight distance from us following a squirrel that was running on the grass, when Pineapple asked me something that no other child of her age in the South Bronx had ever asked of me before. Leaning on her elbows on the picnic table, with a sudden look of serious consideration in her eyes, she seemed to hesitate a moment as if she was not quite sure whether the question in her mind might somehow be a question you are not supposed to ask, then plowed right on and asked it anyway.

"What's it like," she asked me, peering through the strands of beaded cornrows that came down over her eyes, "over there where you live?"

"Over where?" I asked.

"Over—*you* know . . . ," she said with another bit of awkwardness and hesitation in her eyes.

I asked her, "Do you mean in Massachusetts?"

She looked at me with more determination and a bit impatiently, I thought, but maybe also recognized that I was feeling slightly awkward too.

"You know . . . ," she said.

"I *don't* know," I replied.

"Over there—where other people are," she finally said.

Pineapple was usually very blunt and clear—she sometimes inadvertently hurt other children's feelings by her tendency to make unsparingly direct remarks—so her use of that ambiguous and imprecise expression "other people" didn't seem like her at all.

I asked her if she could explain which "other people" she was thinking of. At that point a wall went up. "*You* know," was all she said—"where *you* live . . . where the other people are. . . ."

I didn't try to press her further about who she meant by "other people" after that. I think she felt it would be rude to say "white people," which is what I was convinced she meant, and I have no memory of whether, or how, I tried to answer her. She and I have since had many talks in which she posed the racial question more explicitly. Pineapple is a shrewd teenager now and she has seen a good deal of the world beyond the Bronx and doesn't feel she has to mince her words in talking to a grown-up friend whom she has known now for so many years.

That evening, however, I repeated what Pineapple said to Martha Overall, the pastor of St. Ann's, who pointed out to me how little contact with white people, other than the principal and teachers at the school and some of the grown-ups working at the church, most of these children ever had. "They don't have any friends who are white children. When I take them with me sometimes to Manhattan to go shopping at a store for something special that they want or to a movie maybe on one of their birthdays, and they find themselves surrounded by a lot of white kids, many of the younger ones get very scared. It's an utterly different world for them. In racial terms, they're almost totally cut off."

One of the consequences of their isolation, as the pastor has observed, is that they have little knowledge of the ordinary reference points that are familiar to most children in the world that Pineapple described as "over there." In talking with adolescents, for example, who were doing relatively well in school and said they hoped to go to college, I have sometimes mentioned colleges such as Columbia, Manhattanville, Cornell, or New York University, and found that references like these were virtually unknown to them. The state university system of New York was generally beyond their recognition too. The name of a community college in the Bronx might be familiar to them—or, for the boys, perhaps a college that was known for its athletic teams.

Now and then, in an effort to expand their reference points, the pastor takes a group of children to an interracial gathering that may be sponsored by one of the more progressive churches in New York or to a similar gathering held in New England, for example. I have accompanied the St. Ann's children on a couple of these trips. The travel involved is usually fun, and simply getting outside the neighborhood in which they live is an adventure for most of the children in itself. But the younger children tend to hold back from attempting to make friends with the white children whom they meet, and many of the teenage kids behave with a defensive edginess, even a hint of mockery, not of the white kids themselves but of a situation that seems slightly artificial and contrived to them and is also, as they surely recognize, a one-time shot that will not change the lives they lead when they return to the South Bronx.

It might be very different if these kids had known white children early in their lives, not only on unusual occasions but in all the ordinary ways that children come to know each other when they go to school together and play games with one another and share secrets with each other and grow bonded to each other by those thousands of small pieces of perplexity and fantasy and sorrow and frivolity of which a child's daily life is actually made. I don't think that you change these things substantially by organizing staged events like "Inter-racial Days." Even the talks that certain of the children are selected to deliver on these rare occasions often have a rather wooden sound, like pieties that have been carefully rehearsed, no matter how sincere the children are. Not that it's not worth holding such events. They energize politically the adults who are present and sometimes, although frankly not too often, long-term friendships may be made. But token days are not the ebb and flow of life. They ease our feelings of regret about the way things have to be for the remainder of the year. They do not really change the way things are.

Many Americans I meet who live far from our major cities and who have no first-hand knowledge of realities in urban public schools seem to have a rather vague and general impression that the great extremes of racial isolation they recall as matters of grave national significance some 35 or 40 years ago have gradually, but steadily, diminished in more recent years. The truth, unhappily, is that the trend, for well over a decade now, has been precisely the reverse. Schools that were already deeply segregated 25 or 30 years ago, like most of the schools I visit in the Bronx, are no less segregated now, while thousands of other schools that had been integrated either voluntarily or by the force of law have since been rapidly resegregating both in northern districts and in broad expanses of the South.

"At the beginning of the twenty-first century," according

to Professor Gary Orfield and his colleagues at the Civil Rights Project at Harvard University, "American public schools are now 12 years into the process of continuous re-segregation. The desegregation of black students, which increased continuously from the 1950s to the late 1980s, has now receded to levels not seen in three decades. . . . During the 1990s, the proportion of black students in majority white schools has decreased . . . to a level lower than in any year since 1968. . . . Almost three fourths of black and Latino students attend schools that are predominantly minority," and more than two million, including more than a quarter of black students in the Northeast and Midwest, "attend schools which we call apartheid schools" in which 99 to 100 percent of students are nonwhite. The four most segregated states for black students, according to the Civil Rights Project, are New York, Michigan, Illinois, and California. In California and New York, only one black student in seven goes to a predominantly white school.

During the past 25 years, the Harvard study notes, "there has been no significant leadership towards the goal of creating a successfully integrated society built on integrated schools and neighborhoods." The last constructive act by Congress was the 1972 enactment of a federal program to provide financial aid to districts undertaking efforts at desegregation, which, however, was "repealed by the Reagan administration in 1981." The Supreme Court "began limiting desegregation in key ways in 1974"—and actively dismantling existing integration programs in 1991.

"Desegregation did not fail. In spite of a very brief period of serious enforcement . . . , the desegregation era was a period in which minority high school graduates increased sharply and the racial test score gaps narrowed substantially until they began to widen again in the 1990s. . . . In the two largest educational innovations of the past two decades—standards-based reform and school choice—the issue of racial segregation and its consequences has been ignored."

"To give up on integration, while aware of its benefits," write Orfield and his former Harvard colleague Susan Eaton, "requires us to consciously and deliberately accept segregation, while aware of its harms. . . . Segregation, rarely discussed, scarcely even acknowledged by elected officials and school leaders"—an "exercise in denial," they observe, "reminiscent of the South" before the integration era—"is incompatible with the healthy functioning of a multiracial generation."

Racial isolation and the concentrated poverty of children in a public school go hand in hand, moreover, as the Harvard project notes. Only 15 percent of the intensely segregated white schools in the nation have student populations in which more than half are poor enough to be receiving free meals or reduced price meals. "By contrast, a staggering 86 percent of intensely segregated black and Latino schools" have student enrollments in which more than half are poor by the same standards. A segregated inner-city school is "almost six times as likely" to be a school of concentrated poverty as is a school that has an overwhelmingly white population.

"So deep is our resistance to acknowledging what is taking place," Professor Orfield notes, that when a district that has been desegregated in preceding decades now abandons integrated education, "the actual word 'segregation' hardly ever comes up. Proposals for racially separate schools are usually promoted as new educational improvement plans or efforts to increase parental involvement. . . . In the new era of 'separate but equal,' segregation has somehow come to be viewed as a type of school reform"—"something progressive and new," he writes—rather than as what it is: an unconceded throwback to the status quo of 1954. But no matter by what new name segregated education may be known, whether it be "neighborhood schools, community schools, targeted schools, priority schools," or whatever other currently accepted term, "segregation is not new . . . and neither is the idea of making separate schools equal. It is one of the oldest and extensively tried ideas in U.S. educational history" and one, writes Orfield, that has "never had a systematic effect in a century of trials."

Perhaps most damaging to any effort to address this subject openly is the refusal of most of the major arbiters of culture in our northern cities to confront or even clearly name an obvious reality they would have castigated with a passionate determination in another section of the nation 50 years before and which, moreover, they still castigate today in retrospective writings that assign it to a comfortably distant and allegedly concluded era of the past. There is, indeed, a seemingly agreed-upon convention in much of the media today not even to use an accurate descriptor such as "racial segregation" in a narrative description of a segregated school. Linguistic sweeteners, semantic somersaults, and surrogate vocabularies are repeatedly employed. Schools in which as few as three or four percent of students may be white or Southeast Asian or of Middle Eastern origin, for instance—and where *every other child* in the building is black or Hispanic—are referred to, in a commonly misleading usage, as "diverse." Visitors to schools like these discover quickly the eviscerated meaning of the word, which is no longer a descriptor but a euphemism for a plainer word that has apparently become unspeakable.

School systems themselves repeatedly employ this euphemism in descriptions of the composition of their student populations. In a school I visited in fall 2004 in Kansas City, Missouri, for example, a document distributed to visitors reports that the school's curriculum "addresses the needs of children from diverse backgrounds." But as I went from class to class I did not encounter any children who were white or Asian—or Hispanic, for that matter—and when I later was provided with the demographics of the school, I learned that 99.6 percent of students there were African-American. In a similar document, the school board of another district, this one in New York State, referred to "the diversity" of its student population and "the rich variations of ethnic backgrounds. . . ." But when I looked at the racial numbers that the district had reported to the state, I learned that there were 2,800 black and Hispanic children in the system, one Asian child, and three whites. Words, in these cases, cease to have real meaning; or, rather, they mean the opposite of what they say.

One of the most disheartening experiences for those who grew up in the years when Martin Luther King and Thurgood Marshall were alive is to visit public schools today that bear their names, or names of other honored leaders of the integration struggles that produced the temporary progress that took place in the three decades after *Brown,* and to find how many of these schools are bastions of contemporary segregation. It is even more disheartening when schools like these are not in segregated neighborhoods but in racially mixed areas in which the integration of a public school would seem to be most natural and where, indeed, it takes a conscious effort on the part of parents or of school officials in these districts to *avoid* the integration option that is often right at their front door.

In a Seattle neighborhood, for instance, where approximately half the families were Caucasian, 95 percent of students at the Thurgood Marshall Elementary School were black, Hispanic, Native American, or of Asian origin. An African-American teacher at the school told me of seeing clusters of white parents and their children on the corner of a street close to the school each morning waiting for a bus that took the children to a school in which she believed that the enrollment was predominantly white. She did not speak of the white families waiting for the bus to take their children to another public school with bitterness, but wistfully.

"At Thurgood Marshall," according to a big wall-poster in the lobby of the school, "the dream is alive." But school assignment practices and federal court decisions that have countermanded long-established policies that previously fostered integration in Seattle's schools make the realization of the dream identified with Justice Marshall all but unattainable today.

"Thurgood Marshall must be turning over in his grave," one of the teachers at the school had told the principal, as he reported this to me. The principal, understandably, believed he had no choice but to reject the teacher's observation out of hand. "No, sister," he had told the teacher. "If Justice Marshall was still roamin' nowadays and saw what's goin' on here in this school, he would say 'Hallelujah' and 'Amen!'" Legal scholars may demur at this, but he had a school to run and he could not allow the ironies of names, or history, to undermine the passionate resolve he brought to winning victories for children in the only terms he was allowed.

In the course of two visits to the school, I had a chance to talk with a number of teachers and to spend time in their classrooms. In one class, a teacher had posted a brief summation of the *Brown* decision on the wall; but it was in an inconspicuous corner of the room and, with that one exception, I could find no references to Marshall's struggle against racial segregation in the building.

When I asked a group of fifth grade boys who Thurgood Marshall was and what he did to have deserved to have a school named after him, most of the boys had no idea at all. One said that he used to run "a summer camp." Another said he was "a manager"—I had no chance to ask him what he meant by this, or how he'd gotten this impression. Of the three who knew that he had been a lawyer, only one, and only after several questions on my part, replied that he had "tried to change what was unfair"—and, after a moment's hesitation, "wanted to let black kids go to the same schools that white kids did." He said he was "pretty sure" that this school was not segregated because, in one of the other classrooms on the same floor, there were two white children.

There is a bit of painful humor that I've heard from black schoolteachers who grew up during the era of the integration movement and have subsequently seen its goals abandoned and its early victories reversed. "If you want to see a *really* segregated school in the United States today, start by looking for a school that's named for Martin Luther King or Rosa Parks." In San Diego, there is a school that bears the name of Rosa Parks in which 86 percent of students are black and Hispanic and less than 2 percent are white. In Los Angeles, there is a school that bears the name of Dr. King, 99 percent black and Hispanic, and another in Milwaukee where black children also make up 99 percent of the enrollment. There is a high school in Cleveland named for Dr. King in which black students make up 99 percent of the student body, and the graduation rate is only 38 percent. In Philadelphia, 98 percent of children at a high school named for Dr. King are black. At a middle school named for Dr. King in Boston, black and Hispanic children make up 98 percent of the enrollment.

In New York City, there's a primary school that's named for Langston Hughes (99 percent black and Hispanic), a middle school that's named for Jackie Robinson (96 percent black and Hispanic), and a high school named for Fannie Lou Hamer, one of the great heroes of the integration movement in the South, in which 98 percent of students are black or Hispanic. In Harlem, there is yet another segregated Thurgood Marshall School (also 98 percent black and Hispanic), and in the South Bronx dozens of children I have known, including Pineapple's older sister and her cousin, went to a middle school named in honor of Paul Robeson in which less than half of 1 percent of the enrollment was Caucasian.

There is a well-known high school named for Martin Luther King in New York City too. The school, in which I've had the chance to visit classes many times, is like Seattle's Marshall School in that it isn't sited in a deeply segregated inner-city section of the city but is, in this instance, in an upper-middle-class white neighborhood where it was built in the belief, or hope, that it would attract white students by permitting them to walk to school while only their black and Hispanic classmates would be asked to ride the bus or come by train. When the school was opened in 1975, less than a block from Lincoln Center in Manhattan, as The New York Times observes, "it was seen as a promising effort to integrate white, black and Hispanic students in a thriving neighborhood that held one of the city's cultural gems." Even from the start, however, parents of the neighborhood showed great reluctance to permit their children to enroll at Martin Luther King and, despite "its prime location and its name, which itself creates the highest of expectations," notes The Times, the school before long came to be a destination for black and Hispanic students who could not obtain admission into more successful schools. It stands today as one of the most visible and problematic symbols in the nation of an expectation rapidly receding and a legacy substantially betrayed.

The principal of Martin Luther King in autumn of 2000, which was the first time I visited the school, was Ronald Wells, a tall, distinguished-looking man who had grown up during the civil rights campaigns and whose commitment to the values of that era had not wavered with the years. A religious man who was ordained in the United Church of Christ and was, in the year we met, the only black male principal in the Manhattan high school district, he told me that his family roots were in the South and that his mother came from Charlotte, where the *Brown* decision was successfully enforced for many years and where the integration of the public schools became a fact of life for an entire generation.

From the moment that one walks into the school, one is compelled to look into the heart of history. "I have a dream," read the words of Dr. King that are displayed across the rear wall of the lobby, "that one day . . . the sons of former slaves and sons of former slave-owners will be able to sit down together at a table of brotherhood." But, at the time of my initial visit, student enrollment at the school was 54 percent African-American and 42 percent Hispanic. Only 3.8 percent of the 2,600 students in the building were Asian, white, or "other."

"We used to have more Vietnamese and Polish students . . . , a few Russian immigrants as well," the principal informed me. "Now almost none." A growing portion of the student population was Dominican, he said, and traveled to the school from Washington Heights, a neighborhood to the north of Harlem, which is a long ride for a teenager to take out of a neighborhood with countless segregated schools in order to attend another segregated school—"busing," it turns out, for purposes entirely different from the one with which the word, derided frequently today as an unwelcome strategy for racial integration, is historically identified.

Segregated schools like Martin Luther King are often tense, disorderly, and socially unhappy places, and when episodes of student violence occur, the inclination of the parents of white children to avoid such schools is obviously reinforced. Martin Luther King has had its share of violence across the years, and it was in the news again in January 2002 when two of its students were the victims of a shooting in a hallway of the building on the anniversary of the day when Dr. King was born. The mayor of New York noted the irony of timing and some of the media reminded readers that the legacy of Dr. King had been one of peace. He had been a "man of peace," "preached peace," "taught about peace," as the city's newspapers observed. There was less reference to the "other" important legacy of Dr. King. Although some press accounts alluded to the unsuccessful efforts to attract white students to the school, no headlines pointed to the segregated status of the school as a dishonor to *that* portion of his legacy.

The media discussed some of the strategies that might reduce the likelihood of violence recurring at the school. An advocate for small schools argued that a large school in itself, where students' "personal circumstances" are not known to teachers, makes it harder to keep weapons out of a building. ("Small schools are safer because people get to know the kids and have relationships with them," he said.) Architectural aspects of the school were mentioned as potential problems too. The school had "numerous nooks and crannies," which might have encouraged misbehavior, said one news account, and "its twelve doors make it easier for people to sneak in."

The impression one derived from much of this was that a smaller segregated and unequal school, if better designed, perhaps with fewer doors, might represent a practical solution to the problems that had led to shootings at the school. All this is true to some degree. The school *was* subsequently broken up into a number of much smaller schools, and some of the tensions in the corridors and other common areas diminished as a consequence. Still, reading these reflections on the violence that had erupted at the King, one might have hoped that there had been some reference to the fact of virtual apartheid in itself as one, at least, of many governmentally determined forces that contribute to the social turbulence of adolescents in so many schools like this.

Almost all reflections of this nature tend to be dispatched quite easily these days (this is "victim-thinking," we are sometimes told), and almost everything that we have learned from empathetic social scientists who have examined the direct and indirect emotional and psychological effects of segregated schooling through the course of many years is pretty much dismissed as well. Only rarely are considerations of the possible distortions wrought upon the spirits of these children by the fact of concentrated poverty and racial isolation in themselves admitted to the table of acceptable deliberations when a strategy for overcoming student anguish and controlling student desperation is pursued. That which can't be named as a potential cause cannot be touched upon in looking for a plausible solution. The search for less provocative solutions makes it possible perhaps for those who shepherd the debate to stay away from problematic places.

High school students with whom I get to talk in deeply segregated neighborhoods seem far less circumspect and far more open in their willingness to look into those problematic places. "It's like we're being hidden," said a fifteen-year-old girl named Isabel I met some years ago in Harlem, in attempting to explain to me the ways in which she and her classmates understood the racial segregation of their neighborhoods and schools. "It's as if you have been put in a garage where, if they don't have room for something but aren't sure if they should throw it out, they put it there where they don't need to think of it again."

I asked her if she truly thought America did not "have room" for her or other children of her race. "Think of it this way," said a sixteen-year-old girl sitting beside her. "If people in New York woke up one day and learned that we were gone, that we had simply died or left for somewhere else, how would they feel?"

"How do you think they'd feel?" I asked.

"I think they'd be relieved," this very solemn girl replied.

The name above the doorway of a school has little power to revise these sensitive perceptions. Still, we have these many schools bearing distinguished names that cannot fail to resonate with history. For visitors, the name of Thurgood Marshall on the doorway of a school inevitably stirs a certain expectation and reminds us of the court decision with which Marshall's name is linked forever in our memory. No matter how the meaning of *Brown v. Board of Education* may be retroactively revised, or blurred, or rendered indistinct, which seems to be almost obligatory in the speeches that are given at events commemorating the decision, the question it addressed and the resounding answer it delivered are a part of our collective memory as well.

"Does segregation of children in public schools solely on the basis of race, even though the physical facilities and other 'tangible' factors may be equal," asked the court in 1954, "deprive the children of the minority race of equal educational opportunities? We believe it does." To separate black children from white children of their age and qualifications on the basis of their race, the court went on, "generates a feeling of inferiority as to their status in the community that may affect their hearts and minds in a way unlikely ever to be undone. . . . In the field of public education, the doctrine of 'separate but equal' has no place. . . . Separate educational facilities are inherently unequal."

Like it or not—and many sectors of opinion in our northern cities that applauded this decision 50 years ago appear to like it less and less, or not at all—the court made no accommodation for the possibilities of a redemptive version of apartheid education. Some of us, exhausted by the battle or attempting to allay the disappointment that we feel, may look for almost any way by which to squirm around this. Some hard-nosed intellectuals may counsel us to "reconsider" it. Conservative appointees to the courts may openly deride it, as does Justice Clarence Thomas, and do what they can in order to dismantle the remaining efforts that derive from that decision. But ethicists and theologians and most pastors of our synagogues and churches make it clear that they respect it. Textbooks still, in general, extol it as a symbol of our nation's onward stride to ethical advancement. And students at good high schools read these words in classes about government or history and are not likely to be told by teachers that they represent merely an inconvenient, if sincere, intention which the nation now rejects but are more often taught to view the words of *Brown* as evidence of something good, progressive, and enlightened in our social history.

So we are obliged, in this respect, to live with the ideals and names of heroes and with words of court decisions that official culture honors but official actions and the policies of school boards and the preferences of highly influential sectors of our urban populations fiercely disavow. From coast to coast, indeed, in recent years, middle-class white city-dwellers have not merely fled from schools in which large numbers of black and Hispanic children are enrolled but sometimes openly demanded that their school officials carve out new domains of pedagogic isolation to provide their children with exclusive opportunities which they believe that they deserve.

"Well-organized parent groups" in New York City, noted The New York Times in an account of this phenomenon published five years ago, are asking school officials for permission "to exclude thousands of poor black and Hispanic students who travel long distances" in order to attend schools in their neighborhoods. "The wealthier parents," said The Times, "covet" these buildings as potential sites in which they can create new schools of higher quality to serve their own immediate communities. "The proposed new schools are intended," said the paper, to provide the residents of "upscale New York City neighborhoods" an opportunity to give their children "an education on [a] par with the best suburban high schools."

In the 1960s and 1970s, noted The Times, the boundaries of school attendance zones had sometimes been redrawn "to promote racial integration," but the schools where this had taken place, the paper said, had "lost their distinct neighborhood character" and many "produced lackluster academic results"—which, if this seemingly direct connection was correct, appeared to indicate that school desegregation had not been in the best interests of the children of New York. As carefully as this final point was handled in The Times' account, it seemed to validate the gravitation of the relatively privileged to schools that represent protected enclaves, whether they are newly founded schools or simply public schools that are reserved for children of a middle-class or affluent community. In words that have been heard time and again from those who have defended class and racial insularity in urban schools while managing to make it seem that race and class were not involved, parents in these neighborhoods, according to another story in The Times, indicated they were simply "searching for an old-fashioned sense of community, in which their children walk to school together, learn together and play together, almost as if they lived in a small town instead of a huge city."

Some of the New York City neighborhoods in which these trends have been observed were bastions of progressive thinking 35 or 40 years ago. Some of the white activists who went to Mississippi and to other southern states during the 1960s to participate in civil rights campaigns to uproot segregation grew up in these neighborhoods. The press and clergy in New York were proud of these young people. They are honored sometimes even now at the commemorations of the anniversaries of certain demonstrations, certain marches, certain confrontations in the South and, sometimes, on the anniversaries of *Brown*. There are ironies like these in many other cities of our nation.

"How did New York, with its image as a pioneer in civil rights," ask Orfield and Eaton, "become the epicenter of segregated public education?" Segregation in the schools of New York City and its suburbs, they reply, has been accomplished by a number of forces that include discrimination, court decisions, immigration trends, and government-enforced school boundaries, but most specifically by "one of the nation's highest levels of housing segregation." Residential segregation in the New York City area, they note, remains today at about the same level as in 1960, a remarkable statistic that belies the myth of gradual but steady progress that is frequently suggested by the media. Segregation, moreover, whether in cities or in suburbs, "does not stem primarily [from] preferences" of segregated people. A Gallup poll for Newsday, they observe, showed that only one in ten black people in the suburbs of Long Island, just to the east of New York City, "wanted to live in all-black areas," although the overwhelming number do live in such areas. But, they continue, there have been "no serious government proposals" in New York or in the nation that address the spread of segregation to the suburbs and, "outside the South," states "do little to enforce fair-housing laws."

In suburban Roosevelt on Long Island, as a consequence, nearly 100 percent of students at the high school are black or Hispanic. A twenty-minute drive away, at Plainview High, black and Hispanic students make up only 1 percent of the enrollment while 97 percent of students at the school are white. In numerous other districts in the areas surrounding New York City, black and Hispanic children go to public schools in which they find themselves as isolated as are children of their color in the Bronx.

"We cannot be satisfied," said Dr. King in perhaps his best-remembered speech, delivered on the mall in Washington in August 1963, "as long as the Negro's basic mobility is from a smaller ghetto to a larger one." He was speaking of the movement of black people from small towns to urban areas and made a specific reference to New York in nearly the next sentence. What might not have been easily conceivable to Dr. King or any of his colleagues on that hopeful day in Washington was that a time would come before too long when a reverse mobility—from larger ghettos into smaller ghettos—would become the rule of order in large sections of the North and South alike, as hundreds of thousands of black people moved from inner-city districts to the promised land of a suburban life, only to find their children and themselves entrapped again in the same isolation they had fled.

Many educators make the argument today that, given the demographics of large cities like New York and their suburban areas, our only realistic goal should be the nurturing of strong, empowered, and well-funded schools in segregated neighborhoods—an argument with which, in any given and specific local situation, it would seem impossible to disagree. Even if we have to doubt the likelihood that genuine empowerment and anything approaching full equality will ever be achieved on a broad scale, or long sustained, in the dynamics of the dual system as it stands, one also feels compelled to hope these reservations will be proven wrong and, therefore, to do everything we can to reinforce the efforts of the principals and teachers who devote their lives to working in these schools.

Black school officials in these situations have sometimes conveyed to me a bitter and clear-sighted recognition that they're being asked, essentially, to mediate and render functional an uncontested separation between children of their race and children of white people living sometimes in a distant section of their town and sometimes in almost their own immediate communities. Implicit in this mediation is a willingness to set aside the promises of *Brown* and, perhaps while never stating this or even thinking of it clearly in these terms, to settle for the promise made more than a century ago in *Plessy v. Ferguson*, the 1896 Supreme Court ruling in which "separate but equal" was accepted as a tolerable rationale for the perpetuation of a dual system in American society.

Equality itself—equality alone—is now, it seems, the article of faith to which increasing numbers of the principals of inner-city public schools subscribe. And some who are perhaps most realistic do not even ask for, or expect, complete equality, which seems beyond the realm of probability for many years to come, but look instead for only a sufficiency of means—"adequacy" is the legal term most often used today—by which to win those practical and finite victories that may appear to be within their reach. Higher standards, higher expectations, are insistently demanded of these urban principals, and of their teachers and the students in their schools, but far lower standards certainly in ethical respects appear to be expected of the dominant society that isolates these children in unequal institutions.

At an early-morning assembly at Seattle's Thurgood Marshall School, the entire student body stood and chanted, "I have confidence that I can learn!" exactly 30 times. Similar sessions of self-exhortation are familiar at innumerable inner-city schools: "Yes, I can! I know I can!" "If it is to be, it's up to me." In some schools, these chantings are accompanied by rhythmic clapping of the hands or snapping of the fingers or by stamping on the floor. It usually seems like an invigorating way to start the day. At the same time, politically conservative white people visiting these schools often seem to be almost too gratified to hear black and Hispanic children speaking in these terms. If it's up to "them," the message seems to be, it isn't up to "us," which appears to sweep the deck of many pressing and potentially disruptive and expensive obligations we may otherwise believe our nation needs to contemplate.

And, in plain honesty, when we invite these children to repeat in unison that "if it is to be, it's up to me," we are asking them to say something which, while they have no way of knowing this, is simply not the truth. It is, indeed, an odd thing, when one thinks of it, to ask a six- or seven-year-old child to believe. Does a school board or school system have no role in what this child is to be? Do taxpayers have no role in this? Do Congress and the courts and local legislators have no role in setting up the possibilities of what is "to be," or not to be, within these children's opportunities to learn? Why are the debates about state distribution of resources for our schools so heated, and the opposition to a fairer distribution on the part of wealthy districts so intense, if citizens do not believe that fiscal policies enacted by the government have a decisive role in the determination of the destinies of children?

One of the reasons for these incantations in the schools that serve black and Hispanic children is what is believed to be the children's loss of willingness "to try," their failure to believe they have the same abilities as do white children in more privileged communities. It is this attribution of a loss of faith in their potential and, as an adaptive consequence, a seeming "will to fail"—a psychological pathology—that justifies the hortatory slogans they are asked to chant and the multitude of posters, loaded with ambitious verbs such as "succeed," "attain," "achieve," that are found on classroom walls and sometimes even painted on the outside of a school.

Few teachers that I know who work with kids in inner-city schools question whether this self-doubt is real—nor whether, especially among pre-teens and adolescents, and particularly boys, this sense of doubt is reinforced by pressure from those of their peers who have succumbed already to the cynicism that is commonly a cover-up for fear. Auto-hypnotic slogans that attempt to counter these peer pressures—"I'm smart! I know that I'm smart," which I have heard repeatedly in urban elementary schools, but rarely in suburban schools where the potential of most children is assumed—have come to be the modern mantras of self-help for children in these segregated institutions.

"This is not to say," as the tough-minded and insightful author Ellis Cose observes, "that self-help programs don't work. Some work stunningly well." At the same time, he writes, "effective solutions to ghetto pathologies cannot be crafted by blacks walled off from a larger America." It is notable in this respect that, in all the many writings and proposals dedicated to the alteration of self-image among inner-city youth and the reversal of debilitating pressures from their peers, the suggestion is virtually never made that one of the most direct ways to reduce the damage done to children by peer pressure is to change the *make-up* of their peers by letting them go to schools where all their classmates are not black and brown and poor, and children and grandchildren of the poor, but where a healthy confidence that one can learn is rooted in the natural assumptions of Americans who haven't been laid waste by history.

When I was standing with the children at the Thurgood Marshall School and counting the number of times they chanted the word "confidence," I remember looking at the faces of the boys who stood the closest to me in the gym in which the morning chants were taking place and wondering what impact this was having on them inwardly. When you're among a group of children, you inevitably want to hope that rituals like these might really do some good, that they may make a difference that will last beyond the hour of exhilaration and hand-clapping. Still, these exercises are place-markers. They tell us we are in a world where hope must be constructed therapeutically because so much of it has been destroyed by the conditions of internment in which we have placed these children. It is harder to convince young people they "can learn" when they are cordoned off by a society that isn't sure they really can. That is, I am afraid, one of the most destructive and long-lasting messages a nation possibly could give its children.

CHAPTER 2

Hitting Them Hardest When They're Small

"Dear Mr. Kozol," said the eight-year-old, "we do not have the things you have. You have Clean things. We do not have. You have a clean bathroom. We do not have that. You have Parks and we do not have Parks. You have all the thing and we do not have all the thing. . . . Can you help us?"

The letter, from a child named Alliyah, came in a fat envelope of 27 letters from a class of third grade children in the Bronx. Other letters that the students in Alliyah's classroom sent me registered some of the same complaints. "We don't have no gardens," and "no Music or Art," and "no fun places to play," one child said. "Is there a way to fix this Problem?" Another noted a concern one hears from many children in such overcrowded schools: "We have a gym but it is for lining up. I think it is not fair." Yet another of Alliyah's classmates asked me, with a sweet misspelling, if I knew the way to make her school into a "good" school—"like the other kings have"—and ended with the hope that I would do my best to make it possible for "all the kings" to have good schools.

The letter that affected me the most, however, had been written by a child named Elizabeth. "It is not fair that other kids have a garden and new things. But we don't have that," said Elizabeth. "I wish that this school was the most beautiful school in the whole why world."

Elizabeth had very careful, very small, and neatly formed handwriting. She had corrected other errors in her letter, squeezing in a missing letter she'd initially forgotten, erasing and rewriting a few words she had misspelled. The error she had left unaltered in the final sentence therefore captured my attention more than it might otherwise have done.

"The whole why world" stayed in my thoughts for days. When I later met Elizabeth I brought her letter with me, thinking I might see whether, in reading it aloud, she'd change the "why" to "wide" or leave it as it was. My visit to her class, however, proved to be so pleasant, and the children seemed so eager to bombard me with their questions about where I lived, and why I lived there rather than New York, and who I lived with, and how many dogs I had, and other interesting questions of that sort, that I decided not to interrupt the nice reception they had given me with questions about usages and spelling. I left "the whole why world" to float around unedited and unrevised within my mind. The letter itself soon found a resting place up on the wall above my desk.

In the years before I met Elizabeth, I had visited many elementary schools in the South Bronx and in one northern district of the Bronx as well. I had also made a number of visits to a high school where a stream of water flowed down one of the main stairwells on a rainy afternoon and where green fungus molds were growing in the office where the students went for counseling. A large blue barrel was positioned to collect rain-water coming through the ceiling. In one make-shift elementary school housed in a former skating rink next to a funeral parlor in another nearly all-black-and-Hispanic section of the Bronx, class size rose to 34 and more; four kindergarten classes and a sixth grade class were packed into a single room that had no windows. Airlessness was stifling in many rooms; and recess was impossible because there was no outdoor playground and no indoor gym, so the children had no place to play.

In another elementary school, which had been built to hold 1,000 children but was packed to bursting with some 1,500 boys and girls, the principal poured out his feelings to me in a room in which a plastic garbage bag had been attached somehow to cover part of the collapsing ceiling. "This," he told me, pointing to the garbage bag, then gesturing around him at the other indications of decay and disrepair one sees in ghetto schools much like it elsewhere, "would not happen to white children."

A friend of mine who was a first-year teacher in a Harlem high school told me she had 40 students in her class but only 30 chairs, so some of her students had to sit on windowsills or lean against the walls. Other high schools were so crowded they were forced to shorten schooldays and to cut back hours of instruction to accommodate a double shift of pupils. Tens of thousands of black and Hispanic students were in schools like these, in which half the student body started classes very early in the morning and departed just before or after lunch, while the other half did not begin their schoolday until noon.

Libraries, once one of the glories of the New York City system, were either nonexistent or, at best, vestigial in large numbers of the elementary schools. Art and music programs had for the most part disappeared as well. "When I began to teach in 1969," the principal of an elementary school in the South Bronx reported to me, "every school had a full-time licensed art and music teacher and librarian." During the next decade, he recalled, "I saw all of that destroyed."

School physicians were also removed from elementary schools during these years. In 1970, when substantial numbers of white children still attended New York City's schools, 400 doctors had been present to address the health needs of the children. By 1993, the number of doctors had been cut to 23, most of them part-time—a cutback that affected most acutely children in the city's poorest neighborhoods where medical provision was perennially substandard and health problems faced by children most extreme. During the 1990s, for example, the rate of pediatric asthma in the South Bronx, already one of the highest in the nation, was exacerbated when the city chose to build a medical waste incinerator in their neighborhood after a plan to build it on the East Side of Manhattan was abandoned in the face of protests from the parents of that area. Hospitalization rates for these asthmatic children in the Bronx were as much as 20 times more frequent than for children in the city's affluent communities. Teachers spoke of children who came into class with chronic wheezing and, at any moment of the day, might undergo more serious attacks, but in the schools I visited there were no doctors to attend to them.

Political leaders in New York tended to point to shifting economic factors, such as a serious budget crisis in the middle 1970s, rather than to the changing racial demographics of the student population, as the explanation for these steep declines in services. But the fact of economic ups and downs from year to year, or from one decade to the next, could not convincingly explain the permanent shortchanging of the city's students, which took place routinely in good economic times and bad, with bad times seized upon politically to justify these cuts while, in the good times, losses undergone during the crisis years had never been restored.

"If you close your eyes to the changing racial composition of the schools and look only at budget actions and political events," says Noreen Connell, the director of the nonprofit Educational Priorities Panel in New York, "you're missing the assumptions that are underlying these decisions." When minority parents ask for something better for their kids, she says, "the assumption is that these are parents who can be discounted. These are kids that we don't value."

The disrepair and overcrowding of these schools in the South Bronx "wouldn't happen for a moment in a white suburban school district like Scarsdale," says former New York State Commissioner of Education Thomas Sobol, who was once the superintendent of the Scarsdale schools and is now a professor of education at Teachers College in New York. "I'm aware that I could never prove that race is at the heart of this if I were called to testify before a legislative hearing. But I've felt it for so long, and seen it operating for so long, I know it's true. . . ."

During the 1990s, physical conditions in some buildings had become so dangerous that a principal at one Bronx school, which had been condemned in 1989 but nonetheless continued to be used, was forced to order that the building's windows not be cleaned because the frames were rotted and glass panes were falling in the street, while at another school the principal had to have the windows bolted shut for the same reason. These were not years of economic crisis in New York. This was a period in which financial markets soared and a new generation of free-spending millionaires and billionaires was widely celebrated by the press and on TV; but none of the proceeds of this period of economic growth had found their way into the schools that served the truly poor.

I had, as I have noted, visited many schools in other cities by this time; but I did not know children in those schools as closely as I'd come to know, or soon would know, so many of the children in the New York City schools. So it would be these children, and especially the ones in elementary schools in which I spent the most time in the Bronx, whose sensibilities and puzzlements and understandings would impress themselves most deeply on my own impressions in the years to come, and it would be their questions that became my questions and their accusations and their challenges, when it appeared that they were making challenges, that came to be my own.

This, then, is the accusation that Alliyah and her classmates send our way: "You have. . . . We do not have." Are they right or are they wrong? Is this a case of naïve and simplistic juvenile exaggeration? What does a third grader know about these big-time questions about what is fair and what is not, and what is right and what is wrong? Physical appearances apart, how in any case do you begin to measure something so diffuse and vast and seemingly abstract as having more, or having less, or having not at all?

In a social order where it seems a fairly common matter to believe that what we spend to purchase almost anything we need bears some connection to the worth of what we get, a look at what we think it's in our interest to invest in children like Alliyah or Pineapple may not tell us everything we need to know about the state of educational fair play within our nation, but it surely tells us *something* about what we think these kids are worth to us in human terms and in the contributions they may someday make to our society. At the time I met Alliyah in the school-year 1997–

1998, New York's Board of Education spent about $8,000 yearly on the education of a third grade child in a New York City public school. If you could have scooped Alliyah up out of the neighborhood where she was born and plunked her down within a fairly typical white suburb of New York, she would have received a public education worth about $12,000 every year. If you were to lift her up once more and set her down within one of the wealthiest white suburbs of New York, she would have received as much as $18,000 worth of public education every year and would likely have had a third grade teacher paid approximately $30,000 more than was her teacher in the Bronx.

The dollars on both sides of the equation have increased since then, but the discrepancies between them have not greatly changed. The present per-pupil spending level in the New York City schools is $11,700, which may be compared to a per-pupil spending level in excess of $22,000 in the well-to-do suburban district of Manhasset. The present New York City level is, indeed, almost exactly what Manhasset spent per pupil 18 years ago, in 1987, when that sum of money bought a great deal more in services and salaries than it can buy today. In dollars adjusted for inflation, New York City has not yet caught up to where its wealthiest suburbs were a quarter-century ago.

Gross discrepancies in teacher salaries between the city and its affluent white suburbs have remained persistent too. In 1997, the median salary for teachers in Alliyah's neighborhood was $43,000, as compared to $74,000 in suburban Rye, $77,000 in Manhasset, and $81,000 in the town of Scarsdale, which is only about 11 miles from Alliyah's school. Five years later, in 2002, salary scales for New York City's teachers rose to levels that approximated those within the lower-spending districts in the suburbs, but salary scales do not reflect the actual salaries that teachers typically receive, which are dependant upon years of service and advanced degrees. Salaries for first-year teachers in the city now were higher than they'd been four years before, but the differences in median pay between the city and its upper-middle-income suburbs had remained extreme. The overall figure for New York City in 2002–2003 was $53,000, while it had climbed to $87,000 in Manhassett and exceeded $95,000 in Scarsdale.

Even these numbers that compare the city to its suburbs cannot give an adequate impression of the inequalities imposed upon the children living in poor sections of New York. For, even within the New York City schools themselves, there are additional discrepancies in funding between schools that serve the poorest and the wealthiest communities, since teachers with the least seniority and least experience are commonly assigned to schools in the most deeply segregated neighborhoods. The median salary of teachers in Pineapple's neighborhood was less than $46,000 in 2002–2003, the lowest in the city, compared to $59,000 in one of Manhattan's recently gentrified communities, and up to $64,000 in some neighborhoods of Queens.

None of this includes the additional resources given to the public schools in affluent communities where parents have the means to supplement the public funds with private funding of their own, money used to build and stock a good school library for instance, or to arrange for art and music lessons or, in many of these neighborhoods, to hire extra teachers to reduce the size of classes for their children.

This relatively new phenomenon of private money being used selectively to benefit the children only of specific public schools had not been noted widely in New York until about ten years ago when parents of the students at a public school in Greenwich Village in Manhattan raised the funds to pay a fourth grade teacher, outside of the normal budget of the school, when class size in the fourth grade otherwise was likely to increase from 26 to

32, which was the average class size in the district at the time but which, one of the parents said, "would have a devastating impact" on her son. The parents, therefore, collected $46,000—two thirds of it, remarkably, in just one night—in order to retain the extra teacher.

The school in Greenwich Village served a population in which less than 20 percent of students were from families of low income, a very low figure in New York, compared, for instance, to Pineapple's neighborhood, where 95 percent of children lived in poverty. The Greenwich Village school, moreover, was already raising a great deal of private money—more than $100,000 yearly, it was now revealed—to pay for music, art, and science programs and for furniture repairs.

The chancellor of the New York City schools initially rejected the use of private funds to underwrite a teacher's pay, making the argument that this was not fair to the children in those many other schools that had much larger classes; but the district later somehow came up with the public funds to meet the cost of hiring the extra teacher, so the parents won their children the advantage they had sought for them in any case.

As it turned out, the use of private subsidies to supplement the tax supported budgets of some schools in affluent communities was a more commonly accepted practice than most people in the city's poorest neighborhoods had known. The PTA at one school on the Upper West Side of Manhattan, for example, had been raising nearly $50,000 yearly to hire a writing teacher and two part-time music teachers. At a school in a middle-class section of Park Slope in Brooklyn, parents raised more than $100,000 yearly to employ a science teacher and two art instructors. In yet another neighborhood, parents at an elementary school and junior high had raised more than $1 million, mostly for enrichment programs for their children.

In principle, the parents in poor neighborhoods were free to do fund-raising too, but the proceeds they were likely to bring in differed dramatically. The PTA in one low-income immigrant community, for instance, which sponsored activities like candy sales and tried without success to win foundation grants, was able to raise less than $4,000. In the same year, parents at P.S. 6, a top-rated elementary school serving the Upper East Side of Manhattan, raised $200,000. The solicitation of private funds from parents in communities like this had come to be so common, said the president of the New York City Board of Education, "you almost expect a notice from the schools saying there's going to be tuition." A good deal of private money, moreover, as The Times observed, was "being collected under the table" because parents sometimes feared that they would otherwise be forced to share these funds with other schools. "We can do it," said the leader of the parent group at one of the schools where lavish sums of private money had been raised, "but it is sad that other schools that don't have a richer parent body can't. It really does make it a question of haves and have-nots."

In view of the extensive coverage of this new phenomenon not only by New York City papers but by those in other cities where the same trends are observed, it is apparent that this second layer of disparities between the children of the wealthy and the children of the poor is no secret to the public any longer. Yet, even while they sometimes are officially deplored, these added forms of inequality have been accepted with apparent equanimity by those who are their beneficiaries.

"Inequality is not an intentional thing," said the leader of the PTA in one of the West Side neighborhoods where parents had been raising private funds, some of which had been obtained as charitable grants. "You have schools that are empowered and you have schools that have no power at all. . . . I don't bear any guilt for knowing how to write a grant," he said, a statement that undoubtedly made sense to some but skirted the entire issue of endemic underbudgeting of public schools attended by the children of poor people who did not enjoy his money-raising skills or possible connections to grant makers.

A narrowing of civic virtue to the borders of distinct and self-contained communities is now evolving in these hybrid institutions which are public schools in that they benefit from the receipt of public funds but private in the many supplementary programs that are purchased independently. Boutique schools within an otherwise impoverished system, they enable parents of the middle class and upper middle class to claim allegiance to the general idea of public schools while making sure their children do not suffer gravely for the stripped-down budgets that have done great damage to poor children like Alliyah and Pineapple.

"There are cheap children and there are expensive children," writes Marina Warner, an essayist and novelist who has written many books for children, "just as there are cheap women and expensive women." When Pineapple entered P.S. 65 in the South Bronx, the government of New York State had already placed a price tag on her forehead. She and her kindergarten classmates were $8,000 babies. If we had wanted to see an $18,000 baby, we would have had to drive into the suburbs. But the governmentally administered diminishment of value in the children of the poor begins even before the age of five or six when they begin their years of formal education in the public schools. It starts during their infant years and toddler years when hundreds of thousands of children in low-income neighborhoods are locked out of the opportunity for preschool education for no reason but the accident of birth and budgetary choices of the government, while children of the privileged are often given veritable feasts of rich developmental early education.

In New York City, for example, affluent parents pay surprisingly large sums of money to enroll their youngsters in extraordinary early-education programs, typically beginning at the age of two or three, that give them social competence and rudimentary pedagogic skills unknown to children of the same age in the city's poorer neighborhoods. The most exclusive of the private preschools in New York, which are known to those who can afford them as the "Baby Ivies," cost as much as $22,000 for a full-day program. Competition for admission to these pre-K schools is so intense that "private counselors" are frequently retained, at fees as high as $300 hourly, according to The Times, to guide the parents through the application process.

At the opposite extreme along the economic spectrum in New York are thousands of children who receive no preschool opportunity at all. Exactly how *many* thousands is almost impossible to know. Numbers that originate in governmental agencies in New York and other states are incomplete and imprecise and do not always differentiate with clarity between authentic pre-K programs that have educative and developmental substance and those less expensive childcare arrangements that do not. But even where states do compile numbers that refer specifically to educative preschool programs, it is difficult to know how many of the children who are served are of low income since admissions to some of the state-supported programs aren't determined by low income or they are determined by a complicated set of factors of which poverty is only one.

There is another way, however, to obtain a fairly vivid sense of what impoverished four-year-olds receive in segregated sections of our cities like the Bronx. This is by asking kids themselves while you are with them in a kindergarten class to tell you how they spent their time the year before—or, if the children get confused or are too shy to give you a clear answer, then by asking the same question to their teacher.

"How many of these children were in pre-K programs last year or the last two years?" I often ask a kindergarten teacher.

In middle- and upper-class suburbs, a familiar answer is "more than three quarters of them," "this year, almost all of them," or "virtually all. . . ." In poor urban neighborhoods, by comparison, what I more often hear is "only a handful," "possibly as many as a fourth," "maybe about a third of them got *something* for one year. . . ." The superintendent of the district that includes Pineapple's former school estimated in the fall of 2002 that only between a quarter and a third of children in the district had received even a single year of preschool and that less than five percent had been provided with the two years of pre-K instruction that are common in most affluent communities.

Government data and the estimates of independent agencies tend to substantiate the estimates of principals and teachers. Of approximately 250,000 four-year-olds in New York State in 2001–2002, only about 25 percent, some 60,000, were believed to be enrolled in the state-funded preschool program—which is known as "Universal Pre-K" nonetheless—and typically in two-and-a-half-hour sessions rather than the more extended programs children of middle-class families usually attend. Then too, because these figures were not broken down by family income levels and because the program did not give priority to children of low income, it was difficult to know how many children in the poorest neighborhoods had been excluded from the program.

Head Start, which is a federal program, is of course

much better known than New York's Universal Pre-K and it has a long track-record, having been created 40 years ago by Congress at a time when social programs that expanded opportunities for children of low income were not viewed with the same skepticism that is common among many people who set public policy today. In spite of the generally high level of approval Head Start has received over the years, whether for its academic benefits or for its social benefits, or both, 40 percent of three- and four-year-olds who qualified for Head Start by their parents' income were denied this opportunity in 2001, a percentage of exclusion that has risen steeply in the subsequent four years. In some of the major cities, where the need is greatest, only a tiny fraction of low-income children in this age bracket are served. In New York City, for example, less than 13,000 four-year-olds were served by Head Start in 2001; and, in many cases, Head Start was combined with Universal Pre-K, so the children served by Head Start on its own were relatively few.

There are exceptions to this pattern in some sections of the nation. In Milwaukee, for example, nearly every four-year-old is now enrolled in a preliminary kindergarten program, which amounts to a full year of all-day preschool education, prior to a second kindergarten year for five-year-olds, according to the superintendent of Milwaukee's schools. In New Jersey, full-day pre-K programs have been instituted for all three- and four-year-olds in 31 low-income districts, one of the consequences of a legal action to reduce inequities of education in that state. More commonly in urban neighborhoods, large numbers of children have received no preschool education and they come into their kindergarten year without the minimal social skills that children need in order to participate in class activities and without even such very modest early-learning skills as knowing how to hold a pencil, identify perhaps a couple of shapes or colors, or recognize that printed pages go from left to right. A first grade teacher in Boston pointed out a child in her class who had received no preschool and, as I recall, had missed much of his kindergarten year as well, and introduced me to the boy so I could sit beside him for a while and derive my own conclusions, then confirmed my first impression when she told me in a whisper, "He's a sweetheart of a baby but knows almost absolutely nothing about anything that has to do with school!"

Two years later, in third grade, these children are introduced to what are known as "high-stakes tests," which in many urban systems now determine whether students can or cannot be promoted. Children who have been in programs like the "Baby Ivies" since the age of two have been given seven years of education by this point, nearly twice as many as the children who have been denied these opportunities; yet all are required to take, and will be measured and in many cases penalized severely by, the same examinations.

Which of these children will receive the highest scores—those who spent the years from two to four in lovely little Montessori schools and other pastel-painted settings in which tender and attentive grown-ups read to them from storybooks and introduced them for the first time to the world of numbers, and the shapes of letters, and the sizes and varieties of solid objects, and perhaps taught them to sort things into groups or to arrange them in a sequence, or to do those many other interesting things that early-childhood specialists refer to as prenumeracy skills, or the ones who spent those years at home in front of a TV or sitting by the window of a slum apartment gazing down into the street? There is something deeply hypocritical in a society that holds an inner-city child only eight years old "accountable" for her performance on a high-stakes standardized exam but does not hold the high officials of our government accountable for robbing her of what they gave their own kids six or seven years before.

There are obviously other forces that affect the early school performance of low-income children: levels of parent education, social instability, and frequently undiagnosed depression and anxiety that make it hard for many parents I have known to take an active role in backing up the efforts of their children's teachers in the public schools. Still, it is all too easy to assign the primary onus of responsibility to parents in these neighborhoods. (Where were these parents educated after all? Usually in the same low-ranking schools their children now attend.) In a nation in which fairness was respected, children of the poorest and least educated mothers would receive the most extensive and most costly preschool preparation, not the least and cheapest, because children in these families need it so much more than those whose educated parents can deliver the same benefits of early learning to them in their homes.

The "Baby Ivies" of Manhattan are not public institutions and receive no subsidies from public funds. In a number of cities, on the other hand, even this last line of squeamishness has now been crossed and public funds are being used to underwrite part of the costs of preschool education for the children of the middle class in public institutions which, however, do not offer the same services to children of the poor. Starting in spring 2001, Chicago's public schools began to operate a special track of preschool for the children of those families who were able to afford to pay an extra fee—nearly $6,000—to provide their children with a full-day program of about 11 hours, starting at the age of two if parents so desired. In a city where 87 percent of students in the public schools were black or Hispanic, the pay-for-preschool program served primarily white children.

Almost all these preschools were "in gentrified or gentrifying neighborhoods," The Chicago Tribune reported. "The fresh paint and new toys" in one of these programs on the North Side of Chicago were not there simply "to make preschool a happier place for the new class of toddlers" but "to keep their parents from moving to the suburbs." These and other "gold-plated academic offerings" which the city was underwriting to attract or to retain the children of the middle class had already begun to slow the "brain drain" from the public schools, The Tribune said. In the same year in which the pay-for-pre-K program was begun, 7,000 children from low-income families, many of whom were deemed to be "at risk," were waiting for preschool spaces that the city was unable to provide.

Undemocratic practices like these, no matter how strategically compelling they may seem, have introduced a radical distorting prism to an old, if seldom honored, national ideal of universal public education that affords all children equal opportunity within the borders of a democratic entity. Blurring the line between democracy and marketplace, the private subsidy of public schools in privileged communities denounces an ideal of simple justice that is often treated nowadays as an annoying residue of tiresome egalitarian ideas, an ethical detritus that sophisticated parents are encouraged to shut out of mind as they adapt themselves to a new order of Darwinian entitlements.

"We wouldn't play Little League this way," a parent in a wealthy district in Ohio told me when she was reflecting on the inequalities of education funding in that state. "We'd be embarrassed. We would feel ashamed." Perhaps in order to deflect these recognitions, or to soften them somewhat, many people, even while they do not doubt the worth of making very large investments in the education and the preschool education of their children, somehow—paradoxical as it may seem—appear to be attracted to the argument that money may not really matter that much after all.

No matter with what regularity such doubts about the worth of spending money on a child's education are advanced, it is obvious that those who *have* the money, and who spend it lavishly to benefit their own kids, do not do so for no reason. "If it doesn't matter," said a black physician working in the Bronx about the parallel inequities in medical provision made for privileged white children on the one hand and for poor children of color on the other, "then cancel it for everybody. Don't give it to them, deny it to us, then ask us to believe it's not significant."

This is the persistent challenge that the advocates for children in severely underfunded districts pose to those who are disposed to hear; yet shockingly large numbers of well-educated and sophisticated people have been able to dismiss such challenges with a surprising ease. "Is the answer *really* to throw money into these dysfunctional and failing schools?" I'm often asked. "Don't we have some better ways to make them 'work'?" The question is posed in a variety of forms. "Yes, of course, it's not a perfectly fair system as it stands. But money alone is surely not the sole response. The values of the parents and the kids themselves must have a role in this as well. . . . Housing, health conditions, social factors"—"other factors" is a term of overall reprieve one often hears—"have got to be considered too. . . ." These latter points are obviously true but always seem to have the odd effect of substituting things we know we cannot change in the short run for obvious things like cutting class size and constructing new school buildings or providing universal preschool that we actually could do right now if we were so inclined.

Frequently these arguments are posed as questions

that do not invite an answer since the answer seems to be decided in advance. "Can you really buy your way to better education for these children?" "Do we know enough to be quite sure that we will see an actual return on the investment that we make?" "Is it even clear that this is the right starting-point to get to where we'd like to go? It doesn't always seem to work, as I am sure that you already know . . . ," or similar questions that somehow assume I will agree with those who ask them.

Some people who ask these questions, while they live in wealthy districts where the schools are funded at high levels, don't send their children to these public schools but choose instead to send them to expensive private day-schools. At some of the well-known private prep schools in the New York City area, tuition and associated costs are typically more than $20,000. In their children's teenage years they somtimes send them off to boarding schools like Andover or Exeter or Groton, where tuition, boarding, and additional expenses rise to more than $30,000. Often a family has two teenage children in these schools at the same time; so they may be spending over $60,000 on their children's education every year. Yet here I am one night, a guest within their home, and dinner has been served and we are having coffee now; and this entirely likable, and generally sensible, and beautifully refined and thoughtful person looks me in the eyes and asks me whether you can really buy your way to better education for the children of the poor.

Civility, of course, controls these situations. One rarely gets to give the answer one would like to give in social settings of this kind. And sometimes, too, the people who have asked these questions make it apparent, in an almost saddened afterthought, that they are not appeased entirely by the doubts they've raised, because before the evening's over and once every other argument is made and the discussion at long last begins to wind down to its end, a concessionary comment seems to find its way into the conversation. "Well, that's how it is. . . . Life isn't fair. . . . We do the best we can, in other ways. . . ." Sometimes, then, a charitable activity is named. "Our daughter's private school insists that every student do a service project for one year. . . ." "They tutor children at an elementary school in one of the disadvantaged neighborhoods . . . ," or something else that's decent, philanthropic, and sincere like that, which smoothes the edges of the evening.

References to service programs, mentoring and tutoring and such, provide at least a hint of what fair-minded people often wish that they could do on a more comprehensive basis if the means for doing it did not seem so politically complex or threaten to exact too high a toll on their immediate self-interest. Most honest grown-ups, after all, do not really get a lot of solace out of saying that "life isn't fair," especially if they can see the ways they benefit from the unfairness they deplore. Most also understand that a considerably higher level of taxation for our public schools, if equitably allocated on the basis of real need, would make it possible for far more children from poor neighborhoods to enter the admissions pool for the distinguished colleges and universities their own children attend. Some of their children might encounter stiffer competition. Children like Pineapple and Alliyah might get in instead.

There are others, however, who appear to suffer no uneasiness at all about these contradictions and appear to be convinced—at least, it *sounds* as if they are—that money well-invested in the education of the children of their social class makes perfect sense while spending on the same scale for the children of the very poor achieves, at best, only some marginal results, or maybe none at all. "An equal society," President George W. Bush told the National Urban League in August of 2001, would begin with "equally excellent schools." Simply increasing federal assistance to the public schools, however, had not been effective, he told his audience. It was, he said, like "pumping gas into a flooded engine," by which he seemed to mean that inner-city "engines" (schools) had too much gas (too many dollars) flooding them already.

It was an odd metaphor, I thought. It would have been fair to ask the president how schools like Phillips Academy in Exeter or Andover, the latter of which he had himself attended, were able to absorb some $30,000 yearly for each pupil without "flooding" their own engines. Did they have perhaps a bigger engine to begin with? Did the beautifully developed infrastructure of these schools permit them to deploy large sums of money more effectively than did the schools with rotting window frames and no school libraries? "I'll believe money doesn't count the day the rich stop spending so much on their own children," says former New York City principal Deborah Meier, who subsequently became the principal of an elementary school in Boston; but Mrs. Meier's commonsense reaction is resisted widely among those who are in power now in Washington.

It is sometimes claimed by those who share the president's beliefs that it is possible to point to certain urban districts in which annual per-pupil spending now approximates the levels found in some adjacent middle-class communities but that the children in these districts still do not perform at nearly the same levels as the children in these neighboring communities. Highly selective examples commonly are used to press this point; and the subsequent argument is made that these examples demonstrate "the limited effects" of higher levels of investment in the education of low-income children.

There are several reasons why I've never found this a convincing argument. First, it tends to obviate almost all recognition of the consequences of the previous decades of low funding in these districts: the cumulative deficits in school construction and in infrastructure maintenance, for instance. It also ignores the deficits in preschool education and the effects of prior years of mediocre schooling on the educational levels of the parents of the children in these neighborhoods. Nor does it even contemplate the multiple effects of concentrated poverty and racial isolation in themselves.

Equitable funding levels under these conditions would not merely approximate the spending levels found in wealthier communities; they would far exceed them. And the benefits to be derived from equitable funding could not properly be measured on a short-term basis, since it would take many years before the consequences of so many prior years of organized shortchanging of the children, and their parents and grandparents, in a segregated district could be plausibly reversed. The examples of high-spending urban districts used to press the case against increasing our investment in poor children are, in any case, atypical. Nationwide, as we will document in detail in a later chapter, the differential in per-pupil spending between districts with the highest numbers of minority children and those with the fewest children of minorities amounts to more than $25,000 for a typical class in elementary school. In Illinois, the differential grows to $47,000, in New York to more than $50,000. From any point of elemental fairness, inequalities like these are unacceptable.

Those who search for signs of optimism often make the point that there are children who do not allow themselves to be demoralized by the conditions we have seen but do their work and keep their spirits high and often get good grades and seem, at least, to have a better chance than many of their peers to graduate from high school and go on to college—and, in any case, whether they do or not, refuse to let themselves be broken or embittered by the circumstances they may face.

I have portrayed a number of such powerfully resilient children in my recent book about the South Bronx, Ordinary Resurrections, and in an earlier book titled Amazing Grace. Other writers have portrayed such children elsewhere. There are also academic studies that examine qualities of character in inner-city children who transcend the difficult conditions of their lives, stumble at times, face disappointment and discouragement, but nonetheless persist against the odds and ultimately manage to prevail.

Studies like these may give us valuable lessons about differences in individuals who can, or cannot, overcome adversities. Since all of us must face adversities, they are instructive to us also; and, besides, these studies generally highlight fascinating children who display the kinds of qualities that almost any grown-up would admire. But this—the luminosity of one, the moral toughness of another, the sheer high-jumping brilliance of a third, the kindly impulse sometimes of an affluent person from outside of their community to reward exceptionalities like these—ought not to afford us too much easy consolation for the structural inequities that make these victories so rare. We do not ask most children in America to summon up heroic qualities like these in order to prevail. They prevail and learn their lessons and, more frequently than not, enjoy the years they spend in public school, and usually have at least a reasonable chance of going on to college if they like, not because they represent miraculous exceptions to the norm among their peers, but as a matter of the ordinary expectations that are held for children in a middle-class or upper-middle-class community.

These expectations are not simply those, moreover,

that can be attributed to the ambitions and the value systems of the parents of these children but are rooted in demonstrable advantages in what their schools provide to them: experienced instructors, reasonably small classes, well-appointed libraries, plenty of computers with sophisticated software, at the secondary level often college-level history and literature and science programs, and extensive counseling facilities, as well as the aesthetic benefits of cheerful buildings and nice places to have lunch and, in a lot of secondary schools, lovely quadrangles and courtyards where the adolescents can relax and work with one another in small groups and, especially important for the younger children, green expansive spaces to go out and play at recess so that they return to class invigorated and refreshed.

This nation can afford to give clean places and green spaces and, as one of Alliyah's classmates put it, "fun places to play" to virtually every child in our public schools. That we refuse to do so, and continue to insist that our refusal can be justified by explanations such as insufficiency of funds and periodic "fiscal crises" and the like, depends upon a claim to penury to which a nation with our economic superfluity is not entitled. If we were forced to see these kids before our eyes each day, in all the fullness of their complicated and diverse and tenderly emerging personalities, as well as in their juvenile fragility, it would be harder to maintain this myth. Keeping them at a distance makes it easier.

CHAPTER 3

The Ordering Regime

As racial isolation deepens and the inequalities of education finance remain unabated and take on new and more innovative forms, the principals of many inner-city schools are making choices that few principals in schools that serve suburban children ever need to contemplate. Unable to foresee a time when black and Hispanic students in large numbers will not go to segregated public schools and seeing little likelihood that schools like these will ever have the infrastructure and resources of successful white suburban schools, many have been dedicating vast amounts of time and effort to create an architecture of adaptive strategies that promise incremental gains within the limits inequality allows.

New vocabularies of stentorian determination, new systems of incentive and new modes of castigation, which are termed "rewards and sanctions," have emerged. Curriculum materials that are alleged to be aligned with governmentally established goals and standards and particularly suited to what are regarded as "the special needs and learning styles" of low-income urban children have been introduced. Relentless emphasis on raising test scores, rigid policies of nonpromotion and nongraduation, a new empiricism and the imposition of unusually detailed lists of named and numbered "outcomes" for each isolated parcel of instruction, an oftentimes fanatical insistence upon uniformity of teachers in their management of time, an openly conceded emulation of the rigorous approaches of the military, and a frequent use of terminology that comes out of the world of industry and commerce—these are just a few of the familiar aspects of these new adaptive strategies.

Although generically described as "school reform," most of these practices and policies are targeted primarily at poor children of color; and although most educators speak of these agendas in broad language that sounds applicable to all, it is understood that they are valued chiefly as responses to perceived catastrophe in deeply segregated and unequal schools.

"If you do what I tell you to do, how I tell you to do it, when I tell you to do it, you'll get it right," says a South Bronx principal observed by a reporter from The New York Times in laying out a memorizing rule for math to an assembly of her students. "If you don't, you'll get it wrong."

This is the voice, this is the tone, this is the rhythm and didactic certitude one hears today in inner-city schools that have embraced a pedagogy of direct command and absolute control. "Taking their inspiration from the ideas of B. F. Skinner . . . ," says The Times, proponents of scripted rote-and-drill curricula articulate their aim as the establishment of "faultless communication" between "the teacher, who is the stimulus," and "the students, who respond."

The introduction of Skinnerian approaches, which

are commonly employed in penal institutions and drug-rehabilitation programs, as a way of altering the attitudes and learning styles of black and Hispanic children is provocative, and it has stirred some outcries from respected scholars. To actually go into a school in which you know some of the children very, very well and see the way that these approaches can affect their daily lives and thinking processes is even more provocative.

On a chilly November day four years ago in the South Bronx, I entered P.S. 65, the elementary school in which I met Pineapple for the first time when she was in kindergarten. Her younger sister Briana was now a student here, as were some 25 or 30 other children I had known for several years; but I hadn't visited the building since Pineapple graduated, and there had been major changes since that year.

Silent lunches had been instituted in the cafeteria and, on days when children misbehaved, silent recess had been introduced as well. On those days, the students were obliged to stay indoors and sit in rows and maintain silence on the floor of a small room that had been designated "the gymnasium." The school still had a high turnover of its teachers (Briana's classroom was in chaos on the day that I was there because her teacher had just walked out of the building without warning and it would be several weeks before another teacher could be found), but the corridors were quiet and I saw no children outside of their classrooms.

The words "Success For All," which was the brand name of a scripted program used within the school, were prominently posted at the top of the main stairway and, as I would later find, in almost every room. Also displayed throughout the building were a number of administrative memos that were worded with unusual directive absoluteness. "Authentic Writing," said a document called "Principles of Learning" that was posted in the corridor close to the office of the principal, "is driven by curriculum and instruction." I didn't know what this expression meant and later came back to examine it again before I left the school.

I entered the fourth grade of Mr. Endicott, a man in his mid-thirties who had arrived here without training as a teacher, one of about 15 teachers in the building who were sent into this school after a single summer of short-order preparation. As I found a place to sit in a far corner of the room, the teacher and his young assistant, who was in her first year as a teacher—Mr. Endicott was in his second year—were beginning a math lesson about building airport runways. "When we count the edges around the runway," said a worksheet that was on the children's desks, "we find the perimeter. When we count the number of squares in a runway, we find the area. . . . Today we are going to conduct an inventory of all the different perimeters. . . ."

On the wall behind the teacher, written in large letters: "Portfolio Protocols: 1. You are responsible for the selection of [your] work that enters your portfolio. 2. As your skills become more sophisticated this year, you will want to revise, amend, supplement, and possibly replace items in your portfolio to reflect your intellectual growth." To the left side of the room: "Performance Standards Mathematics Curriculum: M-5 Problem Solving and Reasoning. M-6 Mathematical Skills and Tools. . . ."

My attention was distracted by some whispering among the children sitting to the right of me. The teacher's response to this distraction was immediate: His arm shot out and up in a diagonal in front of him, his hand straight up, his fingers flat. The young co-teacher did this too. When they saw their teachers do this, all the children in the classroom did it too.

"Zero noise," the teacher said, but this instruction proved to be unneeded. The strange salute the class and teachers gave each other, which turned out to be one of a number of such silent signals teachers in the school were trained to use, and children to obey, had done the job of silencing the class.

"Active listening!" said Mr. Endicott. "Heads up! Tractor beams!"—the latter meaning, "Every eye on me."

On the front wall of the classroom in handwritten words that must have taken Mr. Endicott long hours to transcribe: a list of terms that could be used to praise or criticize a student's work in mathematics. At Level Four, the highest of four levels of success, a child's "problem-solving strategies" could be described, according to this list, as "systematic, complete, efficient, and possibly elegant," while the student's capability to draw conclusions from the work she had completed could be termed "insightful . . . , comprehensive." At Level Two, the child's capability to draw conclusions was to be described as "logically unsound"—at Level One, "not present." Approximately 50 separate categories of proficiency, or lack of such, were detailed in this wall-sized tabulation.

An assistant to the principal remained with me throughout the class and then accompanied me wherever else I went within the school. Having an official shadow me so closely is a bit unusual in visits that I make to public schools. Principals who feel relaxed and confident about their teachers typically invite me to sit in on classes without constant supervision and to visit classes that have not been pre-selected. Also unusual, I realized later, was that Mr. Endicott, whom I had met before, did not say hello to me until nearly the final moments of the class and didn't actually acknowledge I was there except by stopping by my desk and handing me the worksheet on perimeters.

A well-educated man, he later spoke to me about the form of classroom management that he was using as an adaptation from a model of industrial efficiency—"it's a kind of 'Taylorism' in the classroom," he explained, referring to a set of theories about management of factory employees introduced by Frederick Taylor in the early 1900s. "Primitive utilitarianism" is another term he used in trying to describe the ethos that appeared to underlie these management techniques. His reservations were, however, not apparent in the classroom. Within the terms of what he had been asked to do, he had, indeed, become a master of control. It is one of the few classrooms I had visited up to that time in which almost nothing even hinting at spontaneous emotion in the children or the teacher surfaced in the time that I was there.

I had visited classes that resembled this in Cuba more than 20 years before; but in the Cuban schools the students were allowed to question me, and did so with much charm and curiosity, and teachers broke the pace of lesson plans from time to time to comment on a child's question or to interject a casual remark that might have been provoked by something funny that erupted from a boy or girl who was reacting to my presence in the class. What I saw in Cuban schools was certainly indoctrinational in its intent but could not rival Mr. Endicott's approach in its totalitarian effectiveness.

The teacher gave the "zero noise" salute again when someone whispered to another child at his table. "In two minutes you will have a chance to talk and share this with your partner." Communication between children in the class was not prohibited but was afforded time-slots and was formalized in an expression that I found included in a memo that was posted near the door: "An opportunity . . . to engage in Accountable Talk."

Even the teacher's words of praise were framed in terms consistent with the lists that had been posted on the wall. "That's a Level Four suggestion," said the teacher when a child made an observation other teachers might have praised as simply "pretty good" or "interesting" or "mature."

There was, it seemed, a formal name for every cognitive event within this school: "Authentic Writing," "Active Listening," "Accountable Talk." The ardor to assign all items of instruction or behavior a specific name was starting to unsettle me. It's understandable that teachers need to do this in their lesson plans and that terms like these are often used in teacher education and in programs of professional development; but in this class, in part because of all the postings of these items on the walls, it seemed the children too were being asked to view their own experience, even the act of sharing an idea, as namable as well.

The adjectives had another odd effect, which was a kind of hyping-up of every item of endeavor. "Authentic Writing" was, it seemed, a more important act than what the children in a writing class in any ordinary school might try to do. "Accountable Talk" was something more self-conscious and significant than merely useful conversation.

These naming exercises and the imposition of an all-inclusive system of control on every form of intellectual activity consumed a vast amount of teaching time but seemed to be intrinsic to the ethos here: a way of ordering cognition beyond any effort of this sort I'd seen in the United States before. The teacher, moreover, did not merely name and govern every intellectual event with practiced specificity; he also issued his directions slowly, pacing words with a meticulous delivery that brought to my mind the way the staff attendants spoke to the Alzheimer's patients at my father's nursing home.

As I sat there, somewhat mesmerized by Mr. Endicott's articulation of his phrasing and his strict reliance on official words, the naming rituals began to strike me as increasingly bizarre. Even the act of telling a brief story, for example, had been given a new name: To write a story, according to a "standards" listing posted on the wall ("English Language Arts Number E-2," subtopic "D"), was to "produce a narrative procedure." The object-noun, although it did not fit the verb, appeared to lend a semi-scientific aura to the utterly pedestrian—"narrative procedure," unlike "story," seeming to suggest something empirical and technical. The verb ("produce") meanwhile seemed to escort the act of writing out of any realm of the aesthetic into an industrial arena. "Production" is inherently a different matter than tale-telling.

I remember, too, another aspect of my visit that distinguished this from almost any other class I'd visited up to this time: Except for one brief giggle of a child sitting close to me which was effectively suppressed by Mr. Endicott, nothing even faintly frivolous took place while I was there. No one laughed. No child made a funny face to somebody beside her. Neither Mr. Endicott nor his assistant laughed, as best I can recall. This is certainly unusual within a class of eight-year-olds. In most classrooms, even those in which a high degree of discipline may be maintained, there are almost always certain moments when the natural hilarity of children temporarily erupts to clear the air of "purpose" and relieve the monotone of the instructor. Even the teachers, strict as they may try to be, cannot usually resist a smile or a bit of playful humor in return.

Nothing like that happened in the time that I was in this class. When I'm taking notes during a visit to a school and children in a class divert themselves with tiny episodes of silliness, or brief epiphanies of tenderness to one another, or a whispered observation about something that they find amusing, like a goofy face made by another child in the class, I put a little round face with a smile on the margin of my notepad so that I won't miss it later on. In all the 15 pages that I wrote during my visit in this classroom in the Bronx, there is not a single small round smile.

When I was later looking at my notes, I also noticed that I couldn't find a single statement made by any child that had not been prompted by the teacher's questions, other than one child's timid question about which "objective" should be written on the first line of a page they had been asked to write. I found some notes on children moving from their tables to their "centers" and on various hand-gestures they would make as a response to the hand-gestures of their teachers; but I found no references to any child's traits of personality or even physical appearance. Differences between the children somehow ceased to matter much during the time that I observed the class. The uniform activities and teacher's words controlled my own experience perhaps as much as they controlled and muted the expressiveness of children.

Before I left the school, I studied again the definition of "Authentic Writing" that was posted in the corridor. Whatever it was, according to the poster, it was "driven by curriculum. . . ." That was it, and nothing more. Its meaning or its value was established only by cross-reference to another schoolbound term to which it had been attached by "drive" in passive form. Authenticity was what somebody outside of this building, more authoritative than the children or their teachers, said that it shall be.

Teachers working in a school like this have little chance to draw upon their own inventiveness or normal conversational abilities. In the reading curriculum in use within the school, for instance, teachers told me they had been forewarned to steer away from verbal deviations or impromptu bits of conversation, since each passage of instruction needed to be timed (Mr. Endicott had a wind-up timer in his room) and any digression from the printed plans could cause them problems if a school official or curriculum director happened to be in the building at the time. Supervisors from the organization that designed and marketed the scripted reading program came into the classroom also to police the way that it was being used—"police" being the word the teachers used in speaking of these periodic visitations.

The pressure this imposes upon teachers to stick closely to the script leaves many with uncomfortable feelings of theatricality. Teachers tell me that they feel they're reading "lines" from a commercial playbook written by an unnamed author with a gift for keeping to a continuity of theme, and attempting now and then to pump vitality into the lines by artifacting their enthusiasm.

Sometimes it seems to do the job of moving children through their lessons almost automatically, and when it does the teacher may be praised for what I've heard described as "managerial proficiency," but it's a curious proficiency, contrived and glazed, as even school officials who enforce these policies will frequently concede. Emphasis, reiteration, and assertiveness in pushing what is only half-believed, or not believed at all, too often take the place of sending out authentic signals of conviction that a child listens for. Thus, "authenticity," no matter how much it's promoted to the children by the posters in the halls, is pretty much denied to those who teach them.

All teaching is theatrical to some degree. Almost all teachers have the obligation at some point or other to present materials or lessons that don't terribly excite them and they learn to simulate enthusiasms they don't always feel; but in a relatively normal teaching situation these are improvised theatrics and the teachers are allowed to come up with their own inventive ways of capturing the interest of their students. And there are also many portions of the day in which the teacher teaches something that she actually selects, and truly cares about, in which case there need be no theatricality at all. The difference in too many schools like P.S. 65 is that nearly the entire schoolday comes to be a matter of unnatural theatrics that cannot be improvised to any real degree without the risk of teachers being criticized by their superiors.

When I later met and talked at length with Mr. Endicott and other teachers at his school, they spoke about this feeling of enforced theatricality, but they reminded me of the high state of vigilance they must maintain in order not to be spied out in deviation from the schoolwide norms. Anxiety-ridden days were common among teachers at the school, they said ("the school, admittedly, is not a mellow place," said Mr. Endicott), and children, not surprisingly, picked up some of the same anxiety as well.

Anxiety, for the children, was intensified, according to a fifth grade teacher, by the ever-present danger of humiliation when their reading levels or their scores on state examinations were announced. "There must be penalties for failure," as the architects and advocates of programs such as these increasingly demand, and penalties for children in this instance were dispensed not only individually and privately but also in the view of others, for example in a full assembly of the school.

"Level Fours, please raise your hands," the principal requested at one such assembly. In front of nearly all their schoolmates, those very few who were described as "Level Fours" lifted their arms and were accorded dutiful applause. "Level Threes, please raise your hands . . . ," the principal went on, and they too were rewarded with applause. "Level Twos . . . ," she asked, and they were given some applause as well. What lesser portion of applause, one had to wonder, would be given to the Level Ones, who were the children reading at rockbottom? The Level Ones, as it turned out, got no applause at all. "The principal didn't ask the Level Ones to raise their hands," according to the teacher who described this series of events to me. "It was like the Level Ones weren't even there."

Most grown-ups can remember moments in their years of schooling when a principal might draw attention to the children in a class who had received good grades and, for example, at a school assembly or a meeting of the PTA, might name the children in each grade who made the honor roll because they got straight A's, or A's and B's, which was the cut-off point for honor roll when I was a student. Few principals, however, would have shamed the children who had managed to come up with only C's and D's—nor, in my memory at least, did principals address us by our letter-grades or numbers, as if these defined not only how well we had done but also who we were. You "got" a B. You "got" a D. But you did not *become* that B or D. Calling the children "Level Fours" or "Level Ones" is something rather new, and children who are labeled in this manner soon begin to use these labels to refer to one another or themselves.

"Reginald is a Level One," Pineapple's sister said, a little scornfully, I thought, when she was telling me about the children in her room that year. "Melissa and Shaneek are Level Threes."

"How are you doing this time?" I inquired.

She wrinkled her nose and looked at me unhappily. "I'm just a Level Two."

Since that day at P.S. 65, I have visited nine other schools in six different cities where the same Skinnerian curriculum is used. The signs on the walls, the silent signals, the curious salute, the same insistent naming of all cognitive particulars, became familiar as I went from one school to the next.

"Meaningful Sentences," began one of the listings of proficiencies expected of the children in the fourth grade of an elementary school in Hartford (90 percent black, 10 percent Hispanic) which I visited a short time later. "Noteworthy Questions," "Active Listening," and other designations like these had been posted elsewhere in the room. Here too, the teacher gave the kids her outstretched arm, with hand held up, to reestablish order when they grew a little noisy, but I noticed that she tried to soften the effect of this by opening her fingers and bending her elbow slightly so it did not look quite as forbidding as the gesture Mr. Endicott had used.

Over her desk, I read a "Mission Statement," which established the priorities and values for the school. Among the missions of the school, according to the printed statement, which was posted also in some other classrooms of the school, was "to develop productive citizens" who have the skills that will be needed "for successful global competition," a message which was reinforced by other posters in the room. Over the heads of a group of children at their desks: a sign anointing them "Best Workers of 2002."

Another signal now was given by the teacher, this one not for silence but in order to achieve some other form of class behavior, which I could not quite identify. The students gave exactly the same signal in response. Suddenly, with a seeming surge of restlessness and irritation—with herself, as it appeared, and with her own effective use of all the tricks that she had learned—she turned to me and, in a burst of furtive anger, she said, "I can do this with my dog. . . ."

I had had a thought like that at P.S. 65 in watching Mr. Endicott. He, however, temporarily at least, seemed to take pride in how well he could do it, while this teacher seemed to feel almost alarmed. She also spoke with sharp discernment of the race-specific emphasis of the curriculum. "If we were not a segregated school," she said, "if there were middle-class white children here, the parents would rebel at this curriculum and they would stop it cold—like that!"

There was no single wall-sized chart of stipulated ways

to praise or criticize a child in this Hartford classroom, nothing like the list that Mr. Endicott had copied on his wall, although there were many smaller lists and charts of subdivided competencies worded in official phrases and identified by numbers on the walls of this and other classes in the building. Teachers who are forced to spend so many hours in compiling these lists and charts and matching mini-skills with numbers for each lesson that they teach have told me that they sometimes feel reduced, as one Massachusetts teacher worded it, to "servile tabulation." They also note that as a consequence of the continuous cross-referencing between the learnings of the children and the state-mandated skills and numbers that are posted on the walls, there is little sense that anything a child learns has an inherent value of its own. Its value is established only if it is connected to a grievously extended skein of namable "objectives" that have been determined outside of the school and are aligned with items that will show up later on a standardized exam.

The teacher cannot simply say, "I read an early lyrical poem of William Butler Yeats with my third graders and discovered that they loved it." Instead, she must position what she did within a recognized compartment: "I used a poem of William Butler Yeats in order to deliver Elementary Standard 37-A," or something of that sort, which she must then identify by naming the intended outcome for the reading of the poem, which might be something as specific as "the recognition of analogies" or, depending on grade level, "understanding meter in an unrhymed poem."

The listing of objectives in a lesson plan is, of course, a normal practice among teachers in most public schools. If they did not do this, utter randomness and impulse would prevail. It isn't the practice in itself, it's the remorselessness with which the practice is applied to almost every little possibility for natural discovery, and pleasure in discovery, that many teachers in these schools make clear that they dislike. By giving every particle of learning an official name, we strip it of uniqueness. By forcing it to fit into the right compartment of significance or meaning, we control its power to establish its own meanings or to stir the children to pursue a small exhilaration in directions that may lead them to a place the experts haven't yet had time to name. Fascination and delight, no matter what lip-service we may pay to them, become irrelevant distractions. Finding "where it goes" and what it "demonstrates" and how it can be "utilized" become the teacher's desolate obsessions.

Teachers who come into elementary education with some literary background tell me that they sometimes feel they are engaging in a complicated kind of treachery when they are forced repeatedly to excavate a piece of poetry or any other literary work of charm or value to extract examples of official skills that have some testable utility. Most administrators even in these highly regimented schools pay tribute on occasion to the worth of art, or of aesthetics, for their own sake; but this notion does not hold up well within a setting in which even Eeyore's sorrowful pronouncements or the soft perplexities of Pooh have to be treated as a kind of "quarry" from which named and numbered competencies have to be hacked out and held up to the bright light of curricular illumination. There is an awful gravitation to the commonplace in this.

Teachers also tell me that these numbering and naming rituals are forcing them to sacrifice a huge proportion of their time to what are basically promotional, not educational, activities. Hours that might otherwise have been devoted to instruction are consumed in restless efforts to position little chunks of subdivided knowledge in acceptable containers; and the ritual continues often after children are dismissed and teachers are obliged to stay at school until late afternoon in order to compile inventories of the outcomes they have named and, once a year at least, participate in meetings at which every separate inventory must be reconciled and unified into a single statement of collective purpose.

Some of these activities take place in suburban schools as well, but their relentlessness is greatly magnified in inner-city schools that are, for instance, under state review because of disappointing scores. In such schools, enormous documents known as "Improvement Plans" that stipulate specific gains a school must make in a specific period of years, which bring to mind those famous five-year plans for steel production in the Soviet era, and sometimes even longer documents that specify a school's "strategic answers" to these plans, create a massive paper-clutter that takes on a kind of parallel reality that has only an indistinct connection with the actual experience of teaching. The amount of time that this consumes is all the more frustrating when one realizes that most of this is being done under the business-driven banner of "efficient management of time." Nothing could be less efficient than this misappropriation of a teacher's energy and hours.

"There's something crystal clear about a number," says a top adviser to the U.S. Senate committee that has jurisdiction over public education; and this point of view is reinforced in statements coming from the office of the U.S. Education Secretary and the White House. "I want to change the face of reading instruction across the United States from an art to a science," said a top assistant to Rod Paige, the former education secretary, in the winter of 2002. But the longing to turn art to science doesn't stop with reading methodologies alone. In many schools, it now extends to almost every aspect of the operation of the school and of the lives that children lead within it. In some schools, even such ordinary acts of children as their filing to lunch or recess in the hallways or the stairwells are subjected to the same determined emphasis upon empirical precision.

"Rubric for Filing" is the printed heading of a lengthy list of numbered categories by which teachers are supposed to grade their students on the way they march along the corridors in another urban district I have visited. Someone, in this instance, did a lot of work to fit the filing proficiencies of children into no more and no less than 32 specific slots:

"Line leader confidently leads the class. . . . Line is straight. . . . Spacing is tight. . . . The class is stepping together. . . . Everyone shows pride, their shoulders high . . . , no slumping," according to the strict criteria for filing at Level Four.

"Line is straight, but one or two people [are] not quite in line," according to the box for Level Three. "Line leader leads the class," but not "with confidence" this time, and "almost everyone shows pride. . . ."

"Several are slumping. . . . Little pride is showing," says the box for Level Two. "Spacing is uneven. . . . Some are talking and whispering."

"Line leader is paying no attention," says the box for Level One. "Heads are turning every way. . . . Hands are touching. . . . The line is not straight. . . . There is no pride."

The teacher who handed me this document believed at first that it was written as a joke by someone who had simply come to be fed up with all the numbers and accounting rituals that occupy much of the day in many over-regulated schools. It turned out that it was no joke but had been printed in a handbook of instructions for the teachers in the city where she taught.

In some districts, even the most pleasant and old-fashioned class activities of elementary schools have now been overtaken by these ordering requirements. A student-teacher at an urban school in California, for example, wanted to bring a pumpkin to her class on Halloween but knew it had no ascertainable connection to the California standards. She therefore had developed what she called "the MultiModal Pumpkin Unit" to teach science (seeds), arithmetic (the size and shape of pumpkins, I believe—this detail wasn't clear), and certain items she adapted out of language arts, in order to position "pumpkins" in a frame of state proficiencies. Even with her multimodal pumpkin, as her faculty adviser told me, she was still afraid she would be criticized because she knew the pumpkin would not really help her children to achieve expected goals on state exams.

Why, I asked a group of educators at a seminar in Sacramento, was a teacher being placed in a position where she'd need to do preposterous curricular gymnastics to enjoy a bit of seasonal amusement with her kids on Halloween? How much injury to state-determined "purpose" would it do to let a class of children have a pumpkin party once a year for no other reason than because it's something fun that other children get to do on autumn days in public schools across most of America?

"Forcing an absurdity on teachers does teach something," said an African-American professor. "It teaches acquiescence. It breaks down the will to thumb your nose at pointless protocols—to call absurdity 'absurd.' " Writing out the standards with the proper numbers on the chalkboard, even though these numbers have no possible meaning to the students, has a similar effect, he said; and doing this is "terribly important" to the principals in many of these schools. "You *have* to post the standards, and the way you know the children know the standards is by asking them to *state* the standards. And they *do* it—and you want to be quite certain that they do it if you want to keep on working at that school."

Then, on top of all the rest, there are the bulletin

boards one must put up not only in the classroom but throughout the school in order to be sure that state officials who come by from time to time to supervise instruction will see all their goals and standards properly displayed above whatever bits and pieces of a child's writing may be viewed as excellent enough to show to visitors.

These are nothing like the lovingly assembled posters of the work of children that most grown-ups who attended school in decades past are likely to recall. They differ in at least two ways: First, the principals in many of these schools refuse to let the less-than-perfect work of children who are struggling still to live up to the standards be displayed at all. If such less-than-perfect work should be selected for some reason, teachers are pressured to correct mistakes. If the teachers clean up the mistakes, according to a teacher who insists on anonymity in speaking to The New York Times, when officials walk by "with a clipboard" looking for the requisite "five elements of a good bulletin board," as the teacher puts it, "at least they won't take it down because of an eraser mark."

"The prevailing wisdom," says The Times, is that these inner-city schools with "long histories of failure and constant turnover of teachers" cannot afford to tolerate "misspellings or the other errors that in wealthier, more successful schools" might be perceived as "normal and even endearing." This is the same message I received from teachers at Pineapple's former school, in which "display and pretense," as one teacher put it, took priority above the substance of the work itself and where, she said, "the cover of the book" is more important than whatever is inside.

The teacher said her principal had told her that these corridor displays were worth the time that they consumed because the children "would take pride" to see their work displayed for visitors; but the teacher said she disagreed. "I don't think the kids take pride in these displays," she said, "when they can see some of their words have been erased" and been "rewritten in a teacher's hand."

I asked her, "Does that really happen?"

"Yes," she said, "it does." She told me that she, like the teacher that The Times had interviewed, had been assured that there were five—"exactly five"—criteria by which a bulletin board is to be judged. When she refused to doctor writings by her students, she was warned that there would be "a letter" in her file, a warning that another teacher at the school told me that he was given too. "I'm so torn up . . . ," she said. "I'm thinking about law school."

There is a second way in which these wall displays are different from the ones we still routinely find in most suburban schools as well as many urban schools that serve the children of the middle class. Almost any piece of writing by a child that is chosen to be posted on a classroom wall or in a hallway of the school tends to be lost beneath a large heraldic statement of the "standard" or "objective" it is meant to illustrate. I stood once for a long time in a third grade classroom in the Bronx examining a mobile that was hanging from a string above a child's desk, on which a state proficiency was named. It had something to do with English language arts, as I recall, and had a number listed also. Almost imperceptible on the same piece of cut-out paper were about 12 words in child's writing that described a leaf. There was a drawing of the leaf as well. The leaf and writing could have been displayed without the number and the designation that outshadowed them. But the obligation of the teacher to contain specifics in generics and position even tiny particles of children's artfulness within allegedly "productive" patterns, governs almost everything. No little leaf, it seems, will go without its number.

Children pick up these numbering and naming rituals, as we have seen—Pineapple's sister, for example, speaking of the other children in her class as "Level Ones" or "Level

Threes." The overinflated formal designations for their class activities seep into their vocabularies too. Official words supplant the use of natural or even logical expressions when the children try to tell you what they're doing at a given moment of the day, or why they're even doing it at all.

The words "Meaningful Sentences," for instance, have been posted on the walls in many of these schools. Wanting to know how children understand the implications of that big word ("meaningful"), I asked a group of fourth grade students once to tell me what it means. "It means you have to box the word you got in SFA"—Success For All—"and underline it in your sentence," said one child.

"You have to put a starred word in the sentence," said another.

"I understand that part," I told the children, but I said that I was still not clear on what this big word actually means.

The children I was talking to seemed flummoxed by the question and they looked at me, indeed, as if it wasn't a fair question and, instead of giving me an answer, they repeated what they'd said about "starred words" and "boxing."

I asked about another term, "Word Mastery," a more familiar classroom term that also had been posted on the wall.

"If you're told to memorize something and you memorize it right," a child who had been identified to me as one of the best students in the class replied, "you get 100—and that's Mastery. . . ."

When I said I still did not quite get the point of what this word itself was supposed to mean, a boy named Timothy explained it in this way: "Mastery means the number of words that you can master in five days," which was, I learned, the span of days that was assigned to each sub-unit of the scripted plan.

"But what does 'master' mean?" I asked the boy.

He looked at me as if I was way outside of the loop of what most educated people are supposed to know. "It means you get 100," he replied.

The circularity of his response, I later thought, made perfect sense within the context of a very tightly closed containment of ideas and reference points. The children gave me answers in the terms that they had learned in the curriculum. Stating meanings for these words in terms that would make sense *outside* of the curriculum—or, in the case of "meaningful," in any terms they understood at all—was not expected of them. I wrote in my notes: "These children seemed 'locked-in.' Whatever the rationale for all of this, it opens up no doors to understanding." Although the principals and teachers in these schools are constantly reminded to hold out high expectations for low-income children, I thought the expectations here were very low. I thought the intellects of children were debased when they were asked to parrot language that they did not understand and weren't invited to explore and figure out.

The argument is sometimes made that scripted lessons and the other elements of order and control that we have looked at in this chapter are essential strategies for schools in which the teachers frequently are inexperienced and where there is high turnover of faculty. If our urban districts cannot give these schools the continuity of staffing by experienced instructors found in schools that serve more middle-class communities, according to this reasoning, they can at least provide the artificial continuity afforded by a set of scripted lessons that leave little to the competence of teachers and can be delivered by a person who has never studied education and has no familiarity with the developmental needs of children.

The problem with this argument, however, is that

many of the teachers who have been recruited to these schools, while those who are most insecure may be relieved at first to be provided with what are described as "teacher-proof" materials, ultimately reject them intellectually, as did many of the teachers at Pineapple's school; or, if they accept them as a necessary recourse, as did Mr. Endicott, they do so nonetheless with deepest reservations and with torn allegiances, as Mr. Endicott made clear. "My main feeling, 98 percent of my reaction to this methodology," he told me flatly, "is that it's horrific for the teachers and boring for the children . . . , an intellectual straightjacket."

"I love my job because I love my students," said one of the younger teachers at the school, "but I also hate my job because I know I'm buying into something that I don't believe in." Few of these new instructors, as a consequence, remain within these schools for very long. (All of the beginning teachers whom I met at P.S. 65 during the time when Mr. Endicott was there, two of whom were graduates of Harvard, another of Cornell, have since departed from the school.) So a curriculum that was imposed, in part, to compensate for staffing needs of schools that had a hard time in recruiting teachers ends up by driving out precisely those well-educated men and women whom school systems have worked so hard to attract into these neighborhoods.

In a letter in which he spoke about the program in effect at P.S. 65, Mr. Endicott told me that he tended to be sympathetic to the school administrators, more at least than the other teachers I had talked with seemed to be. He said he believed his principal had little choice about the implementation of this program, which had been mandated for all elementary schools in New York City that had had rockbottom academic records over a long period of time. "This puts me into a dilemma," he went on, "because

I love the kids at P.S. 65." And even while, in some respects, he said, "I know that my teaching SFA is a charade . . . , if I don't do it I won't be permitted to teach these children."

Mr. Endicott, like all but two of the new recruits at P.S. 65, was a white person, as were the principal and most of the administrators at the school. Most of these neophyte instructors had, as a result, had little or no prior contact with the children of an inner-city neighborhood; but, like the others that I met, and despite the distancing between the children and their teachers that resulted from the scripted method of instruction, he had developed close attachments to his students and did not want to abandon them. At the same time, the class-and-race-specific implementation of this program obviously troubled him. "There's an expression now," he said. " 'The rich get richer, and the poor get SFA.' " He said he was "still trying to figure out my professional ethics" on the problem that this posed for him.

White children made up "only about one percent" of students in the New York City schools in which this system of indoctrinational instruction was imposed, according to The New York Times. "The prepackaged lessons" were intended "to ensure that all teachers—even novices or the most inept—" would be able to teach reading. As pragmatic and hardheaded as such arguments may seem to be, these are desperation strategies that reason out of the acceptance of inequity. If we did not have a segregated system in which more experienced instructors teach the children of the privileged and the least experienced are sent to teach the children of minorities, these practices would not be needed and could not be so convincingly defended. They are confections of apartheid and, no matter by what arguments of urgency or practicality they have been justified, they cannot fail to further deepen the divisions of society.

"It would be of great concern to me and most of the people I know," says Lucy Calkins, the distinguished literacy specialist at Teachers College in New York, "if we had an educational apartheid system with one method of instruction for poor kids and another for middle-class kids." But, to a very troubling degree in many urban areas today, the truth of the matter is that we already do. We will look at these divisions further in the next two chapters.

CHAPTER 4

Preparing Minds for Markets

Three years ago, in Columbus, Ohio, I was visiting a school in which the stimulus-response curriculum that Mr. Endicott was using in New York had been in place for several years. The scripted teaching method started very early in this school. ("Practice Active Listening!" a kindergarten teacher kept repeating to her children.) So too did a program of surprisingly explicit training of young children for the modern marketplace. Starting in kindergarten, children in the school were being asked to think about the jobs that they might choose when they grew up. The posters that surrounded them made clear which kinds of jobs they were expected to select.

"Do you want a manager's job?" the first line of a kindergarten poster asked.

"What job do you want?" a second question asked in an apparent effort to expand the range of choices that these five-year-olds might wish to make.

But the momentary window that this second question seemed to open into other possible careers was closed by the next question on the wall. "How will you do the manager's job?" the final question asked.

The tiny hint of choice afforded by the second question was eradicated by the third, which presupposed that all the kids had said yes to the first. No written question asked the children: "Do you want a lawyer's job? a nurse's job? a doctor's job? a poet's job? a preacher's job? an engineer's job? or an artist's job?" Sadly enough, the teacher had not even thought to ask if anybody in the class might someday like to be a teacher.

In another kindergarten class, there was a poster that displayed the names of several retail stores: JCPenney, Wal-Mart, Kmart, Sears, and a few others. "It's like working in a store," a classroom aide explained. "The children are learning to pretend that they're cashiers."

Work-related themes and managerial ideas were carried over into almost every classroom of the school. In a first grade class, for instance, children had been given classroom tasks for which they were responsible. The names of children and their tasks were posted on the wall, an ordinary thing to see in classrooms everywhere. But in this case there was a novel twist: All the jobs the kids were given were described as management positions!

There was a "Coat Room Manager" and a "Door Manager," a "Pencil Sharpener Manager" and a "Soap Manager," an "Eraser, Board and Marker Manager," and there was also a "Line Manager." What on earth, I was about to ask, is a "Line Manager"? My question was answered when a group of children filing in the hallway grew a bit unruly and a grown-up's voice barked out, "Who is your line manager?"

In the upper grades, the management positions became more sophisticated and demanding. In a fourth grade, for example, I was introduced to a "Time Manager" who was assigned to hold the timer to be sure the teacher didn't wander from her schedule and that everyone adhered to the prescribed number of minutes that had been assigned to every classroom task.

Turning a corner, I encountered a "HELP WANTED" sign. Several of these signs, I found, were posted on the walls at various locations in the school. These were not advertisements for school employees, but for children who would be selected to fill various positions as class managers. "Children in the higher grades are taught to file applications for a job," the principal explained—then "go for interviews," she said, before they can be hired. According to a summary of schoolwide practices she gave me, interviews "for management positions" were intended to teach values of "responsibility for . . . jobs."

In another fourth grade class, there was an "earnings chart" that had been taped to every child's desk, on which a number of important writing skills had been spelled out and, next to each, the corresponding earnings that a child would receive if written answers he or she provided in the course of classroom exercises such as mini-drills or book reports displayed the necessary skills.

"How Much Is My Written Answer Worth?" the children in the class were asked. There were, in all, four columns on the "earnings charts" and children had been taught the way to fill them in. There was also a Classroom Bank in which the children's earnings were accrued. A wall display beneath the heading of the Classroom Bank presented an enticing sample of real currency—one-dollar bills, five-dollar bills, ten-dollar bills—in order to make clear the nexus between cash rewards and writing proper sentences.

Ninety-eight percent of children in the school were living in poverty, according to the school's annual report card; about four fifths were African-American. The principal said that only about a quarter of the students had been given preschool education.

At another elementary school in the same district, in which 93 percent of children were black or Hispanic, the same "HELP WANTED" posters and the lists of management positions were displayed. Among the positions open to the children in this school, there was an "Absence Manager," a "Form-Collector Manager," a "Paper-Passing Manager," a "Paper-Collecting Manager," a "Paper-Returning Manager," an "Exit Ticket Manager," even a "Learning Manager," a "Reading Manager," a "Behavior Manager," and a "Score-Keeper Manager." Applications for all management positions, starting with the second graders, had to be "accompanied by references," according to the principal.

On a printed application form she handed me—"Consistency Management Manager Application" was its title—children were instructed to fill in their name, address, phone number, teacher, and grade level, and then indicate the job that they preferred ("First job choice. . . . Why do you want this job? Second job choice. . . . Why do you want this job?"), then sign and date their application. The awkwardly named document, the principal explained, originated in a program aimed at children of minorities that had been developed with financial backing from a businessman in Texas.

The silent signals I'd observed in the South Bronx and Hartford were in use in this school also. As I entered one class, the teacher gave his students the straight-arm salute, with fingers flat. The children responded quickly with the same salute. On one of the walls, there was a sign that read "A Million Dollars Worth of Self-Control." It was "a little incentive thing," the teacher told me when I asked about this later in the afternoon.

As I was chatting with the principal before I left, I asked her if there was a reason why those two words "management" and "manager" kept popping up throughout the school. I also summoned up my nerve to tell her that I was surprised to see "HELP WANTED" signs within an elementary school.

"We want every child to be working as a manager while he or she is in this school," the principal explained. "We want to make them understand that, in this country, companies will give you opportunities to work, to prove yourself, no matter what you've done."

I wasn't sure of what she meant by that—"no matter what you've done"—and asked her if she could explain this. "Even if you have a felony arrest," she said, "we want you to understand that you can be a manager someday."

I told her that I still did not quite understand why management positions were presented to the children as opposed to other jobs—being a postal worker, for example, or construction worker, or, for that matter, working in a field of purely intellectual endeavor—as a possible way to earn a living even if one once had been in trouble with the law. But the principal was interrupted at this point and since she had already been extremely patient with me, I did not believe I had the right to press her any further. So I left the school with far more questions in my mind than answers.

When I had been observing Mr. Endicott at P.S. 65, it had occurred to me that something truly radical about the way that inner-city children are perceived was presupposed by the peculiar way he spoke to students and the way they had been programmed to respond. I thought of this again here in these classes in Ohio. What *is* the radical perception of these kids that underlies such practices? How is this different from the way most educated friends of mine would look at their own children?

"Primitive utilitarianism"—"Taylorism in the classroom"—were two of the terms that Mr. Endicott had used in speaking of the teaching methods in effect within his school. "Commodification"—"of the separate pieces of the learning process, of the children in themselves"—is the expression that another teacher uses to describe these practices. Children, in this frame of reference, are regarded as investments, assets, or productive units—or else, failing that, as pint-sized human deficits who threaten our competitive capacities. The package of skills they learn, or do not learn, is called "the product" of the school. Sometimes the educated child is referred to as "the product" too.

These ways of viewing children, which were common at the start of the last century, have reemerged over the past two decades in the words of business leaders, influential educators, and political officials. "We must start thinking of students as workers . . . ," said a high official of one of the nation's teachers unions at a forum convened by Fortune magazine in 1988. I remember thinking when I read these words: Is this, really, what it all comes down to? Is future productivity, from this point on, to be the primary purpose of the education we provide our children? Is this to be the way in which we will decide if teachers are complying with their obligations to their students and society? What if a child should grow ill and die before she's old enough to make her contribution to the national economy? Will all the money that our government has spent to educate that child have to be regarded as a bad investment?

Admittedly, the economic needs of a society are bound to be reflected to some rational degree within the policies and purposes of public schools. But, even so, most of us are inclined to ask, there must be *something* more to life as it is lived by six-year-olds or ten-year-olds, or by teenagers for that matter, than concerns about "successful global competition." Childhood is not merely basic training for utilitarian adulthood. It should have some claims upon our mercy, not for its future value to the economic interests of competitive societies but for its present value as a perishable piece of life itself.

Listening to the stern demands we hear for inculcating worker ideologies in the mentalities of inner-city youth—and, as we are constantly exhorted now, for "getting tough" with those who don't comply—I am reminded of a passage from the work of Erik Erikson, who urged us to be wary of prescriptive absoluteness in the ways we treat and think about our children. "The most deadly of all possible sins" in the upbringing of a child, Erikson wrote, derive too frequently from what he called "destructive forms of conscientiousness." Erikson's good counsel notwithstanding, the momentum that has led to these utilitarian ideas about the education of low-income children has been building for a long, long time and, at least in public discourse as it is presented in the press and on TV, has not met with widespread opposition. Beginning in the early 1980s and continuing with little deviation right up to the present time, the notion of producing "products" who will then produce more wealth for the society has come to be embraced by many politicians and, increasingly, by principals of inner-city schools that have developed close affiliations with the representatives of private business corporations.

"Dismayed by the faulty products being turned out by Chicago's troubled public schools," The Wall Street Journal wrote in 1990, "some 60 of the city's giant corporations have taken over the production line themselves," a reference to the efforts that these corporations had invested in creation of a model school in a predominantly black neighborhood that was intended to embody corporate ideas of management and productivity. "I'm in the business of developing minds to meet a market demand," the principal of the school announced during a speech delivered at "a power breakfast" of the top executives of several of these corporations. "If you were manufacturing Buicks, you would have the same objectives," said a corporate official who was serving as the school's executive director.

Business jargon has since come to be a commonplace in the vocabularies used within the schools themselves. Children in the primary grades are being taught they must "negotiate" with one another for a book or toy or box of crayons or a pencil-sharpener—certainly not a normal word for five- or six-year-olds to use. In many schools, young children have been learning also to "sign contracts" to complete their lessons rather than just looking up and telling Miss O'Brien they will "try real hard" to do what she has asked.

Learning itself—the learning of a skill, or the enjoying of a book, and even having an idea—is now defined increasingly not as a process or preoccupation that holds satisfaction of its own but in proprietary terms, as if it were the acquisition of an object or stock-option or the purchase of a piece of land. "Taking ownership" is the accepted term, which now is used both by the kids themselves and also by their teachers. Most people like to think they "get" ideas, "understand" a process, or "take pleasure" in the act of digging into a good book. In the market-driven classroom, children are encouraged to believe they "own" the book, the concept, the idea. They don't *engage* with knowledge; they possess it.

In the Columbus schools, as we have seen, children are actively "incentivized" (this is another term one hears in many inner-city schools) by getting reimbursements for the acquisition of a skill in terms of simulated cash. At P.S. 65 in the South Bronx, I was shown another Classroom

Bank, out of which a currency called "Scholar Dollars" was disbursed. Some of these things may be dismissed as little more than modern reembodiments of ordinary rituals and phrases known to schoolchildren for decades. We all got gold stars in my elementary school if we brought in completed homework; many teachers give their students sticky decals with a picture of a frog or mouse or cat or dog, for instance, as rewards for finishing a book report or simply treating one another with politeness. Most Americans, I think, would smile at these innocent and pleasant ways of giving children small rewards. But would they smile quite so easily if their own children were provided earnings charts to calculate how much they will be paid for learning to write sentences?

Some of the usages that I have cited here ("ownership," "negotiate," for instance) have filtered into the vocabularies of suburban schools as well, but in most of these schools they are not introduced to children as the elements of acquisitional vocabulary and are more likely to be used, unconsciously perhaps, as borrowings from language that has come to be familiar in the world of pop psychology—"learning to 'take ownership' of one's emotions," for example. It is a different story when they are incorporated into a much broader package of pervasive corporate indoctrination.

Very few people who are not involved with inner-city schools have any idea of the extremes to which the mercantile distortion of the purposes and character of education have been taken or how unabashedly proponents of these practices are willing to defend them. The head of a Chicago school, for instance, who was criticized by some for emphasizing rote instruction which, his critics said, was turning children into "robots," found no reason to dispute the charge. "Did you ever stop to think that these robots will never burglarize your home?" he asked, and "will never snatch your pocket books. . . . These robots are going to be producing taxes. . . ."

Would any educator feel at ease in using terms like these in reference to the children of a town like Scarsdale or Manhasset, Glencoe or Winnetka, or the affluent suburban town of Newton, Massachusetts, in which I attended elementary school and later taught? I think we know this is unlikely. These ways of speaking about children and perceiving children are specific to the schools that serve minorities. Shorn of unattractive language about "robots" who will be producing taxes and not burglarizing homes, the general idea that schools in ghettoized communities must settle for a different set of goals than schools that serve the children of the middle class and upper middle class has been accepted widely. And much of the rhetoric of "rigor" and "high standards" that we hear so frequently, no matter how egalitarian in spirit it may sound to some, is fatally belied by practices that vulgarize the intellects of children and take from their education far too many of the opportunities for cultural and critical reflectiveness without which citizens become receptacles for other people's ideologies and ways of looking at the world but lack the independent spirits to create their own.

Perhaps the clearest evidence of what is taking place is seen in schools in which the linkage between education and employment is explicitly established in the names these schools are given and the work-related goals that they espouse. When badly failing schools are redesigned—or undergo "reconstitution," as the current language holds—a fashionable trend today is to assign them names related to the world of economics and careers. "Academy of Enterprise" or "Corporate Academy" are two such names adopted commonly in the renaming of a segregated school. Starting about ten years ago, a previously unfamiliar term emerged to specify the purposes these various academies espouse. "School-to-work" is the unflinching designation that has since been used to codify these goals, and "industry-embedded education" for the children of minorities has now become a term of art among practitioners.

Advocates for school-to-work do not, in general, describe it as a race-specific project but tend instead to emphasize the worth of linking academic programs to the world of work for children of all backgrounds and insisting that suburban children too should be prepared in school for marketplace demands, that children of all social classes ought to have "some work experience" in high school, for example. But the attempt at even-handedness in speaking of the ways that this idea might be applied has been misleading from the start. In most suburban schools, the school-to-work idea, if educators even speak of it at all, is little more than seemly decoration on the outer edges of a liberal curriculum. In many urban schools, by contrast, it has come to be the energizing instrument of almost every aspect of instruction.

Some business leaders argue that this emphasis is both realistic and humane in cases, for example, where a sixteen-year-old student lacks the skills or motivation to pursue a richly academic course of study or, indeed, can sometimes barely write a simple paragraph or handle elementary math. If the rationale for this were so defined in just so many words by the administrators of our schools, and if it were not introduced until the final years of secondary education at a point when other options for a student may appear to be foreclosed, an argument could certainly be made that school-to-work is a constructive adaptation to the situation many teenage students actually face.

But when this ethos takes control of secondary education almost from the start, or even earlier than that, before a child even enters middle school, as is the case in many districts now, it's something very different from an adaptation to the needs of students or the preferences they may express. It's not at all an "adaptation" in these cases; it's a prior legislation of diminished options for a class of children who are not perceived as having the potential of most other citizens. It's not "acceding" to their preferences. It's manufacturing those preferences and, all too frequently, it's doing this to the direct exclusion of those options other children rightly take as their entitlement.

There are middle schools in urban neighborhoods today where children are required, in effect, to choose careers before they even enter adolescence. Children make their applications to a middle school when they're in the fifth grade. Earlier in this writing, for example, I have spoken of Pineapple's older sister and her cousin, both of whom were students at a South Bronx middle school that bore Paul Robeson's name. "Robeson," however, as I subsequently learned, wasn't the complete name of this school. "The Paul Robeson School for Medical Careers and Health Professions" was the full and seemingly enticing designation that it bore; and, sadly enough, this designation and the way the school described itself in a brochure that had been given to the fifth grade students in the local elementary schools had led these girls into believing that enrolling there would lead to the fulfillment of a dream they shared: They wanted to be doctors.

"An understanding and embracement of medical science and health," said the brochure in a description of the school's curriculum, "is developed through powerful learning opportunities. . . . To be successful at the Paul Robeson School . . . , a student is expected to be highly motivated to broaden their horizons." Not many ten-year-olds in the South Bronx would likely know that this description represented an outrageous overstatement of the academic offerings this middle school provided. Unless they had an older sibling who had been a student there, most would have no way of knowing that the Robeson School, perennially ranking at the lowest level of the city's middle schools, sent very few students into high schools that successfully prepared a child for college and that any likelihood of moving from this school into a medical career, as these girls understood the term, was almost nonexistent.

"It's a medical school," another child, named Timeka, told me when I asked her why she had applied there. "I want to be a baby doctor," she explained, a goal that a number of the girls had settled on together, as children often do in elementary school. But the program at the Robeson School did not provide the kind of education that could lead her to that goal. A cynic, indeed, might easily suspect it was designed instead to turn out nursing aides and health assistants and the other relatively low-paid personnel within a hospital or nursing home, for instance, all of which might be regarded as good jobs for children with no other options, if they continued with their education long enough to graduate; but even this was not the usual pattern for a child who had spent three years at Robeson.

Timeka went from Robeson to another of those "industry-embedded" schools, a 97 percent black and Hispanic school called "Health Opportunities," in which only one in five ninth graders ever reached twelfth grade and from which Timeka dropped out in eleventh grade. I had known Timeka since she was a jubilant and energetic eight-year-old. I used to help her with her math and reading when she was in the fourth grade. She was smart and quick and good with words, and very good in math. If she had gone to school in almost any middle-class suburban district in this nation, she'd have had at least a chance of realizing her dream if she still wanted to when she completed high school. And if she changed her mind and settled on a different dream, or many different dreams, as adolescents usually do, she would have been exposed to an array of options that would have permitted her to make a well-informed decision. The choice of a career means virtually nothing if you do not know what choices you may actually have.

"In recent years, business has taken ownership of school-to-work . . . ," according to an advocate for these career academies. National and regional industry associations, he reports, are "linking students" to "standards-driven, work-based learning opportunities while they are in school" and then, he says, providing students with job offers from participating businesses. One such program has taken place for several years at a high school in Chicago where an emphasis on "Culinary Arts" has been embedded in curriculum. A teacher at the school, where 98 percent of students are black or Hispanic (many of Mexican descent), told me of a student she had grown attached to when she taught her in eleventh grade. The student, she said, showed academic promise—"I definitely thought that she was capable of going on to college"—so she recommended her to be admitted to a senior honors class.

It was a big school (2,200 students) and the teacher said she didn't see this girl again until the following September when she happened to run into her during a class break on an escalator in the building, and she asked her if she'd been admitted to the honors class. The student told her, "No," she said. "I couldn't figure out why." Then, she said, "I realized she'd been placed in Culinary Arts."

Students, she explained, were required "to decide on a 'career path' at the end of freshman year," and "once you do this, your entire program is determined by that choice."

Technically, she said, a student could select a college education as "career path," but this option, she reported, wasn't marketed to many of the students at the school as forcefully as were the job-related programs. The career programs in the upper-level grades, moreover, were blocked out "as a double period every day," the teacher said, which made it harder for the students in these programs who so wished to take an honors class or other academic classes that appealed to them.

The program in culinary arts, in which the students were prepared to work in restaurant kitchens, had been set up in coordination with Hyatt Hotels, which offered jobs or internships to students on completion of their education. The program was promoted to the students so effectively that many who initially may have had academic goals "appear to acquiesce in this"—"they will defend it, once they've made the choice," she said—even though some recognize that this will lead them to a relatively lower economic role in later years than if they somehow found the will to keep on and pursue a college education. "If you talk with them of college options at this point," and "if they trust you," said the teacher, "they will say, 'Nobody ever told me I could do it.' If you tell them, 'You *could* do it,' they will say, 'Why didn't someone tell me this before?' "

She told me she felt torn about expressing her concern that college education as a possible career path for such students was, in her words, either "not presented" or else "undersold," because she said there were outstanding teachers in the work-related programs and she did not want to speak of them with disrespect or compromise their jobs. At the same time, she clearly was upset about this since she spoke with deep emotion of the likelihood that "we may be trapping these young ones" in "low-paying jobs."

The teacher's story of her brief encounter with her former student reminded me of the disappointment I had felt about Timeka. The teacher seemed to blame herself to some degree, wishing, I guess, that she could have remained in closer touch with this bright student in the months since she had been a pupil in her class, perhaps believing that she might have intervened somehow on her behalf. The teacher didn't speak of a career in cooking in a restaurant, or work in a hotel, with any hint of condescension or disparagement. She was simply cognizant of other possibilities her student might have entertained; and she was saddened by this memory.

Some advocates for school-to-work, as we have seen, attempt to frame these job-related programs as essentially egalitarian in spirit, and some even go so far as to suggest that these proposals for refashioning an urban school around a corporate agenda somehow find their genesis in the ideals associated with iconic heroes of progressive education like Thoreau. There are, in fact, some school-to-work academies that do try to embody the progressive concept of combining practical experience with genuinely intellectual instruction. At the same time, it is impossible to overlook the fact that the most powerful advocacy for these programs has been coming not from educational progressives but from business leaders and political conservatives who have, in general, been silent, if not hostile, on the subjects of desegregation and equality of funding in our public schools and whose stated views are often redolent of social Darwinist ideas that cannot by the furthest stretches of imagination be regarded as egalitarian. Indeed, some of the most explicit arguments for school-to-work were made during the years of its inception by a writer named Charles Murray who went on to write a national bestseller called The Bell Curve in which theories of innate genetic differences in intellectual ability between the races were advanced.

"For many children," Murray wrote in 1993, schools provide "their only chance to learn how to be adults companies can train. . . ." In olden days, he said, "public schools prepared students for the workplace by teaching them to come to the same place every day," to "stay there for a prescribed number of hours," and to "follow the teacher's (boss's) instructions." Murray argued that we should restore these practices if children are to learn to be "productive workers." This, he emphasized, is "especially important" for children who grow up in what he termed "disorganized homes"—and "particularly . . . in urban areas." Meanwhile, he foresaw a more expansive kind of education for another group of children, "the thin layer of [the] gifted" who, "like it or not," he said, are those who "will determine whether we remain the world's preeminent nation" in the century ahead. Although he made no reference to the racial origins of those for whom it was especially important to be trained as workers, his reference to "disorganized homes" and "urban areas" inevitably brought to mind the characterization of black children that he has advanced in other writings.

It was an utterly unsentimental argument, unaccompanied by any softening allusions to progressive thinkers like Thoreau. What cannot fail to break one's heart is hearing overburdened school officials in so many of our hypersegregated districts giving voice at times to nearly the same sentiments. It is, when one thinks of it, a triumph of some sort for those who have forever looked with equanimity upon the practice of consigning children of poor people to subordinated economic roles in our society when principals who struggle to defend the interests of these children have been driven to the point at which they see no choice but to support the same utilitarian ideas.

When business and the world of commerce are permitted to invade the precincts of our public schools, not merely in the ancillary and familiar role of civic allies or occasional philanthropists but as participants in the determination of the aims of education and the content of instruction, they bring with them a body of beliefs and biases. Business leaders *tell* the urban school officials, sometimes in so many words, that what they need the schools to give them are "team players." Many of the brightest, most creative, independent-minded, and ambitious kids I know are not "team players" and don't *want* to be and, indeed, would lose the very essence of what makes them full, complex, and interesting people if they were. There will, I am afraid, be fewer fascinating mavericks, fewer penetrating questioners, and fewer powerful dissenters coming from our inner-city schools before too long if this agenda cannot be reversed. Team players may well be of great importance to the operation of a business corporation and they are obviously essential in the military services; but a healthy nation needs its future poets, prophets, ribald satirists, and maddening iconoclasts at least as much as it needs people who will file in a perfect line to an objective they are told they cannot question.

Corporate leaders, when they speak of education, sometimes pay lip-service to the notion of "good critical and analytic skills," but it is reasonable to ask whether they have in mind the critical analysis of *their* priorities. In principle, perhaps some do; but, if so, this is not a principle that seems to have been honored in the schools I have been visiting. In all the business-driven classrooms I have been observing in the past five years, plastered as they are with corporation brand names and with managerial vocabularies, I have yet to see the two words "labor unions." Is this an oversight? How is that possible? Teachers and principals themselves, who are almost always members of a union, seem to be so beaten down by this point that they rarely even question this omission.

It is not unusual these days to come into an urban school in which the principal no longer even calls herself "the principal" but chooses instead to be described as "building CEO" or "building manager." In some of the same schools teachers are described as "classroom managers." So when the children in these classrooms are selected to be "learning managers," "line managers," "score managers," "time managers," or such, there is a thematic continuity within the ranks from principals to kindergarten students. I have never been in a suburban district in which principals were asked to view themselves or teachers in this way. Like the want ads and the earnings charts, these terminologies remind us of how wide the distance has become between two very separate worlds of education.

In a quiet moment after we had visited in several of her classrooms, one of the Columbus principals surprised me when she stopped me in the hallway, placed her hand impulsively against my arm, and spoke with sudden wistfulness about the differences in teaching styles and objectives between schools like hers and those that serve more middle-class communities. Making a brief sarcastic reference to the prominent display of acronymic slogans that surrounded us, she said, "I envy principals in schools where children are encouraged to think independently." She started to speak of "problem-posing," "critical thinking as a necessary part of education. . . ." Then the sentence trailed away, as if the rest of this—her hankering for something that she obviously cared about but did not believe she could allow her teachers to indulge on any routine basis—was self-evident and needed no real explanation.

Other principals have said things like this to me, tentatively, not generally in school, more often in an evening's conversation. It is as if they're looking back at an ideal of education that they valued deeply when they started out in their careers, and value still, but feel they have to set aside in order to respond to the realities before them in the neighborhoods they serve and to deliver those empirical results that are demanded of them. These things are said almost nostalgically.

CHAPTER 5

The Road to Rome

If the education of some children, but not others, is to be regarded henceforth as primarily a matter of commercial training or industrial production and the products of this process are the children with the value that is added to them by the skills that they acquire every year in public school, then product-testing of these juvenile commodities appears to have a simple and unquestioned logic of its own. The specifications for the products are already posted there above their heads on classroom walls, in corridors, on classroom doors. It remains to measure the results.

The debates about standardized examinations have been raging in this nation now for several years. A number of respected educators who have made compelling arguments against the nature of these tests, as well as the effect that they have had on teaching practices, are cited in this chapter and at greater length in the end-pages of this work; their arguments apply to public schools in general, both privileged and poor. But inner-city children are the subject of this book; and my concern is with the special consequences high-stakes testing and the uses that are made of it have had on children whom I actually know. As damaging as the obsessive emphasis on testing often proves to be for kids in general, I believe that the effects are still more harmful in those schools in which the resources available to help the children learn the skills that will be measured by these tests are fewest, the scores they get are predictably the lowest, and the strategies resorted to by principals in order to escape the odium attaching to a disappointing set of numbers tend to be the most severe.

Even in good suburban schools where scores are generally high, I don't know many principals and teachers who believe that the repeated measuring of children's skills by standardized exams has had a positive effect upon the processes of education; I know many more who feel it has the opposite result. But, in the districts in which students as a matter of routine do relatively well, the tests do not entirely suffocate instruction or distort the temperaments and personalities of the instructors. Teachers in the elementary grades within these districts generally feel they can allow themselves the luxury of letting youngsters wander off from time to time into a subject that holds interest for them but has no direct, or even indirect, connection with the competencies to be measured by the state. It is a different story in too many inner-city schools where deviations from a charted road set off alarm bells for the supervisory officials and where teachers who are not eternally "on task"—one of a number of such stolidly directive terms imported from the world of industry—are made to understand that they will bear the burden of responsibility if the percentile gains demanded, for example, by one of those school improvement plans are not attained within the time prescribed.

"If the road does not lead to Rome," said a woman

who was called the "manager" of language arts for the Chicago public schools, "we don't want it followed." Rome, she said, was the examination children would be given at the end of a specific sequence of instruction.

In a summer session for students who had failed a previous exam, little was "left to chance," noted a journalist from Education Week. Teachers were "given binders spelling out precisely what they should be doing every day. . . ." To guarantee that they complied, "three dozen monitors" dropped in on classes periodically.

The purpose of these practices, according to the system's CEO ("superintendent" is no longer used to speak of the administrator in this system), was to guarantee that on a given day everyone is at the same place in the sequence. The Chicago CEO, when asked how he had been attracted to the uniformity of this approach, said that he first struck on the idea while scrutinizing training manuals for the National Guard.

Most teachers I know, who tend to look upon the education of young children through a somewhat softer lens than that of military training, are unsettled by such references to military "manuals" and to military metaphors in general; but if we truly want to know the way to get to Rome as rapidly as possible, the forced march of a group of children, like a line of soldiers under strong command, may seem to be a logical approach. So long as knowledge is considered something like a dot upon a map and learning is considered an assault upon that knowledge (invasion of the subject matter, followed by its capture), then it's hard to quarrel with the model that the CEO had used.

Teaching materials used in many urban districts do resemble "manuals" in the sense that they are not real texts but workbooks narrowly conceived to prime the children for the taking of specific tests. The workbook used by children in Chicago's summer session was, indeed, called Test

Best, with no pretense that it served a function other than the one its title indicated. Similarly, in New York City, when Pineapple was in third grade, she had a mathematics workbook with a title that referred explicitly to getting ready for her high-stakes tests. (Bridging the Test Gap, it was called, a pretty awful and demoralizing title, I thought, for a book we hand to children!) The reason I remember this is that she brought it to me once during the afterschool at St. Ann's Church and asked if I would help her with her homework. When she handed it to me, I asked her, "Where is your real math book?" "This is it!" she answered with her usual ebullience, and she opened the test-preparation booklet to the lesson she had been assigned. It may be there were real math books in her classroom that the students weren't permitted to take home; but the homework she and her classmates had been asked to do that week and in the weeks to come was limited to what was in this manual.

Most Americans whose children aren't in public school have little sense of the inordinate authority that now is granted to these standardized exams and, especially within the inner-city schools, the time the tests subtract from actual instruction. In Peoria, Illinois, a couple years ago, I was visiting an elementary school in which black and Hispanic children made up 90 percent of the enrollment. "Success For All Who Walk Through These Doors," a sign proclaimed to visitors, but there was little education taking place in many of the classes at the time I visited because these were "testing weeks" in which a series of examinations had to be administered.

"Our entire 90-minute literacy block was knocked out all last week in second, third, and fourth grades," said the principal, in order to administer a nationally standardized exam of basic skills. The subsequent week, when I was there, students in the first three grades were taking another set of tests in order to assess what are referred to as "phonemic" recognitions. Then, later in the year, another lengthy period of class instruction would be sacrificed to giving children in the third and fourth grades yet another test ("approximately a week of testing," I was told), this one mandated by the state of Illinois. On top of all of this, a teacher said, students also took a test once every eight weeks that was part of the assessment process for the literacy program.

In some schools, the principals and teachers tell me that the tests themselves and preparation for the tests control more than a quarter of the year. At P.S. 65, during the three months prior to the all-important state exam, fifth grade teachers had to set aside all other lessons from 8:40 to 11:00, and from 1:45 to 3:00, to drill the children for their tests. In addition to this, two afternoons a week, children in the fourth and fifth grades had to stay from 3:00 to 5:00 for yet another session of test preparation. "So, on Wednesdays and Thursdays," said one of the teachers, "students have five hours of test preparation" and "they also have to come to school on Saturdays to get three hours more of this during the last four weeks before exams."

The children were told, she said, that "it's not just 'important' that they pass," but that "passing this—the test—is actually the only thing that *is* important." One of her students "was throwing up and crying, so she couldn't take her test, because she was afraid she'd never be allowed to leave the school because she'd never pass the state exam."

In some cities, these examinations start as early as in kindergarten or first grade. Four years ago in Santa Paula, California, for example, kindergarten children were required to take standardized exams beginning in the last week of September. Two weeks, in all, were taken up by these exams, which school officials said they had to give to qualify for extra funding from the federal government.

The tests were written by the company that also writes the Stanford 9, a standardized exam for older children that was used by many districts at the time. "Our philosophy," said the principal of one school in the district where the bubble-tests were used, is that "the sooner we start giving these students tests like the Stanford 9, the sooner they'll get used to it."

A Los Angeles Times reporter described a four-year-old who "tapped his head with his pencil" and "stared blankly at the test booklet before him," because he did not yet know how to read. "The boy looked desperately to his teacher . . . ," who, however, could not give him help. "Keep going," the teacher told him. "The whole page. All by yourself." Some of the children didn't know "how to hold a pencil. . . . Many didn't know the basics of test-taking, such as moving from one page of questions to the next." Other children in the district, said The Times, cried and wet their pants out of frustration.

"They were clueless," said a first-year teacher at another Santa Paula school. "It's not fair." A kindergarten teacher said she thought her job was to make children love to come to school. "This test does not do that," she observed.

Santa Paula's public schools are populated mostly by Hispanics; only about 15 percent of children in the system are Caucasian. In the two schools that The Times's reporter had observed, Hispanic children made up 95 percent or more of the enrollment. As in other instances where standardized examinations are administered to children in their first few years of school, the burden falls most heavily on children who have had no preschool education. The theft of time this represents—two weeks of testing in the first two months these kids have ever spent in school—is simply one more injury they undergo.

There is a new pedagogic term for introducing children to these testing practices beginning at a very early age. The term, according to a teacher-educator in Ohio, is "front-loading children," a usage that appears to have originated in the world of capital investment. ("Short-term pain for long-term gain," this educator said, is how the term has been explained to her.) No matter how offensive this may be to teachers, school officials often feel they have no choice but to apply these practices during the first two years of school, a tendency that has been forcefully encouraged by directives coming from the Bush administration. In Alabama, for example, in which kindergarten children are required to take standardized exams three times in the academic year, officials in one district did away with "nap time" so that teachers would have extra time to get the students ready for their tests. "If the state is holding us accountable, this is the way we have to do it," said the director of elementary education in the district. "Kindergarten is not like it used to be."

The usual administrative rationale for giving tests like these to children in their elementary years is that the test results will help to show their teachers where the children's weaknesses may lie, so that they can redirect the focus of their work in order to address these weaknesses. In practice, however, this is not the way things generally work, because of the long lapse in time between the taking of these tests and the receipt of scores.

Principals and teachers in some schools have told me that the scores on standardized exams, which are administered most frequently between late winter and the early spring, are not received until the final weeks of June and, in some cases, not until the summer. "I get no help from this at all," a teacher in one Massachusetts district told me. "By the time the scores come back, they're not my students anymore, unless they fail—and then maybe I'll see them in my class again the next September." In some states, test results are given to the teachers far more quickly, and in a number of districts, including New York City, "interim assessments" have been introduced so that teachers can derive some benefit from these exams close to the time at which the children take them; but this is not the pattern in most sections of the nation.

There is an entirely different kind of early testing in which the results are instantly available to teachers because they administer and grade the tests themselves and because the tests, which are not bubble-tests, are given individually to children, so that teachers can observe the difficulties that they face and can assess their strengths and weaknesses during the administration of the test itself. I recently watched a teacher giving one such diagnostic test, known as the "ECLAS," to a student in her second grade. This was not a high-stress situation. The student was relaxed and seemed to like the private time and personal attention that the teacher gave him. Although the teacher had to draw upon her ingenuity to keep the rest of the children occupied with independent work while she was doing this, she did not view it as time stolen from instruction because she considered it a valuable *portion* of instruction.

There is no "test prep" for these kinds of genuine assessments. Teachers would have no reason to drill children in advance because the purpose of these tests is not to judge the child or the teacher but to gather information that is helpful to them both. A teacher, moreover, does not have to wait to be informed by a test-scoring company how well or poorly individual children, or the class in its entirety, are doing. The teacher's observations of her students and the running record that she keeps as they progress through the assessment are what matter, and the information that she gains does not need to be evaluated by a stranger in a distant city working for a testing corporation before it can be considered "accurate" or "useful."

This is not the case with high-stakes standardized examinations, the results of which supplant and overrule the judgments of a teacher. "What worries me most," writes Deborah Meier, "is that in the name of objectivity and science," the heavy reliance upon high-stakes testing has led teachers "to distrust their ability to see and observe" the children they are teaching and derive conclusions *based* upon their observation. "For a teacher who sees a kid day in and day out to admit that she won't know how well he reads" until the day the test scores are delivered by an outside agency "is not good news," she says.

"We cannot trust such tests," she writes, "to determine an individual's competence or the success of any particular school, school district, or state," or to determine the worth of any school reform or set of school reforms. "We can win occasional short-term public relations victories . . . by improving testable skills, but in the end such victories will be at the price of good education. Scores will rise and fall as superintendents come and go; that's the way the game works. And meanwhile we distort the education that we offer as we try to beat the game."

One of the distorting consequences that is taking an especially high toll on children of minorities, she notes, is the increasing practice of compelling children to repeat a grade or several grades over the course of years solely on the basis of their test results and, in some districts, almost wholly independent of the judgments of their principals and teachers. "Test-mandated holdover policies have . . . chilling effects," she says. "Every time we hold a child over, we are substantially reducing the odds of that child graduating anytime in the future"—and when a child is held back twice, the likelihood that he or she will never graduate increases by 90 percent. Even before the standards movement started to impose these nonpromotion practices, writes Mrs. Meier, "half the young black men in America were at least one year overage when they reached eighth grade." Now, with nonpromotion rules mandated by a number of our states and cities, many experts are convinced that the nongraduation rates among black and Hispanic students will increase, and some believe this escalation may already be observed.

There is another way in which the students in increasing numbers of our low-performing urban schools are being penalized by the insistent pressure to deliver higher scores on standardized exams. In many of these schools, traditional subjects such as history, geography, and science are no longer taught because they are not tested by high-stakes examinations and cannot contribute to the scores by which a school's performance will be praised or faulted. Anyone who talks informally with children in some of these elementary schools is likely to discover quickly the effects that this has had in limiting their capability for ordinary cultural discernments.

Once, during a conversation with a group of fifth and sixth grade students who had gone to P.S. 65 or were still enrolled there, I was surprised when I was asked if "Massachusetts," which the children knew is where I live, was "in New York." When I said, "No, it's a different state," they seemed confused. I tried to do a little lesson with them about cities, states, and countries, but I recognized that these distinctions were not clear to them at all. (Two of the children told me that the country that we live in is "the Bronx." Two others said it was "New York." One of the children, when I handed her a dollar bill and asked her to study it awhile, finally ventured that it might be "the United States" but voiced this with a question mark, as if she was not convinced enough to state it as a fact.)

Most of these children, two of them already 12 years old, also found it very hard to make even quite general distinctions about periods of time: "last year," "maybe ten years ago," "a hundred years ago," or "centuries ago." Whether the life of Martin Luther King came after, or before, the War Between the States or the War of Independence or, for that matter, the year when they were born was all a hopeless blur. Leaving these kids so utterly adrift in time and place seemed like an act of state-determined cognitive decapitation.

In some of the same schools, art and music are excluded from the organized curriculum, not solely because of budget cutbacks that have decimated art and music programs, as we've noted in New York, but also, again, because these subjects are not tested by the state examinations and, for this reason, are regarded as distractions from the subject areas that *will* be tested. A principal's ability to claim that children in her school are learning to play violins or to read music, or performing in a dance ensemble or a choral group, or participating in a beautiful theatrical production, will not protect the school from sanctions or humiliation if its scores in math or reading do not satisfy the stipulations of the state. Some principals in urban schools do what they can to introduce or to preserve arts programs by securing private grants and by insisting that some portion of the schoolday be protected from the state's empirical demands; but these are largely marginal activities and nothing like the programs of rich cultural exposure that are prized and celebrated in the schools that serve the children of the privileged.

The virtual exclusion of aesthetics from the daily lives of children in these schools is seldom mentioned when officials boast that they have pumped the scores on standardized exams by three or four percentage points by drilling children for as many as five hours in a day. The scores go up, the scores go down, as new officials and new methods come and go, as Mrs. Meier notes; but the stripping away of cultural integrity and texture from the intellectual experience of children, denial of delight in what is beautiful and stimulating for its own sake and not for its acquisitional equivalents, is a perennial calamity.

The banishment of recess from the normal schoolday is perhaps the ultimate penurious denial. In Atlanta, recess has been systematically abandoned to secure more time for test-related programs since the last years of the 1990s, according to the education writer Susan Ohanian, who has documented practices like these in many districts. "We are intent on improving academic performance," said the superintendent of Atlanta's schools in 1998. "You don't do that," he said, if kids are "hanging on the monkey bars." In 80 percent of the Chicago schools, recess has been abolished also. In Chicago, as in other cities, elementary schools that have no recess are most likely to be those that serve minority communities.

What kind of childhood, it may be asked, are we designing for these children, who already have so little opportunity to play in safety in their neighborhoods, who often live in cramped apartments that have neither porches nor backyards, whose only place to play is frequently the stairwell or the hallways of their building? I can attest to this from years of climbing up the often bullet-pocked and urine-smelling stairways of the buildings in which many of Pineapple's neighbors live and finding children running up and down, and back and forth, to play the little games that they make up with one another in between the landings. Pediatricians and psychiatrists may be disturbed to hear of schools where recess is truncated or abolished in the desperation to carve out a bit more time for drilling children for exams; but from the point of view of businesslike efficiency—"time management" and "maximizing productivity"—it may seem to make no sense to squander time on something that has no apparent benefit beyond the fact that it may be enjoyable and healthy.

Some of the districts that deny their children recess also deny the students they call "Level Ones" or "Level Twos" a good part of their summer holidays. Summer ceases to be a time for play and relaxation or for stimulating education of a different kind from that which is provided in the normal months of school and, instead, becomes a time when children who have not done well on standardized exams are dragged back into classrooms where they're given still more drilling in anticipation of a "retest" in September. These are not sophisticated and exciting summer schools of cultural and intellectual advancement such as those that children of the affluent are likely to enjoy, often in vernal settings in which arts and music, camping and athletics, are included. There is nothing "vernal" or sophisticated in these summer sessions for the children of the poor. These are summer institutes of sweat and drill and tension and anxiety, sited in the same unpleasant buildings where the children spent the other ten months of the year, which would not be needed for most of these children if their schools were not so flagrantly deficient in the first place.

Other districts go still further and distort the timing of the summer break for their entire student population in an effort to accommodate school calendars to testing schedules. In these districts, school begins in late July or early to mid-August, not for any reason of historical tradition (as has sometimes been the case in certain sections of the rural South) but because it gives the district one more month to get the children ready for the state exams that they will take in the late winter. This does not mean children are provided with *more* education, as some might at first assume. The school year in such districts typically ends as much as four weeks earlier than in the schools on normal calendars; so what is gained in August is subtracted in the spring. The only reason for this seasonal manipulation is to make it possible to skew the test results by giving schools more time upfront to prep their students prior to the day they take exams.

The tests, however, like it or not, are hanging there like sharpened swords above the heads of principals and teachers, and since the scores, when they are finally released, are widely publicized in press accounts and on TV (the lowest-scoring schools are often named in horror stories in the tabloid papers—"Halls of Shame . . . the worst of the worst . . . the dirty dozen," for example, says The New York Post above a story on twelve of the city's lowest-scoring schools), educators live in terror of the day the scores come out.

These tensions are increased still more in districts where the top officials are provided cash rewards if they can improve "performance" as it's measured by the test scores in the schools they supervise. Principals too, in many districts, can receive a bonus—up to $15,000 yearly in the New York City schools—if their students' scores improve at certain stipulated rates. Teachers also are awarded bonus pay in many districts if their students make impressive gains, a policy that has its parallel in sales incentives in the business world and has been in place at various times in recent years in parts of Texas, North Carolina, Colorado, California, Pennsylvania, Georgia, Ohio, Florida, and elsewhere.

What does it do to those who enter a profession, as the best of educators do, out of enlightened and unselfish inclinations that are not at all unlike the call to ministry or service that brings others into occupations that are altruistic at their core, then find their frame of reference is distorted by a rivalry for extra money at the cost of fellow educators at another school nearby who are often doing every bit as good a job as they but happen to have a group of kids this year with far more complicated problems than their own or who perhaps have had a string of substitute teachers the preceding years? Teachers in these instances are penalized collectively for long-existing problems over which they did not have control; and, while the cash rewards, in principle, are correlated with the progress children make in any given year, there is often little measurable progress made at first after students in a school have been subjected to long periods in which there was no continuity in their instruction.

Then, too, there is the common situation of a school that has been failing for a long time and is finally shut down—which, in itself, if all the other elements within this scheme were rational and fair, may sometimes be a very good idea. The children no longer have a school; so they're dispersed to other schools nearby. One or another of these schools may have much better scores. Suddenly now, with several hundred new arrivals who have failed their tests for several years, the average scores at the receiving schools, of course, go down. So now, illogically enough, *their* faculties and principals come under scrutiny as well.

This happened a few years ago at one of the better elementary schools in the South Bronx. Five months after the school had taken in 250 children from two nearby schools that had been closed, the fourth grade teachers gave their kids their all-important state exams. The average math and reading scores declined substantially. This was not the fault of teachers or the principal; they had had these new arrivals scarcely more than half the academic year. But I walked into the office of the school one day in mid-July and found the principal in tears. There were her test scores in The New York Daily News!

The name of this school is P.S. 30. Its principal, Aida Rosa, recently recalled that moment poignantly. "The reason I was crying," she explained, "was that those kids that I received were close to zero in their scores when they were sent to me. Then I also took in kids from other failing schools because their parents came to me and asked if I would take them in. They'd cry! So I'd admit them. All these kids were very low achievers, but I could not say no to their mothers. . . ."

In a fair-minded system she would have been honored for the faith that parents placed in her and for the qualities of character that made it hard for her to turn them down; but in the new world order of incentives and humiliations, qualities like these earn no rewards. Numbers become everything. Live by rubrics, die by any accidental dip in yearly scores. And to the winners go the extra $15,000.

In one of our conversations, Mr. Endicott described the system of belief demanded of the teachers by the method of test-driven teaching at his school as "a doxology." The heart of the doxology is the unquestioned faith that there is one straight road, and one road only, to be taken and that every stage along the road must be annunciated—stated on the walls, reiterated by the teacher—in advance. In itself, the naming of an "outcome" or "objective" for each lesson by a classroom teacher, as we've noted earlier, is a familiar practice in most schools. It's hard, indeed, to think of any public schools, even in historically progressive districts, where administrators don't believe that certain outcomes should be stated clearly, that they ought to have some rational connection to the tests their students have to take, and that these goals should be pursued with continuity and firmness by their teachers. In most schools, however, there has also been a compensating recognition that at least some episodes of less manipulated learning, and an atmosphere in which the unanticipated question or the unpredicted answer will at all times be respected and can even be enjoyed and welcomed, are essential parts of healthy education too.

Teachers in these schools are able to leave time for children to reveal themselves in the discursive ways that children do as they meander from the question that a teacher may have asked into an answer that appears at first to be irrelevant and which, as younger children's answers often do, seems to forget where it began. In schools I have been visiting in good suburban districts, where there are typically no more than 18 children in a class, teachers do not need to cut a child off abruptly in these situations but can listen patiently enough to find what often is a bit of hidden treasure at the end of one of these long sentences. Sometimes it's that unexpected revelation that unlocks a secret place of motivation that the teacher otherwise might never see. In overcrowded urban schools where it is common to find 28 to 30 children in a class, teachers do not often feel they can afford—or are specifically advised that they *cannot* afford—the luxury of listening to answers which, for lack of obvious, immediate, and literal responsiveness, do not advance the necessary forward march to those objectives that are posted on the wall.

There are teachers everywhere who won't accommodate themselves to these demands; but in too many instances the road that leads to the Iowa Test of Basic Skills or to whatever other state-determined metric may be used allows no detours for the interesting little storyteller who is piling on the "ands" and "buts" to tell us something which, to him at least, is of the greatest possible importance.

Some children I have known rebel against these testing

protocols and the severe intentionality of teaching methods by which they have been accompanied; and even while they give their teachers what the teachers' script demands, and pick up on official words they're supposed to use, and patiently comply with the test-preparation sessions and the rest, they find their quiet ways to say, "I do not like what you are doing to me now"—or, as educator Herbert Kohl has summarized this message, "I won't learn from you." Many children never let these passages of inner insurrection be observed, except perhaps by growing sullen or withdrawn—or, as in Pineapple's case some years ago, by saving up her anger for a long time and then joining other students in the instigation of a palace revolution that impelled the rattled teacher to give up her script and curse them out and shout them down and, in that sorry instance, flee the class, and flee the school. Other children do not wait so long to show their discontent and they confide it sometimes to their grown-up friends outside of school.

One of the children who has talked with me most openly about the testing tribulations and related miseries that he has undergone was twelve years old when he and I first met in the South Bronx. His name is Anthony. When he introduced himself to me at St. Ann's Church in 1993, he told me he wrote poetry—and, he added, was "also working on a novel"—and shortly after that he handed me what he announced was his "first novel" (22 pages, it was a good story).

He read very widely for a child of that age. He first had been attracted to the poetry of Edgar Allan Poe, in part because he knew the poet had once lived in the South Bronx. By the age of thirteen, he had discovered Mark Twain on his own. A year later, he was starting to become entangled in what he would later call "my battle with Charles Dickens." He tended to overreach his reading skills at times; he'd plunge into almost anything that captured his attention, then confess to me he had decided "not to finish it for now" because it proved to be too hard.

Still, his comprehension of the books he finished, and even of the ones he read only in part, was usually pretty good and he would often startle Reverend Overall and me by the incisive, sometimes even supercilious comments he would make about a book he thought that he would like but which then "disappointed" him, a word he liked to use, I think, because it seemed to indicate this was the writer's fault and not a matter of his own distraction or impatience. His scores on standardized exams, however, were about as bad as they could be. By the judgment of the many adults who would come with me to visit at the church and whom he'd often instantly appropriate for long digressive conversations, which they obviously enjoyed, he was a precocious boy with an endearing eccentricity; but in the number ratings of the New York City public schools, Anthony would probably have been decreed to be a "Level Two" in language arts and a "Level One" in math.

"Whenever I went into those bubble-tests," he told me recently, "I knew that I was done for! I'd suddenly become 'clamped-up.' I'd feel, 'I have to get out of this room.' I'd think, 'I hate to do this test, so I'm not going to be able to do well on it. . . .' Number two pencils! The points would always break. The truth is I just hated all of it. I felt beaten down by so much else that went on in the South Bronx at that time"—those were the years when HIV infection decimated families in the neighborhood, and Anthony's uncle died of AIDS a few months after we had met—"the test was one more beating."

The middle school that he attended was a violent, impersonal, unhappy institution where the principal was so caught up in his attempts to reestablish order that he scarcely seemed to have the time to get to know his pupils. When I stopped by one day to ask him a few questions about Anthony, he could not find his records and at first could not remember who he was. After shuffling some papers for a time, he said, "Is he the one with pimples?"

After three years at the school, he went to a newly founded high school in the Bronx that had been praised in press accounts when it had opened and where academic levels were reported to be higher than in other high schools in the area; but his intellectual originality and curiosity and the very traits, indeed, of earnest independence that had led him into writing poetry and lengthy narratives at such an early age created problems for him at the school. He would daydream often, and write poetry or stories in his notebook, while sitting through a course that he found boring. As a result, he frequently was taken out of class and put into a program of detention he described as "isolation." A few of the teachers seemed to like him and tried to speak up for him; but it was clear that the administration of the school thought little of his gifts. The principal told the pastor of St. Ann's, when she went up to question her, that on the basis of his test scores it did not seem likely he would ever go to college.

Now and then, a child like Anthony attracts the interest of a sensitive person from outside the neighborhood who is prepared, and has the means, to help him to escape from what appears to be a dead-end situation. A generous man whom Reverend Overall and I had come to know decided to give Anthony this opportunity. A few months after he had sat in what he called "the isolation chamber" at his school in the South Bronx, Anthony was being interviewed by the headmaster of a good New England boarding school. What didn't come across in scores on standardized exams did come across, it seems, during that interview. He was accepted with the understanding that he must repeat one grade, which he agreed to, willingly.

He never did give up his independent spirit or his sometimes maddening irreverence for a literary work or school assignment that displeased him for some reason; but he worked hard, and teachers in his classes, which were half the size of classes he'd been used to up to then, were able to give him extra help during a class, and after class, as well as in the evenings. It was a great struggle for him at the start, not only academically; but he made friends, looked for support to faculty advisers and the ever-vigilant headmaster, and he kept on writing poetry.

Two years later, when he was in the eleventh grade, Anthony called me late one night in great excitement to report that Dr. Robert Coles—"the writer," he explained in case I did not know—had visited the school to give a lecture and that he had had a chance to question him. I will not attempt to summarize the long narration Anthony provided, which had many complicated twists and turns, as does most of his written work as well. The question he had asked had been about a book that Dr. Coles had written which described a child he had known during the early days of civil rights who had to face tremendous challenges and had to learn to rise above the prejudice and opposition she encountered in her efforts to obtain an education at an integrated public school. In his question, Anthony had drawn upon a poem he loved by Edgar Allan Poe and asked the doctor if he thought this child finally found what she was searching for in life, which Anthony referred to as "her El Dorado." According to Anthony, Coles replied that he had never thought of El Dorado as "a place but as a path" and that he believed this child's path was "good and true," as Anthony reported this, and that "she found 'the way' " and, as he put it, "found it on her own, because she followed her own heart, as you might say, and so she found her El Dorado."

I cannot easily describe the satisfaction that I heard within his voice when he reported this to me. He seemed to take the deepest pleasure in that answer, and he spoke of it repeatedly in weeks to come. I was glad he'd had this chance to question Dr. Coles and, even more, that he'd responded as he did to what the doctor had replied. He often misses what most others think to be "the main point" of an essay he has read or lecture he has heard, which may be one reason why the comprehension questions on a standardized exam sometimes befuddled him. Instead, he tends to fasten on a piece of what he's read or heard that corresponds to something he already cares about and finds his own unusual back-channel to the essence of the work or to the meaning of the man, which leaves him with a sense of intimate association. One result of this, I think, is that his memories of these encounters with a person, or a passage of prose writing, or a poem, linger in his mind for weeks to come, as I discover when he later weaves a detail or a phrase he struck upon into a talk we have on something that appears to be entirely unrelated.

"Not the place but the path, not the goal but the way," he wrote to me a few months later, recollecting Dr. Coles's response. I recognized the gratitude he felt to Dr. Coles for reaffirming his belief that pre-established "destinations" were not everything but that "the journey" had some meaning too. I remember thinking how disruptive this idea would be in many of the classrooms that I visit nowadays. The destination shapes the journey in those classrooms, excavating mysteries, invalidating unpredictables, eclipsing whim, excluding risk, denying pilgrimage.

Anthony was able to escape this; most children in his situation can't. He completed boarding school successfully and was accepted at a four-year college where he studied sociology and literary history. He has since entered graduate school, where he intends to study to become a teacher. Numbers do not tell us all we need to know about our children.

* * *

Thomas Sobol, the former state commissioner of education in New York, who oversaw the early phases of the standards movement from the last years of the 1980s to the middle 1990s, told a group of future teachers in New York not long ago that he was troubled by the unexpected consequences to which much of this had led. "Standards," "testing," and "accountability" have come to be "the current orthodoxy," he observed. "People say we need these . . . standards to remain competitive in a global economy. They say that we have been too lax. They say that students will rise to meet the expectations of their elders and that teachers will work harder if their feet are held to the fire. They say we will reform our schools by demanding more, and holding students and teachers accountable for the results. . . .

"For the record," he went on, "I believe in high standards"—a point, it's worth observing, on which almost every teacher I know fairly well would certainly concur, despite the inclination of some of their harshest critics to assume that those who question the obsessive character of this agenda are in favor of "low standards" and are temperamentally attracted to the goal of mediocrity. "But history teaches us," said Dr. Sobol, "that every good idea contains the seeds of its own heresy" and "much of what is going on in the name of standards and accountability verges on the heretical. . . .

"We are giving kids less and calling it more," "limiting what we teach" to what "we can easily measure," pushing our students "to focus on memorizing information, then regurgitating fact." The student's job, he said, should not be only "to absorb information, but to make connections, find new patterns, imagine new possibilities. . . ." But imagination and inquiry are "not a big item" in the testing and accountability agenda, he went on. "Choosing the right answer to someone else's question is what counts."

Reflecting on "a stifling uniformity of practice" that

the testing movement has imposed on many public schools—with the result, he said, that "thinking, feeling people" are not given "room to think and feel"—he spoke of aspects of a child's education that cannot be measured by exams. "Education involves the heart as well as the mind. . . . Learning entails play and risk-taking as well as ordered study." But, he said, "we don't have time for these things anymore." As our students "cram away" in preparation for exams, what we are giving them now in many places is "a stripped-down curriculum" and "instruction devoid of passion and of meaning."

Despite the stirrings of resistance to these policies, he said, "the juggernaut rolls on. . . . Few of us expect it to disappear suddenly, but many of us expect it to change." Those who work in public schools cannot "long endure the pressure" they are under now, and "the political system simply won't permit" us to deny diplomas to large numbers of our high school students, "turning them out into the streets. . . ." At some point, he said, "in five years, or ten, or twenty, the rules and practices of the standards era will begin to seem old-fashioned. . . . Someday the frenzy will be over. Someday we will come to understand that we have been eating poisoned grain."

A teacher who heard him said that he seemed close to tears as he implored them not to do the same. "Raise your voices," he advised these neophyte instructors—even if you should "be shouted down. Future generations demand it. . . . Your integrity demands it."

In his lecture, Dr. Sobol did not differentiate between the consequences that the testing juggernaut, as he had worded it, has had in inner-city schools and those in wealthier communities, although a passing mention he had made of places where "all learning" has been "focused on the test" (and where, he added, "children no longer read literature—they read disconnected sentences" and "answer practice questions based upon them") seemed to be a reference to the schools in which the drill-curricula are now most likely to be found. He did, moreover, note that we do not give all our students opportunities to learn what they would need to know in order to succeed within the terms of the agenda he had just described. Those who do not have such opportunities, he said, "are usually poor and disproportionately of color," and he termed inequities like these "beyond illegal and unfair—they are immoral."

I disagreed with only two points in his talk. I thought the tests-and-standards movement, as it had emerged during the middle and late 1980s, had been loaded with a coarse utilitarian toxicity and a demeaning anti-human view of childhood right from the start. I also did not share his faith that our political system would reject a set of policies that sends so many thousands of our students to the streets "without high school diplomas," as he'd stated this. The political system has permitted millions of poor children to be sent into the streets without diplomas now for many generations—numbers that are almost certain to increase under the do-or-die agenda that has been enforced by nonpromotion policies. (Many of such students too, as we have seen, are being channeled into training programs that prepare them for the workforce so that they will not, in any case, be "in the streets" where their potentially disruptive presence might arouse political anxiety.)

Still, the revelations he had offered to these future teachers, and the eloquence with which he voiced them, seemed extraordinary, coming as they did from a respected leader in their field who had participated in the early phases of a movement he had subsequently come to question. When I later had a chance to meet with Dr. Sobol in New York, I had the thought of asking Anthony if he would like to come with me. It didn't work out, because I didn't have the time to plan it with him in advance. It was simply a last-minute notion that occurred to me because I thought that Dr. Sobol would have liked this nonconforming and intelligent young man who had been forced to pay a painful price at first for certain of those unexpected consequences the commissioner so powerfully condemned, but had never buckled under, never settled for the predetermined road, and had prevailed at length and found his own way to defend and to affirm his own unique ideals. They are both dissenters, in this sense; I thought they would have taken to each other.

CHAPTER 6

A Hardening of Lines

The demarcations between separate worlds of education are assuming sharper lines. There is a new emboldenment among the relatively privileged to isolate their children as completely as they can from more than token numbers of the children of minorities. In some cities, as we've seen, young middle-class white families have successfully been pressuring their school boards to carve out almost entirely separate provinces of education for their children.

Even before this new phenomenon had been observed, many of the better elementary schools in major cities like New York already had in place admissions policies that clearly favored children of the "savvy parents," as the press in New York City frequently describes well-educated, well-connected people. Applications to a number of these schools, for instance, must be filed very early (12 months prior to admission in some cases) and, by the time less knowledgeable parents even hear about one or another of these schools, they often find that every place is taken by the children of those families that may have acquaintances whose children have attended the same school and who advise them on the strategies that can improve a child's chances of admission.

Then, too, parent applicants are often asked to write or to express their "educational philosophy" and also sign a contract to participate in certain forms of educational support the school expects a parent to provide—both of which, in principle, a parent who has had only a ninth or tenth grade education in a mediocre school can do as well as somebody who went to a good college, even though all parties know this isn't really so and that the outcomes are effectively prefigured in advance. Children as young as three and a half or four are also given tests and interviews as part of the admissions process for some of these schools, and educated parents coach their children for these interviews and frequently enroll them in expensive pre-test programs which are not provided by the schools themselves but must be purchased privately.

Competition for these better schools is "fierce," writes New York author Katha Pollitt in describing strategies she used to guide her daughter through the process of admission to one of the highest-rated schools within the New York City system. In looking for a kindergarten for her child, she reports, "a school's heat"—by which she means its growing popularity among the families of the middle class and upper middle class—"could be gauged . . . by the preponderance of white faces," among parent volunteers for instance, and the "paleness of the students" who were entering the early grades. "The fifth grade might look like Trinidad," she says, "but the kindergarten looked more like Bavaria."

What, she asks, do parents do to win their kids a place in one of the top-rated schools? "They do what I did,"

Pollitt writes. They get a friend, ideally one with children in the school they choose, or "someone famous," someone who's "connected," to "put in a word" on their behalf.

"Some go further" and "fake an address," as she reveals, ideally "in an upscale catchment area" that has "an excellent zoned school" (she names a few examples in primarily white neighborhoods) and then "they prep their kids for IQ tests" and interviews. If they want to boost their child's chances even more, they pay for consulting services from private agencies that give them counseling on how to get their children into schools or programs for the talented and gifted.

As a result, says Pollitt, these programs and these schools end up as "disproportionately white enclaves" often sited in a larger school that is "almost entirely minority and largely poor"—"oases of comparative privilege," as she describes them, "in a desert of deprivation."

It's a wonderfully honest revelation, written by a woman with unquestioned liberal credentials who, like many of my friends in New York City, has a history of strong support for civil rights and, unlike some, has never backed away from these beliefs. Still, given the situation as it already exists within New York, this Harvard educated mother writes, "we parents don't have much choice"—except, she says, "to pocket our qualms" and, as she says she did for her own daughter, "knock ourselves out" to get our children what we can.

How do parents who are not so well-informed at first identify the schools that are considered really good? Readers of the city's upscale magazines and daily press will notice references from time to time to guidebooks that provide a lot of detailed information on the best schools in the city from the early elementary level through the secondary years. Descriptions of some of the elementary schools that are most highly praised convey the sense that, while these schools excel in academic terms, they're also pleasant places in which children in the early grades are not subjected to the kinds of rote-and-drill curricula that we have seen.

Hunter College Elementary School, for instance, is described by Clara Hemphill, a shrewd observer of the New York City schools who is the author of a number of these books, as "a relatively laid-back, relaxed, progressive school" with "tables and chairs instead of desks," and kids in blue jeans "on the floor messing with crayons and construction paper," and "unstructured play." "Early reading isn't stressed," she says. "Instead, the school helps children" to "develop skills" to "better understand" a written text once "they do crack the code. . . ." To qualify for admission to this public school, a child must first be taken to a private testing agency: $165 for the IQ test, she notes. "Parents who can't afford to pay may apply for a free test," she says; but many parents are intimidated to make such requests and, more to the point, most of them have never even heard that such exemptions are available.

In addition to interview coaching and test preparation, Hemphill notes another way in which admissions to the better schools are sometimes skewed. Some of these schools have admissions procedures that are "apparently incorruptible," but even in cases where admissions are decided by a lottery, "it's worth letting the principal know who you are," she says, because "sometimes there's a little wiggle room. . . ." It also "doesn't hurt," she adds, "to make friends with . . . someone in the PTA. . . ."

Hemphill also notes, as Katha Pollitt did, that outright lying is a common strategy for gaining entrance to a school regarded as desirable. "If lying is really, truly your only option, the charade involves putting your name on a friend's [electric] bill, buying a phony lease at a stationery store, or making up a persuasive story about how your child really lives with an aunt across the street from the school. . . .

Short of out-and-out lies, which can lead to trouble, you may consider stretching the truth. . . ."

Parents who have studied guides providing such advice are obviously better suited than the parents of the very poor to find the "wiggle room" that Hemphill has alluded to and also are more likely to possess the social skills by which to take advantage of these strategies. (As a matter of reality, not one parent I have talked with in the St. Ann's neighborhood of the South Bronx over the past five years has ever seen one of these guidebooks.) The very low number of poor children who attend some of these schools can therefore not be unexpected. Less than one percent of children, for example, who attend the Hunter College Elementary School, Hemphill observes, are poor enough to qualify for free and reduced price lunches—this, in a city where three quarters of the children in the elementary schools are poor by the same standard.

Children who attend selective elementary schools usually go on to one of the selective high schools of New York. Hunter College High School is one of the most respected. (Students who have gone to Hunter College Elementary School are automatically admitted to the secondary school.) Among the other highly selective secondary schools of New York City, one of the best-known is Stuyvesant High School in Manhattan. The students I've met who have attended Stuyvesant are generally extraordinary students; they win numerous awards and honors, and New York City's civic and political leaders have rewarded them with academic opportunities unknown to children in the schools I visit in the Bronx. Even in a brief recession in the early 1990s when a billion-dollar cut in funding was imposed on New York City's schools across the board, $150 million was discovered to erect a dazzling new building, the most expensive high school ever built in New York City, for the students who attended Stuyvesant. Not a single high school had been built for students in the Bronx since 1973, observers noted at the time.

In spite of the pride that civic leaders take in Stuyvesant's accomplishments, the racial demographics of the school have been a source of great embarrassment to educators in New York. Less than 6 percent of Stuyvesant's enrollment is black or Hispanic, while black and Hispanic children make up 72 percent of citywide enrollment in the public schools. The city has made intermittent efforts to develop programs of tutorial instruction to assist black and Hispanic children in achieving entrance to the school, but these efforts have not been successful. The trend, indeed, has been distinctly retrograde. Twenty-six years ago, in 1979, black students represented nearly 13 percent of Stuyvesant's enrollment; today they represent only a meager 2.7 percent.

These are obviously disturbing numbers. Yet, no matter what uneasiness they cause for some, there is an underlying sense at the same time, at least among the parents of the children who prevail within this competition, that the students who get into schools like Stuyvesant must genuinely deserve to be there; and it is also commonly believed that most of the kids who don't get in could probably not handle the demands they would be facing if they did. Students themselves sometimes adhere to this belief. "I'm not trying to hide the fact that I think I'm better than the rest," a Stuyvesant student told a visiting reporter when the school's new building opened. "We're supposed to be the best kids, and there may be something to that."

Merit, no matter how it may have been attained, is somehow self-confirming. The early advantages one may have had become irrelevant to most of us once a plateau of high achievement has been reached. The years we may have spent when we were three and four years old in a superb developmental preschool, the strategies our parents may have used to win us entrance to a first-rate elementary school, and all the other preferential opportunities that may have introduced us to the channels in which academic competence has been attained—all this falls out of view once we arrive in a position in which we can demonstrate to others, and ourselves, that our proficiencies are indisputably superior to those of other students of our age who may not have had these opportunities.

All students who go to schools like Stuyvesant are not from privileged families; some children of low income (roughly 15 percent of overall enrollment) get into this school and do so as a consequence of nothing other than hard work and tough competitive abilities. Still, there are those racial numbers, and, no matter how they are explained away at times by those who are the proud alumni of this school, they bear a devastating message. Some people blame these racial differences primarily upon the values systems of black children and their parents. The inequalities in educational provision that we give, or do not give, these children from the starting-gate are given less attention.

"New York is a 'tale of two cities,' " wrote David Dinkins, who would later be elected mayor of New York City but at the time he wrote these words, in 1986, was the Manhattan borough president, "and it should come as no surprise that each of these cities has its own school system." Those who defend the bifurcated system, Mr. Dinkins said, make the familiar argument, "Don't change our schools; make the others better." These people "fail to see," he wrote, "that the two systems are inextricably linked; each exists, in part, because of the other."

At the opposite extreme from schools like Stuyvesant and Hunter College High are those deeply segregated high schools to which all but a small handful of the children I have known in the South Bronx have been routinely steered.

Few of these kids were ever told of schools like Stuyvesant when they were in elementary school or, as I generally discover when I question them, even in their final year of middle school. Many, for that matter, do not know that there is another good selective school, the Bronx High School of Science, in the northwest corner of the Bronx not far from the predominantly white neighborhood of Riverdale. "It's off their radar," says the pastor of St. Ann's. "And even if they hear of it, almost none of them would have a chance of getting in."

Most of the children in the neighborhood have ended up at one of the large and low-performing high schools in the Bronx. Others go to smaller schools, renamed "academies," carved out of larger schools but generally housed in the same buildings. By the time they enter schools like these, the results of all their prior years of educational denial are not easily reversed. Overcrowding and distasteful physical surroundings and large class size have their obvious effects as well. Violence, when it breaks out from time to time, is hardly a surprise.

Two fights broke out in two successive weeks in schools that I was visiting three years ago in Harlem and the Bronx at the invitation of a teacher who had taught in one and now was doing outreach work with students at the other. The first was at a middle school in Harlem which the principal, himself a former dropout of the New York City schools, referred to as a "dumping ground" for kids that "other schools don't want" or kids who'd been expelled from other schools. Seventy percent of students at the school were "Level Ones," he told me. "This is usually the last chance for these children."

The school was one of the many "themed academies" that had been newly founded in New York, but it was academic only in its name and it turned out to be a bleak and grimy institution on the top floor of an old five-story building in East Harlem in the lower floors of which an elementary school was housed. Class size averaged 30 students. (I walked into one class that held 31, another that held 32.) Thirteen of the 15 teachers were "provisionals," which meant they were not fully certified to teach. Supplies were scarce. "Three of my classes don't have textbooks," said the principal. "I have to fight and scratch for everything we get."

The steep climb to the top floor of the building was a challenge for the many students who had asthma. I saw two students pull out their inhalers when they came to the top stair. "After lunch, coming up five floors," the principal said, "I'll see five or six of them pulling out their pumps." Some of the teachers also had to sit and catch their breath after they made the climb. I had raced around the corridors and up and down the stairs of many large and multistoried public schools during the previous two years, but this one knocked me flat.

One of the children from the Bronx whom I had known since he was six years old turned out to be a student here. Elio had been a promising and happy child when we met in 1994. He had gone to P.S. 30 and had been a special favorite of his principal, Miss Rosa. He was a favorite also of Fred Rogers, who came up with me to visit at the school and at Saint Ann's, where I had first met Elio. Elio was eight years old when he and Mr. Rogers became friends.

But Elio ran into problems quickly at the same beleaguered middle school that Anthony had earlier attended. His mother tried, without success, to get him transferred to a better school until, in June 2002, the middle school was finally shut down. At that point, his mother agreed to have him transferred to this school in Harlem. When I later asked her why she had agreed to this instead of trying to enroll him in one of the better middle schools that were presumably available under the school choice program in New York, she said that she was given no alternative. "I went to the district office and they gave me that school," she replied. If other choices did exist, she said, they were not mentioned. Nobody had told her that the problems here were every bit as grave as those from which she thought that she had rescued him.

Sixty-five percent of students at this school, according to the principal, were Hispanic; nearly 35 percent were black. "It looks like an institution," he said, pointing to the drabness of the corridors. "I'm giving students rolls of paper to do murals for the walls." Some of the kids who stood around us in the corridors looked wired-up and angry. One hefty girl raced past us, stopped and wheeled around, came back a couple steps and, with a funny mixture of pugnacity and humor, told the principal that she was going to "get" somebody (another girl, I think) who had insulted her, but then conceded, at the principal's suggestion, that this might not prove to be "a very good idea." She seemed to like the principal and bantered with him for a while but would never quite let down her guard. She was wearing a red sweatshirt with the hood drawn tight around her cheeks and ears. "I have an attitude problem," she explained to me, with which the principal good-naturedly agreed.

"If we had the money, ideal class size for these kids would be 15 to 20," said a teacher. "Many are in foster care—their parents may have died of AIDS or are in jail." But even if they had the money for more teachers, said the principal, "we wouldn't have the space," and he unlocked a door to show me that his social studies teacher had to use a storage closet as her office.

Standards posters, lists of numbered mandates, lists of rubrics lined most of the classroom walls. I asked a mathematics teacher if these lists had pedagogic value for his students. "District wants to see it, wants to know I'm teaching this," the teacher answered, rather dryly. When I asked him how he'd found a job in this academy, he told me he had been in business—"real estate, insurance"—for nine years, then for some reason (I believe he lost his job) he needed to find work. "A friend said, 'Bring your college transcript in.' I did. They sent me to the district. The next day I got the job. . . ." I was impressed that he and other teachers in this school who'd never taught before were handling the students in their classes, for the most part, fairly well; but tensions were apparent in the building the entire time that I was there, and vigilance, not only on the part of teachers and the principal, but also on the part of students, never seemed to be let down.

The fight I witnessed started in the schoolyard during recess, but it quickly made its way to the top floor. A tall Hispanic boy who had an ugly open wound above one of his eyes came tearing down the corridor to where I stood beside the principal and Elio and shoved the three of us aside to catch up with the boy who had attacked him, or who he believed attacked him. The wound above his eye was not too deep but it was bleeding, and his eyes were glistening. A teacher finally restrained him.

On the day after my visit, as his mother told me, Elio came close to being beaten up as well. A group of bigger boys attacked him in the schoolyard and pursued him to the street; so he had fled the school, returning only later when the bigger boys were gone. He had learned by now how to defend himself, but in this case he had been wise enough not to fight back when he could see he was outnumbered.

The second fight that I observed broke out at Walton High School in the Bronx while I was talking with a group of seven students who were waiting in the basement cafeteria to get in line for lunch. Built to hold 1,800 kids, the school held 3,400. More than 95 percent of the students were black or Hispanic; 1.5 percent were white.

Lunch within this very crowded building had to be served in shifts beginning at 9:42. The last of the nine shifts began at 2:19. Once seated in the lunchroom, students had to wait for up to 30 minutes before they could get in line. I had been waiting with these kids for 20 minutes when the violence erupted. One of the girls immediately got up and threw her body over my assistant, Amy Ehntholt, who had never been within a New York City school before this week and found herself by chance only a few feet from the smashing fists of boys who climbed up on the table next to hers and slammed their victim flat before a guard in uniform appeared and somehow brought the confrontation to a halt.

The students who were talking with me at my table barely stirred when this occurred. Three were girls and four were boys and only one had any plans for college. When I asked them what they planned to do after they finished school, several answered me sarcastically. Two of the boys answered me with crude obscenities. All but one reported that they had attended segregated schools like this since kindergarten. I didn't get the feeling that these students wanted to offend me by the language that they used. I had the sense instead that they did not know *how* to voice their feelings on a matter fraught with so much anger without using words like these.

That hard edge softened somewhat when I turned to one, and then another, and addressed them individually. When they asked me what I did and why I'd visited their school, I said I was a writer and was trying to find out what daily life was like for students here and what realistic futures they looked forward to. At this point, the show of toughness seemed to become less important to the boys, who had been the most sarcastic at the start, and a more vulnerable quality appeared.

"This subject is upsetting to me," said the oldest-looking of the boys.

I was surprised to see that he had placed his hand across his chest as if he had discomfort there, then raised it to his throat, which was perspiring. He was sitting to my right and now leaned close to me and looked me in the eyes and touched my arm. "You see," he said with a slight stammer in his voice, "I don't have the least idea of where my life is heading, and these questions that you're asking make me scared."

By the time we were allowed to get in line for food, the students spoke of little else except the fact that they were hungry. Things became a good deal more chaotic as we moved up in the line. When one of the students helped to choose my lunch for me—a sandwich and potato chips and chocolate milk—a big and burly white man who was standing just behind the counter grabbed my tray away from me and said I couldn't eat. When a teacher who was watching this stepped forward to explain I was a guest, he grew defiant and insisted that I couldn't have the food and fought with her over the tray.

A spunky-looking girl with a blithe smile who was standing next to me said something rude about the man behind the counter and then asked me, "Would you like to eat here every day?" I said, "Not really," but the truth is I was very hungry by this time and was beginning to get weak, which happens to me more often nowadays when I don't eat than when I was a teacher 28 years old. She grabbed a half-pint chocolate milk container while the man who seemed to be in charge of things still argued with the teacher, and she slipped it in my pocket.

I asked her whether the older students were permitted to go out to local stores to buy their lunch. It was, I guess, a naïve question. "What do you think," she said, "that anyone is going to come back for if they ever let us out?"

A few minutes later, while I talked with faculty members in another basement room nearby, a student in the lunchroom who was angry for some reason filled the place with pepper-spray. Doors and windows had to be thrown open. When I came back into the larger room after my meeting with the teachers, two of the boys who had been waiting for their lunch with me were hanging out around the counter, looking bored and edgy once again. I couldn't tell if they'd had anything to eat by then or not.

I was glad the kids had taken me to lunch with them. Inner-city schools do not, in general, encourage visitors to witness this predictably unpleasant aspect of their students' daily lives. "Lunchroom Hell," as another New York student once described these periods in which they're herded down for squalid feedings in the basements of their schools, does not come up too often in those intellectual deliberations on the reasons for collapsing motivation among students in these schools. A convenient defect of vision makes it possible to bypass shameful physical conditions that are almost guaranteed to coarsen the mentalities of children and to manufacture restlessness and discontent and academic apathy among too many of their peers.

I visited several classes, but the only program I observed that seemed to be well-funded and which had a cheerful setting and small class size was a class called "Virtual Enterprise" in which I spent an hour after lunch.

"Congratulations! You are no longer students—you are employees!" said an introduction to the program I was handed as I came into the room. The students told me they were learning how to organize and work within a small-sized corporation and to market goods like bracelets, scarves, and shoes, and other aspects of production, purchasing, and sales. On an impulse, I asked if they expected that employees of their simulated business would be members of a union.

"Meaning—*what*?" a bright young woman asked me.

I asked the question to some other students but drew mostly puzzled looks until one student said that their employees wouldn't need a union "because they'll be getting 401(k)'s." A Wall Street firm had been advising them on business practices, as the instructor told me when I asked her how the program was designed. "No," she said. "They have not said anything I know of, up to now, concerning unions!"

The teachers who were my hosts at Walton High spoke favorably about the benefits this program offered students who, as one of the instructors pointed out, had "no advantages in terms of family ties or good connections" to the business world, as students in a middle-class community might have; and they argued that the students gained a sense of competence and self-esteem from these activities that might empower some of them to go to college after graduation. It was, however, a very small program and included only 30 students, "an elite group," I was told by one of the older teachers.

In the academic classes that I visited, the girls in general were more involved in working at their lessons than the boys. In a biology class of 28 black and Hispanic students, most of the girls had buckled down to do their lab reports while several of the boys were wandering the room. The instructor had taught at Walton High for many years and was, according to a group of girls who chatted with me at the end of class, one of their favorite teachers; but she had her hands full with a number of the boys whose math and literacy levels were so far below the norm for children of their age that they found it hard to understand the course materials and, as a result, seemed to withdraw from class activities almost entirely. I was sitting near a small boy with a ponytail who wasn't doing any work at all but was engaged in chatting up a pretty girl in half-rim spectacles beside him. "This student has poor writing skills," the teacher said. "She's doing the report for both of them."

There were 33 children in a mathematics class I visited. Some of the classes I observed held fewer students, but the average class size at the school was 34 and teachers and students spoke of classes with as many as 39 or 40 in a room. Throughout the day, teachers introduced me to ambitious and high-spirited young people who, they said, were likely to do well on their examinations and would probably go to college. There are clusters of such students in all schools like Walton High. Still, the pyramid of numbers for enrollment by grade levels told an old sad story that is heard in schools like this in cities everywhere: There were 1,275 ninth grade students in the fall of 1999, but only 400 of these students were enrolled in twelfth grade in October 2002. Of these survivors, according to the school's annual report, only 188—not quite 15 percent of those who'd been in ninth grade three years earlier—met the requirements for graduation in June of their senior year.

Children of recent immigrants, according to school documents, made up only between six and ten percent of students in the school. So "immigration," which has sometimes been presented to the public as an expiating reason for the academic problems and the racial segregation of the New York City system, was not a primary factor in this instance. This was a place of disposition, for the most part, for young people who grew up and went to school in the United States but had never had more than a fraction of a chance to find their way into good schools like Hunter College Elementary School or a secondary school like Stuyvesant. The Bronx High School of Science, I discovered when I took a walk around the neighborhood, is only two long blocks from Walton High. It might as well be in another country.

Later that week, I spent a day at several schools in Roosevelt, one of many segregated suburbs of New York, several of which are situated on Long Island. A district of a mere 3,000 students, 85 percent of whom are black, 15 percent Hispanic, living in an area of only one and a half square miles, Roosevelt is not a municipal jurisdiction in the commonly accepted sense. According to Arthur Eisenberg, director of litigation for the New York Civil Liberties Union, who escorted me throughout my visit there, "It's not a village, not a town. It has no government, no mayor, and no police. . . . It exists exclusively as a school district." Its property taxes are extremely high—among the highest in the state, as Eisenberg observed—but its residential properties, despite the fact that many of its homes are very handsome and well-kept, surrounded by attractive lawns and gardens, have little taxable value and the district lost much of the tax yield from commercial properties when business fled, along with almost all white residents, as African-Americans arrived in hopes of living a suburban life within a mixed community.

In spite of its high tax rates, therefore, and despite the additional funding it received from state and federal sources, Roosevelt had been for many years the lowest-spending district in Nassau County on Long Island. In the school-year 2001–2002, for instance, Roosevelt was spending not quite $12,800 for each pupil while the average expenditure in Nassau County was in excess of $14,600. The predominantly white community of Great Neck spent $19,000 on each student the same year, while the prosperous town of Mineola spent nearly $20,000.

"Roosevelt is New York's Soweto," said a high official of the Roosevelt schools when he described its poverty and demographics to me in a private conversation recently. As often is the case in these historically embattled districts, I encountered a degree of wariness at first among administrators of the system who, no doubt, had ample reason to be cautious and defensive with a visitor from outside the community. I did not have the sense that they were trying to mislead me but, as in similar districts I have visited, I got the feeling that beleaguered leaders were so frightened of additional exposure of the district's critical condition that they now and then conflated wishes and intentions with more accurate realities.

In an early-morning briefing I was given, for example, a woman in charge of pre-K education told me of the preschool program serving Roosevelt's children, which, she said, the district was "aligning" with a newly implemented drill-curriculum adopted by the elementary schools, the same one, it turned out ("Success For All"), that I'd observed in Hartford and Columbus and the Bronx. "We service all of the district's four-year-olds," she said emphatically.

I was surprised by this; and when I therefore asked her for the numbers, she revised what she had said from "all" to a more modest estimate. "We serve 140 children," she at length confirmed, many of whom, she said, did not end up attending Roosevelt's schools but went to private schools or lived in other districts. At that point, another official said that somewhat less than half the children in the system ("maybe between 30 and 50 percent," she said) received what she considered "real pre-K" before they entered kindergarten. One of the principals also noted the extremity of need among the children that her school received. "Every year we have a number of children who come into our first grade without having been to kindergarten *or* pre-K," she said. Her school, she added, served a number of homeless children in the area.

In the first of four schools that I visited, an 80-year-old elementary school with "unresolved asbestos problems," I was told, layers of paint were peeling from the walls and most of the classrooms had no doors. The reason there were no doors, according to the principal, was that the school had been converted to accommodate an open-space approach to learning called "the open classroom" 30 years before. The approach, she said, had proven unsuccessful, but the school had never had the money to restore the doors. So, even though the school had long since gone back to the kind of teaching that takes place in classrooms known as "self-contained," there had been no effort to contain these rooms except by using bookcases or stacks of cubbyholes or blackboards as dividers.

The SFA curriculum was being implemented at the time that I arrived. The little phonics books that are essential to this program were not on display, however, and when I asked a fourth grade teacher where they were, she threw her hands up in the air and told me, "Please don't ask! We haven't yet received materials," even though it was already late November. While waiting for materials, the children had been spending time in mastering the silent signals. In a fifth grade class, as I came in, every arm shot out, with fingers flat, in instantaneous reaction to the "zero noise" salute that had been given by their teacher.

"There is respiratory danger to the students in this carpet," said the director of facilities as we were standing next to an extensive area where "particles of carpet" had been "coming loose" and now were "being breathed by children," in his words. "Commercial carpet of this nature lasts for seven years at maximum," he said. When I asked how old this carpet was, he studied it more closely and then estimated, "Twenty years." Construction of a new school to replace this building would, he hoped, begin in three more years.

The second elementary school I visited was cordoned off by signs that read "RESTRICTED AREA" and "DANGER." One of the two sections of the school, the principal explained, had been condemned 12 months before. Structural problems were observed, and she was told there was a danger of the roof collapsing without warning. The notification got to her at one p.m. that day, "and we were ordered to be out by three."

Teachers had been given only those two hours to pack up materials, she said, and many lost their records, lessons, and supplies. After the move, which took place in the first week of November, she was forced to double up first grades and kindergartens—one of the fifth grades had to "triple up," according to their teacher, with two other classes in the building's cafeteria—until two dozen portables could be installed. At the time of my visit, two thirds of the classes at the school took place in portables.

The portables were clean, well-lighted, and had windows; but the ceilings were lower than in ordinary classrooms, and the rooms felt cramped, and there was scarcely space to walk around the children's desks and chairs, or in between them. Students wore uniforms, and discipline was tight. Standards listings were conspicuously posted. Photographs the principal permitted me to take display the numbers of specific skills I had observed in other classes like these.

In a third grade class of over 30 students that was housed in the portion of the school building itself that was still usable, children read me sentences they'd written about what they liked the best about the new curriculum.

"My favorite skill is silence," said one child.

"No talking," said another.

Another said her favorite skill was "looking at the other person," which is a part of what is known as Active Listening.

In a sixth grade class, the name of Rosa Parks was written on the board. The children gave me good and detailed answers when I asked them what they knew about conditions in the South when she was a young girl.

"Black people had to go to separate bathrooms," said one child.

"Black people had to drink from separate water fountains," said a second.

"Black children had to go to segregated schools in those days," said a third.

"This is the worst place you could ever put a child," said the principal.

There was no sugar-coating in her language as she talked about the infrastructure problems and the other difficulties that her teachers and their students patiently endured. Still, she said that she did not permit herself to yield to disappointment or to wallow in despair. "I need to believe," she told me, as I was about to leave the school, "And still we rise. . . ."

The junior and senior high schools shared a single building, which was not in blatant disrepair but was suffused with a disturbing sense of lethargy and aimlessness the day that I was there. The principal, who had arrived here only two months earlier, did not yet seem to know the building well and was hard-pressed at first to find an academic class that I could visit. She guided me to classrooms without classes and appeared impatient when I voiced the wish to see a class with children in the room. Sometimes, when we walked into a room, she simply looked confused as to the reasons why there were no students there. When I told her, as politely as I could, that I would really like to meet some children, she escorted me into a sewing class for seventh and eighth graders in which boys and girls were making decorative pillows.

"Hold up your pillows. We have visitors," the teacher said.

The civil liberties attorney who was with me seemed to share my puzzlement about the academic purpose of this lesson. When I asked the teacher why the kids were making pillows, she replied that New York State "mandates two years of this."

I felt hesitant to second-guess her, but I somehow did not think that what she said was actually so. It turned out, as a school official told me later, that the only state requirement to this effect in junior high or middle school was that all students take "three quarters of a year of study" in an area known as Home and Careers. He said that he was pretty sure this did not mean they were obliged to take "a sewing class." Two years of *mandatory* sewing classes, other educators told me, would be quite unusual to find in districts of New York that serve primarily white children.

"Hand-sewing skills," the teacher explained, were being taught to seventh graders and "machine skills" to eighth graders.

"Thread machine correctly," said a poster of instructions for the use of a machine. "Check knob settings. Line up the edge of the fabric with the edge of the presser. . . . Turn handwheel toward you so needle goes down in fabric. . . . Drop stitch regulator, stitch forward. STEER STRAIGHT."

The teacher said the children also learned check-writing and were taught the way to do an interview ("shake hands" and "look them in the eyes," she said), the way to read a want ad, and the way to write a résumé.

Only ten eighth graders passed their state exam in English language literacy skills in the preceding June, out of a total of 220 children, said the principal. Not a single boy in the twelfth grade had met the standards to receive the state diploma, which is called the Regents in New York. The attrition rate of students between ninth and twelfth grades was, moreover, very high. According to a series of the school's annual reports, there had been 178 ninth graders at the school in 1999, but there were only 80 twelfth grade students three years later.

The students were proud of the pillows they had made and brought them to me and Mr. Eisenberg so we could look at their designs; some of them were beautiful. If the rest of the curriculum were strong, I guess it might be argued that this class was practical and offered students satisfaction in aesthetic work, and might be useful to a student later on in looking for a job. Still, given the serious academic problems of the students in the school, the sewing lessons struck me as anachronistic.

It proved to be a struggle to convince the principal to let me sit in on an academic class. At last, she let me stick my head into a ninth and tenth grade math class (31 enrolled, the teacher said, but only 22 were present at that hour—it was getting close to two p.m. by now), an economics class that seemed to have some academic substance, and a history class taught by a middle-aged black teacher who delivered to his kids a really solid lesson of the kind one would expect to see in almost any first-rate high school in America.

I left with the confused emotions that I often feel after a visit to a school or district in which academic levels are disturbing and the physical conditions of a number of the buildings are degrading to the children but where most of the people teaching in these buildings seem devoted and hard-working and, as best one can discern from only a day's visit, seem to be doing everything within their power and experience to cope with the calamity that has been handed them. The look of tortured dignity in the eyes of many who had welcomed me remained as one of the most stirring memories of that experience.

More than a year before my visit to these schools, the State Commissioner of Education and the New York Board of Regents had considered dissolution of the district and dispersal of its students to surrounding schools. The New York Times, in an editorial opinion, gave its backing to this plan. Noting that the county that surrounded it had helped impoverish Roosevelt by a policy of "dumping welfare clients" there beginning in the later 1960s (this proved to be a major factor in solidifying segregation in the Roosevelt schools), the paper argued that the district ought to be dissolved in order not to do more damage to its children.

The reaction to this proposal on the part of the surrounding districts, said Richard Mills, the commissioner of education, when we met by chance only a few days later, was "sheer terror." The most virulent resistance had appeared in a predominantly white district named East Meadow that was virtually contiguous with Roosevelt. "KEEP ROOSEVELT STUDENTS OUT OF EAST MEADOW," residents were warned in flyers handed out to kids and parents in East Meadow. The Roosevelt schools are "failing badly," said the flyer, because of "rampant violence" and "drug sales" and "continual assaults" and other problems such as "widespread pregnancies. . . ."

"Do you want this brought to East Meadow?" residents were asked.

If the integration plan went through, the flyer warned, "we will have no choice except to remove our children from the East Meadow schools and move away. But who will buy our homes? People with a lot less money, for much lower prices. Our property values will drop dramatically." The authors of the flyer made an unconvincing effort to insist that this was not a racial issue ("it's all about social class," the flyer claimed), but the language used to speak about the Roosevelt children—"the low-achieving, dysfunctional, criminal bunch from Roosevelt which the state wants to dump on us"—was not unlike the language that inflamed the fears of white communities throughout the South a generation earlier. Similar warnings, I was told by the superintendent of East Meadow's schools, had been displayed on bumper stickers also.

Not long after this, the state officials' tentative suggestion was withdrawn. Instead, having removed the local board of education that had been elected by the residents of Roosevelt and replaced it with appointees subject to state governance, the state set out to put in place the instruments of strict accountability that we have seen in other districts. At the elementary level, these included many of the elements of order and control, including the peculiar managerial curriculum ("consistency management manager applications" and the rest) that I had last seen in Columbus.

If ever there had been an opportunity to end the educational apartheid of a small community of children, this had been it. The tiny population of the Roosevelt schools could, physically at least, have been absorbed with ease into surrounding districts. And despite the angry voices that emerged in districts like East Meadow, responsible civic groups and leaders of the local clergy could, if they had wished, have exercised their ethical authority to shame the hateful and to galvanize the more enlightened people in their towns to find a way to make the Roosevelt children welcome in their schools and their communities. The civil liberties union tried to rally backing for the state commissioner's suggestion, "but we could not do it, even in progressive sectors of the population," I was told. "No civic or political voices came to our support."

In the final event, therefore, the choice was to bring heightened discipline and numbered lists and scripted lesson plans to Roosevelt's children rather than bring Roosevelt's children back into the mainstream of America. There have been changes in the district since. The superintendent in the year I visited, who was a disciple of Rod Paige, at that time the U.S. education secretary, but who had never run a school system before, has been replaced by an experienced administrator who has had success in other districts with long histories of academic failure. The new superintendent, whom I met soon after his appointment, started his career in education as a teacher in the Bronx and seems to have an old schoolteacher's genuine affection for young children and teenagers.

It is possible, as a result, that Roosevelt's schools will undergo some serious improvements in the years ahead and that the learning atmosphere within the system will become far less robotic and more truly academic than before. One can only hope that this may turn out to be true; but the lessons of the past three decades in the Roosevelt district and the lessons we have learned in other separate and unequal districts that have undergone repeated shifts in governance over short periods of time cannot leave us with an easy optimism. Newspaper stories offer now and then what Newsday calls "at least a flicker of hope," but deeper into these news accounts one generally finds more sobering realities. There is a rhythm in these cresting and declining hopes. One sees it in similar districts almost everywhere.

CHAPTER 7

Excluding Beauty

One day when I was teaching fourth grade in the Boston schools, I gave my students an assignment for which I was later criticized by one of the supervising personnel. These were the children who had had 12 substitute teachers in the months before the principal removed me from my other fourth grade class, the one that I was teaching in the auditorium, and sent me into this room for the months that still remained before the end of school.

The assignment I gave them was to describe for me in writing what they saw in front of them each day when they came into school, what they liked, what they did not like in the class, or in the school, and how they felt in general about the situation in which they and I now found ourselves. Because of their limited writing skills, I told them I would not be looking at their spelling and grammar at the start but would be looking for the vividness of details in their papers and the openness with which they would put down their own most private thoughts.

"In my school," began a paper that was handed back to me a few days later, "I see dirty boards and I see papers on the floor. I see an old browken window with a sign on it saying, Do not unlock this window are browken. And I see cracks in the walls and I see old books with ink poured all over them and I see old painting hanging on the walls. I see old alfurbet letter hanging on one nail on the wall. I see a dirty fire exit I see a old closet with supplys for the class. I see pigeons flying all over the school. I see old freght trains throgh the fence of the school yard. I see pictures of contryies hanging on the wall and I see desks with wrighting all over the top of the desks and insited of the desk."

Another child told me this: "I see lots of thinings in this room. I see new teachers omots every day. I can see flowers and children books and other things. I like the 100 papers I like allso cabnets. I don't like the drity windows. And the dusty window shallvalls. . . ."

This was another paper I was given: "I see pictures in my school. . . . I see arithmetic paper a spellings paper. I see a star chart. I see the flag of our Amerrica. The room is dirty. . . . The auditorium dirty the seats are dusty. The light in the auditorium is brok. The curtains in the auditorium are ragged they took the curtains down because they was so ragged. The bathroom is dirty sometime the toilet is very hard. The cellar is dirty the hold school is dirty sometime. . . . The flowers are dry every thing in my school is so so dirty."

Many things have changed in inner-city schools since then; and some remain the same. Physical disrepair and squalor may not be as blatant in most districts now, although there are schools I visit where conditions are a good deal more offensive than the ones my students faithfully described. The child who said, "I see new teachers omots every day," could have been speaking about any one of countless inner-city schools in the United States today. The insult to aesthetics, the affront to cleanliness and harmony and sweetness, are continuing realities as well for children who must go each morning into morbid-looking buildings in which few adults other than their teachers would agree to work day after day.

There is no misery index for the children of apartheid education. There ought to be; we measure almost every other aspect of the lives they lead in school. Do kids who go to schools like these enjoy the days they spend in them? Is school, for most of them, a happy place to be? You do not find the answers to these questions in reports about achievement levels, scientific methods of accountability, or structural revisions in the modes of governance. Documents like these don't speak of happiness. You have to go back to the schools themselves to find an answer to these questions. You have to sit down in the little chairs in first and second grade, or on the reading rug with kindergarten kids, and listen to the things they actually say to one another and the dialogue between them and their teachers. You have to go down to the basement with the children when it's time for lunch and to the playground with them, if they have a playground, when it's time for recess, if they still have recess at their school. You have to walk into the children's bathrooms in these buildings. You have to do what children do and breathe the air the children breathe. I don't think that there is any other way to find out what the lives that children lead in school are really like.

On an October day three years ago, I walked into an elementary school in Oklahoma City, where the schools had been desegregated under a court order about 25 years earlier. The district has become resegregated since, after a federal judge released the city from court oversight in

1991, declaring that a program of compensatory education called "Effective Schools" had proven to his satisfaction that a segregated schooling system need not be unequal and observing also that the city was establishing an "Equity Committee" to provide assurance that an equal education would be given to all children.

Likable children and hard-working teachers and unconscionable overcrowding were apparent from the moment I arrived. Approximately 750 children were enrolled, although the building could accommodate only about 400. The other 350 children were attending class in trailers, some of which reeked of disinfectant on the day that I was there. Ninety percent of the students were Hispanic, black, or Native American. Only about a third of those in kindergarten had been given preschool education: 36 four-year-olds in all, according to the principal, with 70 others on a waiting list.

Whether the Equity Committee still existed was unclear; if so, it did not appear to have fulfilled the expectations of the federal court. Teachers at the school were paid approximately $2,500 less, on average, than were teachers in the other elementary schools within the district and had taught, on average, for less than five years, while teachers elsewhere in the district had been teaching for an average of 12 years. Per-pupil funding was officially reported to be virtually the same as elsewhere in the district (a bit less than $7,000), although the lower salaries that teachers here were paid must have skewed this figure somewhat in reality. In addition to its public funding, the school received a private grant of $27,000 yearly from a petrochemical corporation known as Kerr-McGee, which amounted to approximately $36 yearly for each pupil. An official of the corporation served as chairman of the governing council of the school, a not uncommon arrangement in low-income schools that need to look to private-sector sources for support.

In back of the drab redbrick building, part of which had been erected around 1910, the rest during the 1930s, there was a concrete drainage channel which had come to be a hangout for gang members and where transients gathered in the evenings, said the principal. "A body was found out there some time ago," he noted as we walked across an open area to visit classrooms in the trailers. To the left of the school, across a narrow street, there was a row of rundown wooden houses, but the most dilapidated-looking buildings in the neighborhood were not these houses but the antiquated trailers in which nearly half the children spent their days in school.

Some of the trailers, which the principal described as "barracks classrooms," were so distant from the school that they could not be wired in to school security, the principal explained, and they were burglarized at times as a result. For lunch the children walked to the main building, but the lunchroom was so small that children had to come there in six shifts beginning at ten-thirty. "The kindergarten children are served first," he said, "but it's so early they get hungry later, and they need to have a snack." There were no bathrooms in the trailers. Children had to leave their classrooms and line up outside the bathrooms in another trailer, which, according to the principal, could be "most uncomfortable" in very cold or rainy weather.

The principal, who had come here as a fourth grade teacher ten years earlier, was an affable, blunt-speaking person, somewhat rumpled in his style. He told me that the high-stakes standardized exams his students had to take were "starting to control the teaching—much more than I'd like." There was, as a consequence, no recess at the school. The sacrifice of recess was intended to permit the teachers to increase "their time on task," he said.

The school nonetheless had a much softer and more child-friendly feeling than the other schools I had been visiting in recent months. In a kindergarten class taught by a playful giant of a man known to the kids as "Mr. C" (his actual name, he said, was "very hard for children to pronounce"), I watched a lively reading lesson in which phonics and sight-recognition of familiar words were being taught not from a scripted plan or drill-based phonics text but from a storybook in which the children, who were sitting on a colored rug in front of him, seemed thoroughly engaged.

When one of the children started to chatter just a bit too much, he handled it in a good-natured way. "Let's give our mouth a *little* zip," he said, and drew a finger and thumb across his lips as if they were a zipper, and the child smilingly complied. When a boy gave him a good and careful answer to a question, he reached out his hand, palm flat, and met the child's hand, palm flat as well, then asked the class if they would like to do "the pumpkin rhyme" or sing "the song about the apple tree" and when the class appeared to be divided on the matter, he allowed them to do both.

As tall as he was, he must have seemed tremendous to these five-year-olds, but he was gentle with them and he had a playful personality. When he stood up to tell a story about "monsters" at the end of class, one of the little girls began to laugh so hard that she fell over in her chair and then, of course, although she wasn't hurt, began to cry, which brought the monster story to its end because the teacher had to kneel down on the floor to comfort her.

Of the 21 children in his kindergarten classroom, four were white. That was three more than I'd ever seen in kindergarten classes in the Bronx; but 99 percent of children in the school were poor and, despite the modest benefactions of its corporate big brother, the overcrowding of the building and the squalor of the barracks classrooms struck me as a throwback to another era in our history.

A few days later, at an elementary school in Lexington, Kentucky, I walked into a class of second and third graders who were being taught a lesson about corporate achievement and the workings of the private market by a representative of IBM. After he was done, their teacher ran them through a drill of new vocabulary words they had just learned.

"When we give you money for coming to work," the teacher asked, "what do we call it?"

"Income!" said the children.

"When there's something we want that someone else can sell, what do we call it?"

"Goods!" the class replied.

"When there's something we want that no one has for sale, what do we call it?"

"Scarcity!" the class replied in unison.

The name of the school was Russell Elementary. Historically known as one of Lexington's three "colored schools" (it was known as "Colored School Number 1" when it was opened in 1888), it was now sited in a building that had been erected in 1953, according to an old edition of a local paper, as "the new school home of approximately 350 Negro children." It opened its doors in January 1954 and was dedicated on April 4 of the same year, a scant six weeks before the *Brown* decision would be handed down. Renovated only once since it was built, the school had subsequently fallen into disrepair. The principal showed me gaping holes in several walls and said the basement was condemned for use "because of ventilation problems," so activities like music, which she valued highly, could not take place in the basement any longer.

A resourceful person, it appeared, she had devised a tentative solution to this problem so that children could continue to be given musical instruction. At the bottom of a set of stairs next to an open area beside one of the exits of the building, there was a collection of small violins and cellos. Better-funded schools might have a real performance space. In this school, the children and their music teacher settled for this spot beside the door. It was carpeted, however, and the stairs provided space where a small audience might sit; and even with the serious infrastructure problems that the principal had pointed out, it was a more cheerful school, by far, than any I had visited in recent months.

The instructional approach in use within the school, which was based upon a body of ideas called "multiple intelligences" developed by Howard Gardner, a psychologist at Harvard University, emphasized the interrelationship of art and science with arithmetic and reading and the other elements of elementary school instruction. Children who had special needs were integrated into mainstream classes; and, in part because the school had been awarded magnet status in the district, 20 percent of students in the school were white.

The principal told me she was born in Mississippi and had gone to Jackson State and come of age during the civil rights campaigns in which her father, who was a minister, had been an activist and leader. She was a warm and glowing woman who refused to let her natural expressiveness be tightened up by jargon and did not seem worried in the least to let me see some of the children acting mischievous and foolish in the corridors.

As she was talking with me at one point, a group of second grade girls came down the hall pretending they were birds with arms spread out and fluttering like wings. When they saw the principal, some of them broke out of line to rush her for a hug. They had just come back from recess and were quite excited about something that had happened in the playground. They chattered at her all at once.

The hard edge of the standards-driven juggernaut did not seem to have made more than minor inroads on instructional approaches in this building; and despite the fact that testing pressures were increasing for the teachers at the Russell at the time that I was there, it had not lost that fragile sense of unprotected and unglazed humanity in grown-ups and endearing randomness in children that is often very hard to find in other urban schools today.

A harsher reality was present in the public schools I visited in California. Tensions were greater; pressure to conform to very rigid state curricular requirements was more severe; and physical conditions in most of the schools I visited were more discouraging than those that I had seen in any other section of the country other than in Oklahoma City.

Overcrowding in the California schools was legendary by this time. "Hundreds of thousands of our children are trying to learn in overcrowded, out-of-date [and] unsafe classrooms" or "in temporary trailers" that were staked out in the spaces that had once been playgrounds, as then Governor Gray Davis had observed. Even with the use of trailers, nearly a thousand schools throughout the state were forced to operate on year-round calendars.

In San Bernardino, children at an elementary school called Monterey attended class in staggered shifts right through the year. "At any point, three quarters of the student population is in school," the superintendent told me. Children in three other elementary schools went to class on normal calendars, he said; so the district had to publish separate calendars, one of which was called "continuous," and one "traditional," to indicate two separate school-years for two separate sectors of the population.

At the time of my visit, Monterey was under state review because of very low scores on examinations in preceding years. Half the teachers working at the school two years before had either left or been removed since then, according to the principal. Class size in the younger grades was not too high—I saw 20 children in a first grade class, 19 in a second—but fourth and fifth grade classes averaged 29 and 30, with a few of the classes holding 33 or more. About a quarter of the teachers were uncertified and working under what are termed "emergency credentials." Of the 800 children at the school, all but three received free or reduced price meals. Nearly 90 percent were children of minorities.

Standardized tests in language arts and mathematics started in the first grade at the school, the principal reported. A first grade teacher had ten pages of enumerated standards, correlated with the items to be tested, posted on her wall. "Only two or three of my students," said a kindergarten teacher, "usually have any preschool preparation." The principal estimated that, on average, three quarters of his students had received no pre-K education.

The immediate threat above the teachers' heads at Monterey was an imposing document called "The Immediate Intervention Plan"—not unlike the "School Improvement Plans" imposed on other low-performing schools in other states—which called for "five percent improvement" in the students' scores over a given period of time. If this goal was not achieved, the school would be subjected to a second and more stringent level of state oversight. These state demands for pumping test scores by specific numbers in specific periods of time had grown so arbitrary and invasive, as a school board member told me, that experienced principals were suffering from symptoms of anxiety such as respiratory stress and stomach pains. "One principal," she said, "has asked to be demoted to vice-principal" because "the emotional toll that this is taking has begun to make her ill."

The superintendent spoke of the message he believed the overcrowding of the school conveyed to parents in the neighborhood. "Our parents do not know what 'the best' is," he observed, "but they *want* the best. When we have to assign their kids to summer semesters and to portables while three miles down the road they can see schools with traditional calendars and with sufficient space, I can understand it when they ask, 'Why are our children not important?' "

In a legal action filed by the American Civil Liberties Union and a number of other civil rights and advocacy groups, parents and children asked a question not unlike this of the state of California. In documentation presented to the Superior Court of California in 2001 and 2002, drawing upon depositions taken from teachers and other school employees and from more than 60 students who attended 18 public schools, attorneys described conditions of substandard educational provision that were reminiscent of conditions in the schools of southern districts as they were described in cases tried by Thurgood Marshall and Charles Hamilton Houston and their colleagues in the years preceding *Brown*.

Among the items documented in court papers, according to the Sacramento Bee, were "chemistry labs with no chemicals at all," "literature classes without books," "computer classes where, according to one student, 'we sit there and talk about what we would be doing if we had computers,' " "classes in which students were forced to stand or to sit on bookshelves, cabinets or window sills," because there were more kids than chairs, and classes without regular teachers where, as in one San Francisco school, a substitute teacher let a class watch movies and, as a student at the school reported, "everybody failed" the final exam. At one elementary school whose students were among the plaintiffs in the case, the computer lab became as hot as 92 degrees on summer days, according to another press account, and teachers had to spray their kids with water during class to cool them off enough to do their work.

Some of the most disturbing documentation I was shown by lawyers for the plaintiffs came from children only eight or nine years old who were attending one of the many California schools that suffered rodent infestation. "I saw a rat in room 28," wrote a boy named Daniel in the fourth grade of an elementary school (1,500 children in attendance, 99 percent minority) in the large and sprawling district of Los Angeles. "The room smelled very bad and it made me sick to my stomach. There was blood all over the place."

"I saw a rat," another child wrote. "It was a big fat rat. I saw the fat rat dead. . . . There were nine rats in the classroom."

"I was very scared," wrote a child in the class named Ashley whose friends reported seeing one of the live rats climbing on her chair. "It was hard for me to breathe. I asked the teacher to send me to the nurse."

"Ashley got sick because of dead rats," wrote another child.

At the 75th Street Elementary School in South Central Los Angeles, which I visited with my friend Rebecca Constantino, the director of a small nonprofit agency that donates books to underfunded schools, the presence of rats was only one of a number of health hazards children had to face. Exposed asbestos and the presence of flaking chips of lead-based paint were serious problems too. A letter that was headed "WARNING to 75th Street School Parents," sent home by the teachers, recommended that they take their children to be tested for lead poisoning.

Of the 1,800 children in this year-round school, nearly

1,400 were in session at a given time. Because of the way the schedule was arranged, roughly half the children had no summer break; a child completed one grade in the final week of June and began the next grade three days later. "On Friday afternoon I'm in the first grade. On Monday morning I'm in second grade," as one of the teachers laid out the school calendar.

According to school documents, 99.7 percent of children in the school were black or Hispanic. At the time of my visit, more than a quarter of the teachers were not certified and were working on emergency credentials. "Typical stay for teachers here is three and a half years," an older teacher said. "Once they get their credentials after the third year, many move out to the Valley"—where, she said, there were more middle-class and upper-class communities. As in many overcrowded buildings, discipline was tight. Lining up her children at the classroom door, a first grade teacher said, "Ten-hut!" The children in the line stamped twice. "Are you ready?" asked the teacher. "Yes . . . ma'am!" said the kids in unison. "Pass!" the teacher told them.

Perhaps to compensate for inexperience and instability of staffing, the Success For All curriculum had been adopted here. In a kindergarten class, the children were chanting consonant sounds when I arrived, then read without emotion from a story in a phonics book that had only a rudimentary story-line and no apparent literary qualities but which employed the sounds they were supposed to learn that day.

"Who can tell me who were the main characters?" the teacher asked them after they had come to the conclusion of the story. Three or four children answered this and almost all her questions. Most of the others simply stared at her with faces blank. There were no rich displays of children's work within the room; nor, for that matter, were there many signs or posters that appeared to have been drawn or written by the teacher. The room instead was inundated by externally created posters, signs, and admonitions. It was a plastic-feeling, unamusing setting with no colorful vitality.

In another kindergarten class, there was a poster with a large schematic illustration of a wheel, at the top of which there was an exhortation to the teacher to uphold "CLEAR EXPECTATIONS . . . ACADEMIC RIGOR," under which and spaced around the illustration of the wheel were various subtopics such as "Content Standards" and "Assessment Data" and "Analysis of Student Work." Nothing on the chart explained itself or justified its presence in the room. Why was it here? What was it for? I asked a school official who was standing nearby to explain it to me.

"If it's visually on your screen," she said, "it's going to be more on your intake, and you're liable to move it from your short-term memory to your long-term memory. And this"—she pointed to one of the items on the chart—"enables you to input this into your professional day. So, for example, you might glance at it and think, 'Oh yes, I need to do Analysis of Student Work. It's up there on my wheel.' "

I'm not sure how often this is likely to be true. Once teachers post these charts and mandates on their walls, many tell me that they rarely look at them again and, even if they do, I don't believe they'd often stop and think, "It's time to do Analysis of Student Work." The postings are iconic. They represent part of a paper world that has only a very vague and indirect connection to the things that take place in a classroom or the actual behavior of a teacher.

"This stuff is gobbledygook," my friend Rebecca said. "Teachers are told they have to go along with this since people from the district come around to check. 'Have you got your content standards on the wall? Have you got your wheel of expectations?' The assumption is the teacher is too dumb to know enough to analyze her children's work unless she sees it on a poster. Meanwhile, what you really need are pencils! paper! children's books! or counselors for students in your class who have real problems!"

The school consisted of three tired-looking buildings painted brownish-yellow and surrounded by a metal fence that gave it the appearance of a prison; and even with the year-round calendar it wasn't large enough to hold so many children and was forced therefore to put a row of portables at one end of the playground. "The majority of California schools," according to one of the lead attorneys in the ACLU case, "continue to operate on the traditional school calendar. The vast preponderance of kids who have to go to school on year-round schedules are Hispanic. The next highest racial group of students in these year-round schools are black. The ethnic distinctions here are very obvious. We have detailed documentation that confirms this."

Fremont High School in Los Angeles enrolls almost 5,000 students on a three-track schedule, with about 3,300 in attendance at a given time. The campus "sprawls across a city block, between San Pedro Street and Avalon Boulevard in South Central Los Angeles," the Los Angeles Times observes. A "neighborhood fortress, its perimeter protected by an eight-foot steel fence topped by spikes," the windows of the school are "shielded from gunfire by thick screens." According to teachers at the school, the average ninth grade student reads at fourth or fifth grade level. Nearly a third read at third grade level or below. About two thirds of the ninth grade students drop out prior to twelfth grade.

There were 27 homerooms for the first-year students, nine homerooms for seniors at the time I visited in spring of 2003. Thirty-five to 40 classrooms, nearly a third of all the classrooms in the school, were located in portables. Some classes also took place in converted storage closets—

"windowless and nasty," said one of the counselors—or in converted shop rooms without blackboards. Class size was high, according to a teacher who had been here for six years and who invited me into her tenth grade social studies class. Nearly 220 classes had enrollments ranging between 33 and over 40 students. The class I visited had 40 students, almost all of whom were present on the day that I was there.

Unlike the staggered luncheon sessions I observed at Walton High, lunch was served in a single sitting to the students in this school. "It's physically impossible to feed 3,300 kids at once," the teacher said. "The line for kids to get their food is very long and the entire period lasts only 30 minutes. It takes them 15 minutes just to walk there from their classes and get through the line. They get 10 minutes probably to eat their meals. A lot of them don't try. You've been a teacher, so you can imagine what it does to students when they have no food to eat for an entire day. The schoolday here at Fremont is eight hours long."

For teachers, too, the schedule sounded punishing. "I have six classes every day, including my homeroom," she said. "I've had *more* than 40 students in a class some years. My average class this year is 36. I see more than 200 students every day. Classes start at seven-thirty. I don't usually leave until four or four-thirty. . . ."

High school students, when I meet them first, are often more reluctant than the younger children are to open up their feelings and express their personal concerns; but hesitation on the part of students did not prove to be a problem in this class at Fremont High. The students knew I was a writer (they were told this by their teacher) and they took no time in getting down to matters that were on their minds.

"Can we talk about the bathrooms?" asked a student named Mireya.

In almost any classroom there are certain students who, by force of the directness or unusual sophistication of their way of speaking, tend to capture your attention from the start. Mireya later spoke insightfully of academic problems at the school, but her observations on the physical and personal embarrassments she and her schoolmates had to undergo cuts to the heart of questions of essential dignity or the denial of such dignity that kids in squalid schools like this one have to deal with.

Fremont High School, as court papers document, has "15 fewer bathrooms than the law requires." Of the limited number of bathrooms that are working in the school, "only one or two . . . are open and unlocked for girls to use." Long lines of girls are "waiting to use the bathrooms," which are generally "unclean" and "lack basic supplies," including toilet paper. Some of the classrooms "do not have air-conditioning," so that students "become red-faced and unable to concentrate" during "the extreme heat of summer." The rats observed by children in their elementary schools proliferate at Fremont High as well. "Rats in eleven . . . classrooms," maintenance records of the school report. "Rat droppings" are recorded "in the bins and drawers" of the high school's kitchen. "Hamburger buns" are being "eaten off [the] bread-delivery rack," school records note.

No matter how many times I read these tawdry details in court filings and depositions, I'm always surprised again to learn how often these unsanitary physical conditions are permitted to continue in a public school even after media accounts describe them vividly. But hearing of these conditions in Mireya's words was even more unsettling, in part because this student was so fragile-seeming and because the need even to speak of these indignities in front of me and all the other students seemed like an additional indignity.

"The problem is this," she carefully explained. "You're

not allowed to use the bathroom during lunch, which is a 30-minute period. The only time that you're allowed to use it is between your classes." But "this is a huge building," she went on. "It has long corridors. If you have one class at one end of the building and your next class happens to be way down at the other end, you don't have time to use the bathroom and still get to class before it starts. So you go to your class and then you ask permission from your teacher to go to the bathroom and the teacher tells you, 'No. You had your chance between the periods. . . .'

"I feel embarrassed when I have to stand there and explain it to a teacher."

"This is the question," said a wiry-looking boy named Edward, leaning forward in his chair close to the door, a little to the right of where I stood. "Students are not animals, but even animals need to relieve themselves sometimes. We're in this building for eight hours. What do they think we're supposed to do?"

"It humiliates you," said Mireya, who went on to make the interesting statement that "the school provides solutions that don't actually work," and this idea was taken up by other students in describing course requirements within the school. A tall black student, for example, told me that she hoped to be a social worker or a doctor but was programmed into "Sewing Class" this year. She also had to take another course, called "Life Skills," which she told me was a very basic course—"a retarded class," to use her words—that "teaches things like the six continents," which she said she'd learned in elementary school.

When I asked her why she had to take these courses, she replied that she'd been told they were required, which reminded me of the response the sewing teacher I had met at Roosevelt Junior High School gave to the same question. As at Roosevelt, it turned out that this was not exactly so. What *was* required was that high school students take two courses in an area of study that was called "the Technical Arts," according to the teacher. At schools that served the middle class or upper middle class, this requirement was likely to be met by courses that had academic substance and, perhaps, some relevance to college preparation. At Beverly Hills High School, for example, the technical arts requirement could be fulfilled by taking subjects such as residential architecture, the designing of commercial structures, broadcast journalism, advanced computer graphics, a sophisticated course in furniture design, carving and sculpture, or an honors course in engineering research and design. At Fremont High, in contrast, this requirement was far more likely to be met by courses that were basically vocational.

Mireya, for example, who had plans to go to college, told me that she had to take a sewing class last year and now was told she'd been assigned to take a class in hair-dressing as well. When I asked the teacher why Mireya could not skip these subjects and enroll in classes that would help her to pursue her college aspirations, she replied, "It isn't a question of what students want. It's what the school may have available. If all the other elective classes that a student wants to take are full, she has to take one of these classes if she wants to graduate."

A very small girl named Obie who had big blue-tinted glasses tilted up across her hair interrupted then to tell me with a kind of wild gusto that she took hair-dressing *twice*! When I expressed surprise that this was possible, she said there were two levels of hair-dressing offered here at Fremont High. "One is in hair-styling," she said. "The other is in braiding."

Mireya stared hard at this student for a moment and then suddenly began to cry. "I don't *want* to take hair-dressing. I did not need sewing either. I knew how to sew. My mother is a seamstress in a factory. I'm trying to go to college. I don't need to sew to go to college. My mother sews. I hoped for something else."

"What would you rather take?" I asked.

"I wanted to take an AP class," she answered.

Mireya's sudden tears elicited a strong reaction from one of the boys who had been silent up to now. A thin and dark-eyed student, named Fortino, with long hair down to his shoulders who was sitting on the left side of the classroom, he turned directly to Mireya.

"Listen to me," he said. "The owners of the sewing factories need laborers. Correct?"

"I guess they do," Mireya said.

"It's not going to be their own kids. Right?"

"Why not?" another student said.

"So they can grow beyond themselves," Mireya answered quietly. "But we remain the same."

"You're ghetto," said Fortino, "so we send you to the factory." He sat low in his desk chair, leaning on one elbow, his voice and dark eyes loaded with a cynical intelligence. "You're ghetto—so you sew!"

"There are higher positions than these," said a student named Samantha.

"You're ghetto," said Fortino unrelentingly to her. "So sew!"

Mireya was still crying.

Several students spoke then of a problem about frequent substitute teachers, which was documented also in court papers. One strategy for staffing classes in these three- and four-track schools when substitutes could not be found was to assign a teacher who was not "on track"—that is, a teacher who was on vacation—to come back to school and fill in for the missing teacher. "Just yesterday I was subbing [for] a substitute who was subbing for a teacher who never shows up," a teacher told the ACLU lawyers. "That's one scenario. . . ."

Obie told me that she stopped coming to class during the previous semester because, out of her six teachers, three were substitutes. "Come on now! Like—hello? We live in a rich country? Like the richest country in the world? Hello?"

The teacher later told me that three substitutes in one semester, if the student's words were accurate, would be unusual. But "on average, every student has a substitute teacher in at least one class. Out of 180 teacher-slots, typically 25 or so cannot be filled and have to be assigned to substitutes."

Hair-dressing and sewing, it turned out, were not the only classes students at the school were taking that appeared to have no relevance to academic education. A number of the students, for example, said that they were taking what were known as "service classes" in which they would sit in on an academic class but didn't read the texts or do the lessons or participate in class activities but passed out books and did small errands for the teachers. They were given half-credits for these courses. Students received credits, too, for jobs they took outside of school, in fast-food restaurants for instance, I was told. How, I wondered, was a credit earned or grade determined for a job like this outside of school? "Best behavior and great customer service," said a student who was working in a restaurant, as she explained the logic of it all to ACLU lawyers in her deposition.

The teacher gave some other examples of the ways in which the students were shortchanged in academic terms. The year-round calendar, she said, gave these students 20 fewer schooldays than the students who attended school on normal calendars receive. In compensation, they attended classes for an extra hour, up until three-thirty, and students in the higher grades who had failed a course and had to take a make-up class remained here even later, until six, or sometimes up to nine.

"They come out of it just totally glassed-over," said the teacher, and, as one result, most teachers could not realistically give extra homework to make up for fewer days of school attendance and, in fact, because the kids have been in school so long each day, she said, "are likely to give less."

Students who needed to use the library to do a research paper for a class ran into problems here as well, because, as a result of the tight scheduling of classes, they were given no free time to use the library except at lunch, or for 30 minutes after school, unless a teacher chose to bring a class into the library to do a research project during a class period. But this was frequently impossible because the library was often closed when it was being used for other purposes such as administration of examinations, typically for "make-up tests," as I was told. "It's been closed now for a week because they're using it for testing," said Samantha.

"They were using it for testing last week also," said Fortino, who reported that he had a research paper due for which he had to locate 20 sources but had made no progress on it yet because he could not get into the library.

"You have to remember," said the teacher, "that the school's in session all year long, so if repairs need to be made in wiring or something like that in the library, they have to do it while the kids are here. So at those times the library is closed. Then, if there's testing taking place in there, the library is closed. And if an AP teacher needs a place to do an AP prep, the library is closed. And sometimes when the teachers need a place to meet, the library is closed." In all, according to the school librarian, the library was closed more than a quarter of the year.

During a meeting with a group of teachers later in the afternoon, it was explained to me in greater detail how the overcrowding of the building limited course offerings for students. "Even when students *ask* to take a course that interests them and teachers want to teach it," said one member of the faculty—she gave the example of a class in women's studies she said she would like to teach—"the physical shortages of space repeatedly prevent this." Putting students into service classes, on the other hand, did not require extra space. So, instead of the enrichment students might have gained from taking an elective course that had some academic substance, they were obliged to sit through classes in which they were not enrolled and from which they said that they learned virtually nothing.

Mireya had asked her teacher for permission to stay in the room with us during my meeting with the other teachers and remained right to the end. At five p.m., as I was about to leave the school, she stood beside the doorway of the classroom as the teacher, who was giving me a ride, assembled all the work she would be taking home.

"Why is it," she asked, "that students who do not need what we need get so much more? And we who need it so much more get so much less?"

I told her I'd been asking the same question now for nearly 40 years and still had no good answer. She answered, maturely, that she did not think there was an answer.

Before we left the building, the teacher gave me papers that the students wrote about the various dilemmas that they faced at school. On the plane flying east, I had an opportunity to read them, some of which had been addressed to me, some to their teacher.

Several papers spoke about the lengthy periods of time that had been sacrificed to testing. "For real? I believe we get desturbed about 20 days," a student named Alexis wrote. "I think we spend like a month and a half from school time onely preper for our testing," wrote another. "Sometimes I feel that when we go [to] testing," wrote a girl named Erica, "we are actually missing big part of a class . . . and you never know when a class will make you see life defferently." "There is at least two weeks that is taken away from testing," wrote a boy named Javier. "I think there's more but I'm not Shure. Theres alot of school time that is wasted. . . ." One of the most proficient pieces, with the fewest syntax errors and the most coherent sentences, was by Fortino. "I don't have to go all into detail," he began. "I think it's a school that is in deep shit overall. . . . The biggest problem with Fremont is over population. Teachers are pushed so far that they just give up on their students. Others trie to keep up the fight," he wrote, "but they are lossing slowly."

Many of the students blamed themselves for problems in the school ("the neighborhood is ghetto so that means the students here are ghetto," said a boy named David), and there were several who believed the school might soon improve, or had already started to improve, because, as one boy wrote, a "stricked new principle" had been appointed recently. I was saddened to read these papers after talking with the students for so long, because their writing skills would give no hint of the lucidity of thinking many demonstrated in our conversation.

Some of the students were recent immigrants; but the teacher said a large majority—"two thirds to three quarters"—had attended elementary school here in Los Angeles. The years in which they were in elementary school were the same period of time in which the tough accountability agenda had been gathering momentum, and it had been firmly set in place when most of them had been in middle school. Yet very few could write a sentence at the fourth or fifth grade level and their spelling, which might have made sense phonetically, did not incorporate conventional irregularities; and the syntax in most of their papers was encumbered and disabled and lacked continuity and fluency and was unequal to the meanings it was meant to bear.

Those who are inclined to understate the role of racial bias in perpetuation of the educational inequities the students had described to me at Fremont High have sometimes argued that "it's all more complicated now" because it isn't only African-Americans who go to these substandard schools but children of other ethnic origins as well—"all these diverse minorities," as I have heard it said in more or less those words—and therefore "it's a whole new ballgame that we're playing in today."

I disagree. I would argue that it is the same old ballgame, with Hispanic students and now also many Southeast Asian students of low income placed in very much the same positions in which black kids have been forced to play for well over 100 years, and still are forced to play. And in most places they are playing in the same old run down ballparks with the same inferior equipment and the same inadequate and overburdened supervision that black students in these districts have experienced, and still experience; and often, of course, they undergo the same indignities together. They are drilled in the same rigidified curricula in schools that face the same impermanence of staffing, under exhortations to the same allegedly high expectations that are contradicted by the same degrading physical realities; and when they get to high school, if not sooner, they are channeled all too frequently into the same low level work-related programs of instruction with the same results in limiting their future economic options that we've seen in schools that serve primarily black children.

In the first pages of this book, I spoke of the sewing class for black fifth graders (females only) in the school in which I taught in 1964 and 1965 in Boston. We have also seen the sewing class for seventh and eighth grade students (males and females both) at Roosevelt Junior High School. Courses in hair-dressing ("cosmetology") have also been offered to black females in our nation's segregated schools for decades, starting as long ago as in the 1950s, if not earlier, a caste-determined practice that was rarely questioned by repeated generations of administrators in these systems. Now Hispanic students also, mostly female, are encouraged or required to take classes such as these, as we have seen at Fremont High, while children of the white and middle class are likely to be learning algebra and calculus and chemistry and government and history and all those other subjects that enable them to set their sights on universities and colleges.

"We seein' more than y'all can see," the very small girl named Obie said to me at one point in our conversation. I think she said this when I may have briefly seemed to draw back from Fortino's words about the "owners of the factories" who needed high school girls, as he believed, to learn to sew. There was a flash of anger and defiance in her eyes. Although she said this in a slightly patronizing way, I took a liking to her almost instantly. At the same time, I didn't think that what she said was actually true. I think that most Americans can see the same injustices she and her classmates saw. It isn't the vision of those kids that seemed unusual to me. It is the plain words that they used when they reported what they knew. I was grateful to the students in that class at Fremont High for sticking it out with me for two full hours until late into the afternoon. I felt challenged by their honesty.

CHAPTER 8

False Promises

When I was a teacher in the 1960s, one of the most highly publicized attempts to lift the levels of achievement for black children in de facto segregated schools was under way in New York City. The program, known as Higher Horizons, was the subject of extensive press attention, most of it tremendously enthusiastic at the start. The federal government assisted in the financing of this and other efforts like it elsewhere; and, indeed, as Gary Orfield has observed, far greater sums of money were invested in compensatory programs of this nature in the decades after *Brown,* at least in northern cities, than in programs of desegregation. So it is of interest to look back and see not only how these policies were heralded but what they actually achieved.

According to a U.S. Civil Rights Commission report on racial isolation in the public schools, published in 1967, Higher Horizons had been termed "the most extensive project ever undertaken in the area of education for disadvantaged children." The program had begun in 1959 on a small pilot basis and, when fully implemented three years later, served approximately 60,000 New York City children. Higher Horizons initially spent $50 more per pupil than was spent on children who were not included in the program. Teachers were "encouraged to improve . . . their expectations of the students." Various forms of counseling were offered "in an effort to raise student aspirations." Efforts were also made "to broaden the cultural backgrounds and horizons" of the students by providing visits to museums and libraries. Extra instruction was provided to improve their reading, writing, and arithmetic skills.

A report on the program after its first year, according to The New York Times, "showed gratifying achievements in improving the education of elementary and junior high school children. . . . The students, who are part of this . . . nationally publicized and recognized program, are doing substantially better in their academic work. . . ." The "ingredients of the prescription," said The Times, "hardly a secret formula," were "more and better teachers and—more money." On the latter point, the paper said, "it is encouraging to note that while the extra cost per student was $50 at the beginning of the experiment, it has now settled down to $27. . . ."

Among "significant accomplishments" the program had achieved were "improvement in reading," "a decline in the number of school suspensions because of extreme misbehavior," "better attendance," "good work habits," improvement in "self-discipline," and a "dramatic increase" in cooperation between the school and home. "Third grade pupils in the program showed gains in reading comprehension in six months that exceeded the normal growth for that period by 2.3 months. Pupils in six of the schools scored 3.0 months in reading-grade above third grade children from comparable schools not participating in the program." In one junior high, the paper said, pupil suspensions dropped from 30 to 11 in a single year.

"This is the greatest single experience I have had," said Abraham Ribicoff, the U.S. secretary of health, education and welfare, when he visited a Harlem school in which the program was in operation. "It should be an object lesson for America." And, noting the very small amount of money that was being spent to make the program possible, the secretary praised the program for the benefits that it delivered for so few taxpayer dollars. "What a cheap investment," he observed, "to take a boy and give him some stars in his eyes."

The problem, as it soon turned out, was that the program had become *too* cheap too rapidly. The reduction in investment in each child from the starting point of $50 down to $27 had watered down whatever gains it may have brought in its initial phase. By 1966, the great excitement in the media about "significant accomplishments" had suddenly come crashing to a halt. "Without fanfare . . . ," The Times observed, "the New York City school system last week admitted that the Higher Horizons program is being closed down."

Seven years after it began, the program had been evaluated by independent researchers from New York University. As the Civil Rights Commission noted, the researchers found no measurable improvement in the academic achievement of participating children and, in a follow-up study of the children when they were in junior high, could find no meaningful differences between those children who attended segregated schools that had this program and those in segregated schools that had not been a part of this experiment. Dr. Elliott Shapiro, a respected figure in the education world of New York City at the time and principal of a Harlem elementary school that had participated in the program, testified at a Civil Rights Commission hearing, "Maybe there were some few changes in attitude," which he said were "hard to measure," but "there was really very little change" in levels of achievement.

Other cities—Berkeley, Syracuse, Seattle, and Philadelphia were four that were examined by the Civil Rights Commission—carried out similar efforts during roughly the same time. In none of these cities, the commission notes, did the results appear to be more promising than those that were recorded in New York. "High hopes have reaped an insignificant harvest . . . ," said the superintendent of the Berkeley schools after four years of experience in trying to extract some benefits from a compensatory education program for black children in that city.

The Civil Rights Commission then examined various desegregation efforts carried out in some of the same cities and in other cities where the ethnic demographics were the same or similar to these. None of these undertakings in the major northern cities had been large. "In New York City, for example," the commission said, "about 100 boundary changes" in attendance areas for public schools had been made from 1959 to 1963 in order to promote desegregation. "Despite these changes, the extent of segregation in the city's schools was greater in 1963" than it had been in 1958. Some of the efforts elsewhere in the nation were, however, more extensive. In those cities studied by the Civil Rights Commission in which there were both desegregation programs and compensatory education programs, the former consistently revealed more favorable results in the performance of the students.

Higher Horizons, as the Civil Rights Commission noted, was only one of several projects of compensatory education that were instituted in that era. Even the tiny Roosevelt district on Long Island, already becoming deeply segregated at the time, created a compensatory program,

New Frontiers in Education, which, said The New York Times, was "similar to the Higher Horizons program of the New York City public schools," intended to help children who do not "live up to their . . . potential" by augmenting "cultural experiences" and taking the students on one-day visits outside their community. "The first visit was a tour of the Columbia University campus, followed by a football game and a meeting with some of the football players. . . ." Other visits were made to the United Nations, the Museum of Natural History, and the Hayden Planetarium. "The program has brought dividends in improved report cards . . . ," said The Times; but, as in Berkeley, Philadelphia, and the other districts in which efforts to improve achievement in apartheid settings were attempted, the initial promises turned out to be illusory.

Boston had a similar program, known as Operation Counterpoise, which was advanced, I thought quite shamelessly, by school officials to resist demands from leaders in the black community that even limited efforts at desegregation be attempted. The compensatory program proved to be a dismal failure. (I can testify to this from memory: The school in which I taught was part of Operation Counterpoise and was, according to our school board, "saturated with compensatory programs." The alleged improvements that this program brought were imperceptible to those of us who worked there.) Still, undertakings of this nature, whether they were called "compensatory" or described in other terms, proliferated in the next three decades and, in a variety of forms, continue to proliferate today.

I have a habit of keeping almost every press release, government publication, or promotional brochure that has arrived here in the mail from state and federal agencies, academic institutes, "Education Excellence Commissions," and private-sector "partnerships for education" that have heralded exciting-sounding strategies and projects for the transformation or the radical improvement of our nation's inner-city schools. If, like me, you kept these documents in one enormous and intimidating pile in your office through the course of many years, and if you ever had the will to sit down for an evening and read through these publications and examine carefully the claims and promises that each and all have made, then ask yourself how great an impact any of these projects had over the course of time and how many fewer, for that matter, anyone who works in urban education nowadays is even likely to recall, you might come from such an evening with a justified suspicion that the promises we hear today of new and even better ways to guarantee successful outcomes in our nation's segregated and unequal public schools will one day be reviewed with the same sense of disappointment, if not irony.

Among these documents are several that describe a movement that began some 30 years ago known as "Effective Schools." (There were, and are, innumerable programs with this title, which were often introduced in urban districts as alternatives to integration efforts, as in Oklahoma City.) There were also, as I now discover, "More Effective Schools," a major undertaking that attracted a great deal of media attention in New York, then similar projects that expanded on this concept—an extra syllable was added to the term and "Efficacy" came to be the word of choice during the early 1990s—then "Schools of Excellence," then "Schools of Enterprise" and many other variations on the latter term, which bring us up into the present day.

Numerous blue-ribbon panels that included well-known educators, governors, and usually business leaders have been formed over the years in order to promote these projects or to recommend more sweeping and ambitious ones. Few of the summations issued by these panels mentioned more than passingly the presence of apartheid demographics and severe inequity of funding in our public schools. They were polite and elevated-sounding documents, and their extreme civility of utterance might have been compromised by references to visceral realities like these.

"It would be callous to doubt that a group of able citizens might make sound suggestions" for reform of education, said Fred Hechinger, the education writer of The New York Times, when yet another task force of distinguished people was announced to carry out another major study of potential strategies to bring improvements to the schools in New York's poorest neighborhoods. "Yet realism," he went on, "combined with a working memory, invites the feeling that a familiar performance is about to be repeated." Mr. Hechinger was, in most instances, a courteous observer of the education projects undertaken in the New York City schools. His reference to the "familiar performance" of creating a new task force to release a new report was, even in its mildly sarcastic tone, unusual for him. It is a performance that has been repeated many, many times over the decades since.

Wandering through the galaxies of faded names and optimistic claims, I find something called "Lighthouse Schools," and also "Focus Schools," "Accelerated Schools," "Blue Ribbon Schools," "Exemplary Schools," and "Pilot Schools," all of which were variations on a concept once called "Model Schools" (or "replication models," in a slightly more contemporary term), then "Quality Schools"—and schools of "Total Quality" indeed!—and a profusion of new terms like "quality curriculum" and "quality performance" that began to filter into education publications and the speeches heard at education conferences, then into grant proposals and prospectuses. ("First, go for quality. . . . Second, reward success in producing quality. . . . Education, like private enterprise, can improve by restructuring. . . . Minorities would benefit greatly from restructured learning systems. . . . Such an effort must establish clear goals. . . ."—Quality Education for Minorities, 1990.)

During the same period, another, somewhat more assertive series of reports and books and summit conferences and national symposia began to promulgate a new set of pronouncements as to how to "fix" our schools by codifying lengthy lists of school reforms that "work"—both "fix" and "work" being the operative verbs and both evoking the idea that schools might be perceived as poorly functioning machines that simply needed a corrective checklist to assure their more productive operation.

In 1986, for instance, Education Secretary William Bennett issued a 66-page booklet, called "What Works," that listed 41 attributes of a successful school, including "rigorous" textbooks and curriculum, consistent enforcement of discipline, the memorization of "historical dates," literary passages, and "the correct spelling of words," "moral awareness" and "good character" reinforced by "good adult examples," and an emphasis upon the primacy of phonics. "High teacher expectations," "continuous assessment," and "positive work attitudes," which, said the report, were emphasized by business leaders, were additional components.

Highly praised by educational conservatives, this inventory came to be the template for a series of successive lists of things "that work" which were promoted widely by the media. "Yes, Our Schools Can Be Saved" was the Newsweek headline for a story citing Secretary Bennett on "discovering what works" and heralding the success of a predominantly black high school in the South where, among other instruments of rigor, corporal punishment had been reinstituted and teachers were required to submit their lesson plans each day for an inspection by the principal. "What Works" was the cover headline of an education insert in The New York

Times in January 1992. ("At least seven ideas . . . that work" were listed in one of the featured stories, one of which was projects that "build students' self-esteem," another "corporate involvement.") Similar collections of "what works" proposals were reiterated in the media throughout the next ten years. "How to Fix America's Schools" was the headline on the cover of BusinessWeek in 2001. "Here Are Seven Ideas That Work"—remarkably enough, exactly the same number that The Times identified a decade earlier. As in the reports of many of those various blue-ribbon panels to which Mr. Hechinger referred with a degree of weariness, the possibility that one more thing that "works," or might if it were seriously tried, would be a national assault upon the institution of apartheid education in itself did not seem worthy of consideration in these media accounts. With only a few exceptions, inequality in financing of education went unmentioned also.

An entirely different kind of promise, one that seems much easier to understand in human terms, is the high set of expectations that attach themselves to changes in the topmost personnel—superintendent, CEO, or chancellor, as they are variously known—who come and go so frequently in many of our urban systems, although personnel and program oftentimes are intertwined.

"I served as New York State commissioner eight years," says Thomas Sobol, "and I worked with seven chancellors of New York City's schools. The system just devours them. . . ." He listed the chancellors with whom he'd worked and spoke in particular of one, a man named Richard Green, the city's first black chancellor, who had previously worked in Minneapolis and was received with high praise from the New York media and from the city's private-sector leaders. Soon enough, he started to incur the criticism that he was too cautious, too methodical, and not sufficiently aggressive. He began to have the stricken look of someone who could barely breathe; and this, as it turned out, was literally so. He was asthmatic and the asthma soon became acute and chronic. Facing an audience of business leaders or the press, he often held an inhaler in his hand. During a period of special tension in the spring of 1989, he suffered an attack of asthma and died suddenly.

Sobol told me of a memorial service held for Dr. Green, which took place at a church in Harlem, and he spoke of what he called "a sort of keening, wailing" among those who were assembled, mourning the loss of what he called "this savior who, however, in all honesty, had not had time to do a lot before he died."

His successor served on an interim basis for only about eight months and was succeeded by Joseph Fernandez, a former superintendent of the Miami schools who was greeted with the same extravagance of praise that Dr. Green had been accorded when he had arrived. "New Chancellor, New Hope for Schools," a headline in The Times announced. "It's a thrill," the paper said, "to hear Joseph Fernandez talk about his plans. . . ." The Daily News described Dr. Fernandez as "a terrific choice"—a "good man for [a] tough job"—in an editorial that celebrated his selection. "The revolution has started," said the paper only a few weeks after he took office. A month later, Newsday noted that some critics were complaining that Fernandez was "beginning to behave less like a city schools chancellor and more like a city schools czar. Others worry that he's pushing the system into radical change much too quickly. Still others insist that the changes he seeks contain inherent flaws. Happily, such fears are off the mark." Indeed, said the paper, "the mumblings of unease about Fernandez are encouraging" because they might be indications he was making progress.

Dr. Fernandez, with whom I became acquainted shortly before his premature departure from the New York City system, was an extremely able leader, as were his three immediate successors, two of whom I also had the privilege to know. The overstated language with which his arrival in New York was heralded, however, did him a disservice, attaching to him expectations that no individual, no matter how considerable his gifts, could possibly fulfill. Ignoring the inequities of the divided system he inherited, it set him up as an exemplar of hope largely because of his support for what was then regarded as a forward-looking notion (site-based management of schools). Three years after he arrived, Dr. Fernandez was dismissed, his manner of leadership now retroactively described by some as "arrogant, abrasive or aloof," according to The Times. "He made too many enemies," said Newsday. "His greatest strength—a sometimes imperious distaste for compromise—became his fatal flaw. The Lone Ranger was felled by a ricochet from his own silver bullet."

Exaggerated expectations have exacted an especially high toll on urban school officials who, like Richard Green and Joseph Fernandez, are also minorities. Fernandez's successor, another Hispanic educator with a good track record prior to arriving in New York, was welcomed with high expectations but resigned within two years after a siege of hostile treatment by the city's mayor. His successor, Rudy Crew, a black administrator who was also greeted with a chorus of applause on his arrival in New York, survived in office for four years. Not long after he was fired, he described to me what he believed to be the bludgeoning he had received from New York City politicians and a good part of the city's press. I had disagreed with some of the policies he put in place while he was in New York, but to see a man as decent, strong-hearted, and proud as Dr. Crew sitting across from me at dinner and attempting to control the tremor in his voice as he recalled the sense of visceral insult he had undergone, was terribly disturbing. Right or wrong, he was convinced that much of the harsh treatment he'd received in his last year in office had been tinged with racial condescension; some of the black principals I knew believed that this was true.

James Baldwin had written of black leaders who were given a limited degree of power to control and, if they could, relieve some of the miseries of Harlem 50 years ago. Speaking of "the nicely refined torture a man can experience from having been created and defeated by the same circumstances," Baldwin wrote, "the best that one can say is that they are in an impossible position" and that those "who are motivated by genuine concern maintain this position with heartbreaking dignity." That precarious sense of dignity, often protected by reliance upon hyperbolic claims and a progressively more glazed and fragile smile, may be noted among good black and Hispanic school officials to the present day. Too much is expected of them when they come; too little is accorded to them when they leave. The structures of apartheid and inequity that have defeated them remain unchanged.

In a similar dynamic, certain highly gifted or, in any case, initially impressive urban principals are periodically elected to assume the same role as an incarnation of the possibilities for hope within a context of historic failure which we are encouraged to believe is not systemic but the fault primarily of the ineptitude or lassitude of previous administrators. "With lightning speed," the newly chosen principal has turned a failing school into "a place where students learn"—"no ifs and buts"—instructional time is "maximized," teachers are "utilizing more deliberate techniques," and a poor-performing school is on the way to "a dramatic turnaround," the latter word ("turnaround"), it seems, having become an almost knee-jerk usage in these narratives of hope. Sometimes the dynamic-sounding program introduced by a new principal does have a galvanizing and perceptible effect and one that lasts for more than a few years. In other cases, it is really just an avalanche of words and short-term measures that temporarily establish a degree of calm within the school and sometimes bring a sudden spike in test results or graduation rates, although the academic gains more frequently than not turn out to be short-lived and, in some cases, they have proven to be spurious.

Some will recall the adulation heaped upon a principal in Paterson, New Jersey, in the 1980s, who became the subject of a film and was presented to the public as a salvatory figure who was not afraid to discipline black students with unusual severity and walked the hallways of his high school with a bullhorn and a bat. The principal, whose name was Joe Clark, came to be a favorite of the White House in the Reagan years and was the subject of a cover story in Time magazine, where he was photographed holding his baseball bat in both his hands and looking as if he would not hesitate to use it. Education Secretary Bennett called his school "a mecca of education" after Clark threw out 300 students who were often late for class or had high absence rates, whom he described as "parasites" and "leeches." Two thirds of the students he threw out ended up in the Passaic County Jail, according to a teacher at the school, but average test scores briefly rose a bit because the kids who scored the lowest now were gone.

When I visited the school in 1990, its famous principal had already departed. (He was subsequently appointed the director of a juvenile detention center.) Whatever promise had been represented by his highly visible presence had departed with him. He left behind a grim and stolid school where classes in the language arts took place in a dingy basement, full-grown adolescents I observed had to squeeze their bodies into desks that were the size appropriate for elementary school, and English classes that I visited were stripped of literary content and were used almost exclusively, according to their teachers, to drill students for exams. The average reading level of the students was below sixth grade.

The Paterson "turnaround" had been suspicious from the start. It had sounded too good to be true, and it turned out that this was so; but the general pattern of identifying principals who have a vibrant public presence, and attach themselves to trends and slogans that may be in favor with tough-minded politicians ("cracking down" on troublesome teenagers, for example, and insisting there are "no excuses" for a student's failure), then attributing to each of them the gift of working a near miracle in record periods of time, repeats itself in other urban districts to the present day.

There are hundreds of principals in our urban schools who are *authentic* heroes, few of whom would emulate the posturing and bluster of Joe Clark and most of whom do not receive the notice and support that they deserve. But there is a difference between recognizing the accomplishments of able school officials and the marketing of individuals as saviors of persistently unequal systems. As with the hero children, so too with the hero principals, there is this inclination to avert our eyes from the pervasive injuries inflicted upon students by our acquiescence in a dual system and to convey the tantalizing notion that the problems of this system can be superseded somehow by a faith in miracles embodied in dynamic and distinctive individuals. I don't believe that this is true. I don't believe a good school or a good school system can be built on miracles or on the stunning interventions of dramatically original and charismatic men or women. I don't think anyone really believes this.

* * *

On a significantly more far-reaching scale, there are the promises made by our nation's presidents, which in some notable cases in the past (that of Lyndon Johnson, for example) have delivered very important benefits to children of low income but which, in other and more recent instances, have either been broken very quickly or else been acted upon with a degree of bullish certitude that leaves no room for sensible correction when the consequences turn out to be damaging.

It was only 14 years ago, in 1991, that President George H. Bush announced an education plan known as America 2000, which was described as "a nine-year crusade" to radically reform the nation's schools. The plan was broken down into six "Education Goals," including a commitment to assure "school readiness" for all preschoolers, a pledge to make American children the top-ranking students in the world in math and science by the year 2000, achievement of a high school graduation rate of 90 percent, testing of all students in the fourth and eighth and twelfth grades, assurance that all schools were free of drugs and violence, and universal adult literacy. The president's language in promotion of these goals suggested that transformative results could be expected. "Education and expectation go hand in hand," he told an audience of high school students, "and your world—the whole world—trembles with new possibilities." Speaking to business and education leaders in the White House, he was no less passionate. "To those who want to see real improvement in American education, I say: There will be no renaissance without revolution."

Few substantial new resources were provided to the states and local districts to achieve these goals, however. The only new money Mr. Bush requested for the public schools was $700 million, most of which was earmarked to create a network of new model schools, which were to be known as "New American Schools" and which were intended to be financed partly by the private sector. The White House said these schools, which it called "world-class schools," would "break the mould" of public education, phrases that were used with enervating repetition for the next three years. A number of such schools—not "new schools" for the most part but preexisting schools in which the private sector took a direct role in shaping the curriculum—may still be found today, but they have never had much impact upon other public schools, which was the justification for the program in the first place. And, indeed, before the president left office, many of his goals had more or less dissolved into thin air, and very few people that I knew could still remember what they were.

Some of the goals that Mr. Bush proposed, moreover, as Fred Hechinger observed, were anything but new or "revolutionary" as the president proclaimed. Eight years earlier, in 1983, President Ronald Reagan had "issued a set of goals that included reducing the high school dropout rate" from 30 percent to 10 percent by the school-year that began in 1990. "President Bush now calls for reducing the high school dropout rate from 30 percent to 10," but this time by the year 2000.

Ten years later, President George W. Bush unveiled another ambitious education plan. "No child," we were told this time, in what was partly a recasting of the promises that had been made in 1991, was to be "left behind." This is not to say that the new set of goals, enacted into law in January 2002, did not go far beyond the items in the 1991 proposal. The testing of children, one of the six goals alluded to by George H. Bush, had now assumed a central role in the agenda of his son, which also included strict demands for proof of "adequate yearly progress" in all public schools and penalties, such as the loss of federal funds, for schools that did not meet their goals, as measured by their students' scores on standardized exams. In these cases, schools would also be obliged to pay for tutoring by private companies or to facilitate the transfer of their students, if the parents so requested, to a better school that boasted higher scores.

The latter provision, "the right of transfer," which appeared at first to be an opening for children of poor people to attend good schools in middle-class communities, turned out to be a bit of teasing rhetoric that had no realistic application. In most urban systems there were not enough high-scoring schools to which the children of a failing school could transfer. In some cities like New York, moreover, many of the most successful schools, which tended to be clustered in more privileged communities, had strict selection policies that included interviews and testing, as we've seen. In schools in which there were no such requirements, in any case, enrollments often were already full, and parents in these neighborhoods were not disposed to see their own children excluded so that children from a poorer neighborhood could be enrolled.

In New York City, as a consequence, only 8,000 out of 275,000 eligible students were able to make transfers in 2003–2004. In Cleveland, where nearly 17,000 students qualified to transfer to another school under the new legislation, only 58 children did so. In Chicago, of 19,000 applicants for transfers, only 1,100 were approved. In the vast Los Angeles district, only 175 students were successful in achieving transfers. Nationwide, only one percent of eligible children transferred from a failing school to a higher-performing school under the provisions of the federal law.

If the president had used his leadership to advocate for transfers not only within school districts, but *between* them, the transfer option might have had real meaning and, indeed, if earnestly enforced, it might have opened up the possibilities for mightily expanded racial integration in suburban schools surrounding our core cities. Some of our most segregated urban neighborhoods lie just adjacent to well-funded districts serving middle-class communities. Less than a fifteen-minute bus ride often separates our wealthiest and poorest schooling systems. The president, however, did not choose to use his power to advance this kind of transfer, which would have required great political audacity. As a result, the transfer option up to now has proven all but meaningless.

Playing games of musical chairs with children's lives, when half the chairs are broken and the best chairs are reserved primarily for people of his class and race, is cynical behavior in a president. The cost of building new and safe schools for the children in our urban districts or rebuilding those that can be salvaged, has been estimated by the General Accounting Office at well above $100 billion and, if the rewiring of schools for Internet access is included, at about $200 billion. (This is the cost merely for infrastructure, totally apart from what it would require to provide low-income districts with resources to deliver anything approximating equal education to their children on an annual basis.) Even in more prosperous times, states have been unwilling or unable to address these infrastructure needs. Now, after several years of a sustained recession, any serious attempt to deal with overcrowding and endemic squalor in such schools as Walton High and Fremont High is virtually impossible without a massive new infusion of resources from the federal government.

The president has provided no such new infusion to rebuild or modernize the schools of urban districts and has allocated only half the funds that Congress authorized to enable schools to meet the terms of the new law. Meanwhile, he has immersed the nation's educators in a complicated clutter of accountability demands that have intensified the pressure upon principals in inner-city schools to institute or reinforce the rote-and-drill instructional techniques that are most closely keyed to state exams.

In perhaps the most stunning breach of faith shown by the Bush administration, the fiscal limits that the president has put in place have led to a sharp decline in the proportion of low-income children served by Head Start programs. "Now is the time to make Head Start an early-learning program to teach all our children to read," said Mr. Bush in his acceptance speech at the Republican convention in July 2000. Five years later, the percentage of eligible children who are excluded from this program has risen from 40 percent to 50 percent, the consequence of a White House budget that takes no account of rising rates of child poverty and a growing number of children in the age group Head Start was designed to serve.

"They not only break their promises to children," says Marian Wright Edelman, president of the Children's Defense Fund, "they're actually serving fewer children in absolute numbers than before. Twenty-five thousand of the children served by Head Start up to now will not receive it any longer and, because they are not dealing with the growth of child poverty, half the eligible children have already been locked out. They're acting without morality. They're telling us it's okay to take this from our children while they're giving tax cuts to the millionaires and billionaires. I don't understand people who can do this."

Understandable or not, Mr. Bush continues to insist that his agenda is succeeding. The president, at least, has wisely moved the target date for the completion of his plans so far into the future (to the year 2014) that he will long be out of office by the time a day of reckoning arrives. But if the past may be relied upon to make predictions for the future, we may sensibly expect that much of what is promised in the present set of goals, no matter how they dominate the national attention at the present time, will be retracted, or amended, or diluted, or else more or less forgotten long before that very distant date arrives. The testing protocols, unhappily, may be the only part of this that actually survives.

Idols crumble. New ones are erected and then crumble too. In Houston, Texas, which for several years had been promoted to the nation as "a pillar of the so-called Texas miracle in education," notes The New York Times—former education secretary Rod Paige had been superintendent of the district and had made his reputation there—some people "are questioning whether the miracle may have been smoke and mirrors" all along.

Highly implausible test-score fluctuations in the Houston schools have awakened suspicions of cheating on the part of principals who had apparently been pressured by administrators to do anything they could to boost the scores. At one school, named Wesley Elementary, which, according to Education Week, "gained national acclaim under then superintendent Rod Paige" for what appeared to be spectacular results in students' scores, a recent analysis reveals that students scoring in the highest ten percent statewide when they were in fifth grade dropped to the bottom ten percent the following year in middle school. The 99 percent black and Hispanic school, which was using a scripted reading system and was praised by President Bush for its impressive gains, had been suspected of cheating once before, in 1998, when Mr. Bush was governor of Texas, but the principal insisted it was "racist" to believe the scores were false because this would somehow indicate black and Hispanic children could not learn. Suddenly now, according to The Dallas Morning News, it appears that these suspicions had been justified.

A former fifth grade teacher told The Morning News that teachers were "instructed . . . how to cheat" by walking around their classrooms while the students worked on their exams, stopping behind students who had chosen the wrong answer to a question, and remaining behind such students until they selected the right answer. Further analysis of students' test scores at this school and others indicates that this was not an isolated situation. Nearly 400 Texas schools are now suspected of having cheated too. Investigations have been launched in 23 Houston schools, as well as in dozens of schools in other major districts. In at least one case, a criminal inquiry is under way.

Additional evidence uncovered recently indicates that gains in high school graduation rates in Houston, which had been widely publicized in national reports, also appear to have been overstated or outrightly false. A report by state officials in 2003, according to The New York Times, revealed that "more than half the students" who had disappeared from 16 middle schools and high schools in the year when Mr. Paige was winding up his tenure there should have been identified as dropouts, "but were not." One high school, in the following year, insisted that it had no dropouts—not a single student had dropped out, the principal reported—even though 460 students had disappeared from the enrollment of the school that year. In an internal memo to the principal, a school official had alerted her to the discrepancies between the claims that she was making and the numbers he'd unearthed. "We go from 1,000 freshmen to less than 300 seniors with no dropouts," noted this official. "Amazing!" The principal continued, nonetheless, to claim the high school had no dropouts.

One of the basic elements of the accountability procedures introduced by Mr. Paige had been "incentivizing" principals and faculty to raise their students' scores, attendance rates, and graduation rates by giving them financial bonuses for meeting "school performance goals" within a given year, a practice we have seen in other districts. At the Houston school that claimed it had "no dropouts," for example, $75,000 in cash bonuses had been awarded to the staff for raising test scores and attendance rates and lowering its dropout figures in the year in which 460 students left the school. Now suddenly even the business sector that had forcefully supported this approach had second thoughts about the consequences. "The Houston system's supporters in the business community, some with close ties to the Bush administration," said The Times, "maintain that the city's dropout figures had long defied credibility. . . ."

In the wake of these revelations about Houston, similar revelations surfaced also in New York. Thousands of low-performing students who had left school, or been pushed out of their schools, had been improperly excluded from the dropout figures. School officials had concealed the numbers of such students from the public's scrutiny by labeling these pupils "discharged students," which implied that they had transferred to another school or else enrolled in an "equivalency program" even when there was no evidence for these assumptions. Although official dropout figures for the city's high schools had been listed at about 20 percent, a report released by Advocates for Children now revealed that over 55,000 students—not included in that 20 percent—had been "discharged" in 2000–2001, while less than 34,000 graduated in that year. At one Bronx high school that some of the kids I knew attended, more than 1,000 students were "discharged," out of a student body of 2,500. Only 123 students graduated.

In Chicago too, one of the initial bastions of the tough accountability procedures in which dramatic gains in test scores and in school completion rates had been reported, it turned out that success rates at the high school level had been knowingly inflated by the same misleading practices used in New York and Houston. Chicago for several years had claimed a graduation rate of 70 percent. It was now revealed that more than half the students in the system failed to reach their senior year and win diplomas.

The falsification of statistics in the Houston schools, however, had more national significance because it was on the strength of Houston's "miracle" in bringing business-modeled methods of accountability to bear on public schools that Secretary Paige, once he arrived in Washington, had made the argument that the same model of reform should be imposed on public systems elsewhere. "It was Enron accounting," said a former employee of the Houston system in describing the statistical devices used to fabricate a record of success within a system that had thrown out thousands of young people who, if they remained in school, would mar the image of apparent progress in achievement gains. In this respect, the Texas miracle had its precursor in the Joe Clark miracle in Paterson, New Jersey, and it had been applauded by the same political conservatives who had made Clark a national hero more than 15 years before.

At the heart of the agenda Mr. Bush and his associates have been promoting for our public schools, there lies the "scientific" model of accountability and measurement that consciously applies the practices of business management to guarantee efficiency in operation of a classroom, school, or district, while, in general, bypassing questions about inequality, to the degree that this is possible. As in the case of other promises of school renewal we have seen, the impression has been given to the public that this model of restructuring our public schools is something truly new and represents a radical departure from the undertakings of the past. Yet, in reality, the language and the ideology infusing this agenda are not new; they are, in fact, only the newest rehabilitation of some very old vocabularies and ideas that far predate the various reforms that have been put in place during the last 15 to 20 years and have their roots, indeed, nearly a hundred years ago at the start of the last century.

"Our schools are, in a sense, factories in which the raw products (children) are to be shaped and fashioned into products to meet the various demands of life," wrote Elwood Cubberley, an influential educator of the early 1900s and one of the leading voices for the business model of efficiency in education at that time. "The specifications for manufacturing come from the demands of twentieth-century civilization and it is the business of the school to build its pupils according to the specifications laid down. . . .

"By means of standards and units of the type now being evolved and tested out . . . ," said Cubberley, "it will be possible for any school system to maintain a continuous survey of all the different phases of its work, through tests made by its corps of efficiency experts, and to detect weak points in its work almost as soon as they appear." The function of the expert in efficiency would be "to study the needs of life and the industries, with a view to restating the specification for the manufacture of the educational output," to "study means for increasing the rate of production, and for eliminating the larger present waste . . . ," "to test the product at different stages of manufacture," and "to advise the workers [that is, teachers] as to the results. . . ."

Cubberley's views, as educational historian Raymond Callahan described them in a now largely forgotten book, Education and the Cult of Efficiency, published in 1962, were widely shared by other educators of his day. In a textbook for teachers in training, published in 1910, a prominent educator named William Bagley stated that the problems faced in managing a class ought to be regarded by the teacher as primarily "a problem of economy"—"as a 'business' problem," Bagley emphasized—and that the "first rule of efficient service" for a teacher must be "unquestioned obedience" to his or her superiors. The situation, he wrote, was "entirely analogous to that in any other organization or system" such as business enterprises or "the army" or "the navy."

Utilitarian objectives must be uppermost, a speaker told the members of the National Education Association in 1909. "Acquisition by earning" ought to be made the focus of our schoolchildren's desires, teachers were advised. "Ordinarily, a love of learning is praiseworthy; but when this delight in the pleasures of learning becomes so intense and so absorbing that it diminishes the desire and the power of earning, it is positively harmful. Education that does not promote the desire [for] earning . . . is not worth the getting."

The emphasis on mercenary principles and businesslike efficiency was paralleled, as Callahan observes, by the emergence of eugenics theories and their application to our education system. In a widely read book titled Laggards in Our Schools, published in 1909, an educator named Leonard Ayres argued that "75 percent of Negro children" in the public schools of Memphis ought to be regarded as retarded because they were overage for their grade levels. It was during the same era that "scientific testing" of intelligence came into ascendancy.

"As far as intelligence is concerned, the tests have told the truth . . . ," wrote Lewis Ternan, an educational psychologist and an adherent of the new eugenics thinking. "The whole question of racial differences in mental traits," he argued, "will have to be taken up anew" and studied scientifically as a result of what he held to be the low intelligence of "Indians, Mexicans, and Negroes." Children of these racial groups, he said, "should be segregated" in their classes and be given "concrete and practical" instruction.

"They cannot master abstractions, but they can often be made efficient workers . . . ," he observed. "There is no possibility at present of convincing society that they should not be allowed to reproduce . . . ," he said regretfully.

Ternan was no minor figure in the history of educational psychology. Elected president of the American Psychological Association in 1922, Ternan, like his contemporary Cubberley, was one of the most influential education scholars of his day. His colleague Edward Thorndike, who taught at Teachers College in New York for more than 40 years, was, like Ternan, a convinced believer in eugenics: "One sure service of the able and good is to beget and rear offspring. One sure service (almost the only one) which the inferior and vicious can perform is to prevent their genes from survival."

Equal education, not surprisingly, was no more accepted as a plausible objective in that era than it is, in general, today. "Theoretically," wrote Cubberley, "all the children of the state are equally important and are entitled to have the same advantages; practically, this can never be true. The duty of the state is to secure for all as high a minimum of good instruction as is possible, but not to reduce all to this minimum; to place a premium on those local efforts which will enable local communities to rise above the local minimum as far as possible; and to encourage communities to extend their educational energies to new and desirable undertakings."

Cubberley's conviction that, in practice, all the children of our nation cannot be regarded as if they were equally important would, effectively, become enshrined in formulas for state assistance to school districts in the years to come, which have remained in place, with various modifications, to the present day.

A great deal has obviously changed within the nation's dialogue on public education in the past 100 years—

few scholars or elected politicians would subscribe today, not openly at least, to the eugenics theories that accompanied the birth of IQ testing in this nation, although IQ tests are still employed in the selection process for some of our better public schools, as Katha Pollitt for example noted in New York—but much remains the same. The insistence upon more exacting measurement of "the results" of education practices by the use of methods used in industry and commerce, which is presented to the public as a new and promising discovery ("a reinvention" of our schools, we have been told), the "product" talk, the "outcome" talk, the "scientific-basis" talk, along with the accountant talk ("there's something crystal clear about a number") and the acquisition talk ("how much is my answer worth?"), are certainly not new. And, although the advocates for these ideas today no longer speak of factories as models of production for the workers whom our schools are now expected to turn out, and tend to speak instead in metaphors of "enterprise" that do not always sound exclusively industrial, the truth is that the children of the black and brown and very poor (those very same "Mexicans" and "Negroes" who, as Ternan argued back in 1922, ought to "be segregated" and provided "practical" instruction) are, for the most part, segregated still. And, as thousands of Mireyas and Fortinos in our nation's inner-city schools can testify, they still are counseled far too frequently to seek their future destinies in practical activities like working in a sewing factory or in the kitchen of a hotel restaurant or in the least-remunerated levels of the healthcare industry and other service industries, no matter what the rhetoric we find in school brochures or school improvement plans or in the speeches of a U.S. president.

Experts in desegregation sometimes note that social policy in the United States, to the degree that it concerns the education of black and Hispanic children, has been turned back more than 50 years to where the nation stood in 1954. In other respects, however, the retreat from modern principles of justice has gone back a great deal further into history. The efficiency agenda and the notion that our public schools exist primarily to give the business sector what it asks for, or believes it needs, are anything but new; and the racially embarrassing beliefs by which these notions were accompanied a century ago, although widely disavowed today, are with us still.

"Hold up your pillows," said the teacher in the segregated and unequal junior high in Roosevelt. "We have visitors."

CHAPTER 9

Invitations to Resistance

What do we need to do to alter these realities?

I asked this question to the teachers who met with me after class at Fremont High School in Los Angeles. "We need our teachers marching in the streets," the teacher in whose class I had been visiting replied.

She had been listening with me to the statements of her students for the previous two hours. She had heard Mireya's disappointment about having been obliged to take a sewing class when she had hoped to take an AP class instead. She had heard Fortino's swift reply: "You're ghetto—so you sew!" She had been listening to students like Mireya and Fortino now for many years. The anger in Fortino's voice was now in hers.

"We need to speak the word 'racism' clearly," said an older teacher who had been at Fremont High for more than 15 years.

Other teachers spoke of the indignities imposed on students by the squalor of the building, the shortages of bathroom space, the sense of concentration and compression and containment of their young mentalities. Like many teachers I have met in similarly segregated schools over the past ten years, they taught apartheid's children but they had not given up their condemnation of apartheid and its consequences.

"Before we gave up on integration, we should have tried it," wrote Jack White, a columnist for Time magazine, nearly ten years ago. Public schools, he charged, are "so separate and vastly unequal that *Plessy v. Ferguson,* not *Brown v. Board of Education,* might as well be the law of the land." Indicting "privileged African-Americans" along with white Americans, he said that some "have acquiesced" in giving up the struggle long before it has been won. "Just like many whites, a lot of us walked away from the fight for school integration once we made sure our own progeny would receive its undeniable benefits by enrolling them in high-priced private academies," he said, while, in effect, abandoning "most poor black children," who remain "stuck in decrepit ghetto classrooms."

"Herewith," he went on, "a radical proposal. . . . Revive the civil rights movement, which went into limbo long before some of its most important goals were accomplished. . . . The genteel race mixing that goes on among the elite is no substitute for a determined national effort to include poor nonwhite children in America's bounty—and if it takes a new round of sit-ins to put the issue back on the national agenda, so be it.

"Such a campaign," he continued, "would be disruptive and strongly opposed, but then so was the battle to desegregate lunch counters. America has never made progress on racial issues unless there was enough agitation to force society to take action." Honor among privileged blacks and whites alike, he said, "depends on rediscovering our commitment to treating all children fairly. If it takes new turmoil to bring that about, that is a price we should be willing to pay."

White's essay bears the headline "Why We Need to Raise Hell." It brings to my mind the restlessness and anger of a New York City teacher I have known and visited repeatedly in class since 1995. A conscientious and devoted teacher, Louis Bedrock has been working at P.S. 30 in the Bronx for 16 years. In school, you would not sense his feelings of political impatience; he does his best to make his fifth grade class a happy and protective place for children. His wrath emerges when he's leaving school, or walking in the neighborhood, or when the weekend comes.

An intellectual who gave up teaching at the college level to devote his life to teaching in the Bronx, he speaks with unforgiving anger of the policies of city planners in New York during preceding decades that effectively cut off communities of color in the Bronx in ways that rendered permanent their demographic isolation. He grows incensed about newspaper stories that politely circumvent these structural realities and calls me on the phone sometimes at night to vent his feelings.

Mr. Bedrock is a teacher of my generation—he came of age during the high point of the civil rights campaigns—but there are many younger teachers coming into inner-city schools who have been steeped in civil rights ideals as well. I am thinking of dozens of those ardent young idealists whom I meet, graduates of colleges like Brown and Spelman, Reed and Swarthmore, and state universities in Madison and Amherst and Ann Arbor for example, where they've studied teacher education but also immersed themselves in social history and social justice programs and the history of civil rights. Once in the classroom, they do not shut these lessons from their minds but try their best to keep faith with the principles that have inspired them.

These are not teachers who believe that *Brown* is something to commemorate at arm's length with a glimpse of antique videos of men and women of their age in demonstrations in the southern states from 45 or 50 years before and snippets of nostalgic or heroic writings about children walking into all-white schools escorted by platoons of federal marshals or police. They do not accept the notion that apartheid is a faded vestige of a distant past. They can't, because they see it daily in their classrooms, and they know that too much sentimental celebration of the heroism of the past can be exploited as an exemption from the heroism that is needed now.

There are principals who speak out on these matters too. In Seattle, teachers told me of a high school principal named David Engle who gave up his job in protest at a federal court decision that turned back the clock on racial integration by removing what was known as a "tie-breaker" in admission policies for public schools, which had been instituted in the 1970s and permitted schools to factor in a child's race in order to promote desegregation. The principal resigned from integrated Ballard High School in the spring of 2002 when it grew apparent that the racial mix of students at the school would be diminished greatly as a consequence. In the previous fall, the entering ninth grade class at Ballard High was nearly equally divided between whites (55 percent) and nonwhites (45 percent). Immediately after the court decision, the nonwhite population dropped to 32 percent. The same effect was seen in middle schools and elementary schools. At one of the Seattle elementary schools that had been integrated up to now, the number of minority children in the kindergarten classes dropped from 37 percent to 11 percent in just one year.

"The racial divide is widening in Seattle," Engle said

in an address to students at his school when he announced his resignation. He said he recognized that his decision would not counteract the ruling of the court but that he wanted to inspire students to take action on their own convictions and "to understand the moral, political, and symbolic landscape of our city." He said he had been influenced by the memory of Rosa Parks's refusal to give up her seat to a white man in Montgomery, Alabama, when the buses there were segregated in the 1950s. "As a privileged leader of a school at the center of the new racial controversy," Engle told the students, "I have decided I could not dodge this decision."

When he later spoke to me about the motives that had led him to resign, he said he had been stirred by statements that his students often made about the degree to which they valued the diversity of Ballard High. "Almost to a kid, they'd say, 'I like who goes to school with me.' " Teenagers, he said, "watch us constantly. They look for signals as to which direction we, their educators, may be heading. . . ."

His resignation sent a message other educators in the city voiced as well. "That's going in the wrong direction," said the assistant principal of another high school from which nonwhite children now were being turned away. "We want to increase the number of students of color . . . , not decrease it." In a statement released by the principals of 17 other high schools, Engle's colleagues in Seattle said, "We want to be very clear that we support the ideals upon which David acted. This is not about one principal. . . . It is about all of us." The superintendent predicted there would be "enhanced . . . racial segregation in our schools." He said he found this "very troubling to me personally."

Other superintendents voice the same concern, although they do not often do this publicly. The superintendent of the Indianapolis public schools, a highly regarded leader among urban educators whose name is Duncan Pritchett, told me in the summer of 2004 that an integration program that had been in place for 20 years was being phased out as a consequence of a federal court decision. "There's no question integrated education has been a benefit to our community," said Pritchett. "I've seen it with my own eyes." When the integration program started in the 1980s, Pritchett said, "I remember the initial fears that people of both races felt, because they had no understanding of each other." Over time, he said, "the fear dissolved. The kids did it. They worked it out much faster than the grown-ups. You could see it very quickly in the way they played with one another in the playgrounds. Over the next few years, all these things became more natural. I don't mean that we did not have problems, but they tended to be few and far between and, for the most part, they were not 'race problems' but 'kid problems. . . .' "

Pritchett told me he grew up in Washington, D.C., and was a teenager at the time when Martin Luther King came there to speak in August 1963. "I remember 'I Have a Dream.' I was a part of that. I was *there,*" he said, "and I have never wavered in my faith that Dr. King was right in his beliefs."

"Over the long haul," said Pritchett, "segregated schools will not be equal to the schools attended by the middle class." No matter what inducements are held out at first to placate or win over people in the black community, "kids of color will get less and less. History teaches us this if we are willing to learn anything from history. We're going to see the same 50-year cycle that began with *Brown* all over again, I am afraid. That certainly is the way that things seem to be heading. . . ."

Knowing that Indianapolis is one of the most politically conservative communities in the United States, I asked Dr. Pritchett if it would endanger his position if I quoted him by name. "This is my last year in Indianapolis," he said. "I don't know where I'll be working next. But I could care less what anyone might say. If we who are working in these schools don't advocate for children, then who will?"

Some of the high-ranking school officials who have spoken to me as Dr. Pritchett did are not willing to be quoted and identified by name because of the precarious positions that they hold in cities where such views would be unwelcome. But if there is ever to be another major struggle in this nation to confront not only pedagogies targeted exclusively at children of apartheid, but apartheid in itself, we may hope that educators such as these will have a role in leading it.

At every opportunity I have to talk with advocates and educators who share any part of my beliefs about these matters nowadays, I ask the same repeated questions: Where should teachers, superintendents, principals, and others who are troubled by the silence of our nation's leaders on this issue look for recourse and for reinforcement of their discontent? What body of political objectives are sufficiently within the realm of realistic hope to be worth striving for? Where, within the limits of the possible, should we direct whatever time and energy we have? I posed these questions recently to Gary Orfield, who has written a number of important books and co-authored several major studies on desegregation and resegregation that we have examined earlier. Four floors over Brattle Street in Cambridge at his office in the Harvard Graduate School of Education, Orfield answered me with some of the most vigorous, demanding, and not always academic answers I have heard from anyone in academic life for many years.

"A political movement is a necessary answer," he

began. "We cannot look to the courts to do it in the present age. We cannot look to the two political parties, the Republicans and Democrats, to do it. We need to reach out to a broader sector of the nation to initiate a struggle." Entirely apart from teachers and administrators such as those I've noted here, he urged me to reflect on one too frequently forgotten sector of the population: those hundreds of thousands of successful black adults who can witness to the consequences of desegregated schooling from their own experience as students.

"We now have far more educated black adults who have participated in desegregated schooling and who don't want to go back. We also have a lot more white adults who have experienced school integration and have seen it work successfully." Most of these people are not "doing anything politically today," he said, "but we should challenge them to act. . . ." To those who look upon the prospect of reenergizing the desegregation struggle as highly improbable, given the temper of the times, Orfield gave an answer that a generation of sometimes exhausted-seeming liberals and many of the younger teachers that I know need very much to hear. "Political movements aren't so hard to start," he said he tells his listeners. "There are people right here in this room who could begin a movement in this city if they have the will and the resolve."

I told him of the highly skeptical response I generally get when I make statements like that to an audience of civic leaders in a city like Chicago or New York. How can one even dream of racial integration, I am asked, in a district in which 75 to more than 85 percent of students are black or Hispanic and most middle-class white parents do not send their children to the public schools, or not beyond the elementary grades.

"You can do it *anyway* in certain schools and certain urban neighborhoods," he said. But more important, he went on, is the participation of the suburbs; and he launched into a strong defense of an approach to integrated schooling that I had myself experienced in Massachusetts many years before but of which one hears only infrequently these days. Pointing to a number of desegregation programs, all but a few initially court-ordered, in which inner-city children are enrolled in the suburban districts while some of the children from the suburbs go to school within the central cities, Orfield noted that as many as ten million black, Hispanic, and white children have attended school together in these programs, most of which have histories of long-sustained support among the parents and the students of participating suburbs. "Once you do it," he said, "you find that almost everything that people feared was false—the apprehension disappears. Then there is this wonderful discovery that people make: Children whom they thought to be so different from their own kids aren't so different after all. . . ."

A quiet-spoken man with a sly smile in his eyes, Orfield shifted his focus for a time from the interdistrict busing programs he'd described to strategies, still more explicitly political, that could directly challenge residential segregation in the widening belt of suburbs that surround the cities in which hypersegregated schooling is most likely to be found. He arrowed in immediately on Section Eight, the major form of federal housing subsidies for families of low income, which, as it is used today, tends not to reduce but to intensify the segregation of an urban neighborhood because minority families who receive a Section Eight certificate are almost always induced by housing agencies to look for housing in the segregated neighborhood in which they live. (This is a nearly universal practice in the Bronx, as I have documented in Amazing Grace.)

"We should give recipients of Section Eight intensive counseling on where to look for housing far beyond the limits of their neighborhood," he said; and he went on to speak of an approach, known as "the Gautreaux Remedy," which has been implemented in Chicago now for many years and has enabled inner-city families to find housing in more than 100 smaller cities, towns, and villages in the Chicago area. As limited as the program is in context of the population size and demographics of Chicago, Orfield nonetheless insisted it had been successful, and is still successful, "and ought to be expanded and attempted elsewhere."

He spoke as well of the inducements that the federal government or state and local governments could give home-builders in the suburbs to build multi-family housing units for which Section Eight certificates would be accepted, and of pressures that fair-minded citizens should bring to bear on town committees to revise their zoning laws in order to permit this, and the need for statewide laws that would *compel* municipalities to do this, none of which will sound particularly new to anyone involved for decades in fair housing litigation but the sum of which took on a powerful momentum in his confident and steadfast words. It was that note of confidence, the sheer amount of hopeful energy that he conveyed, that was, to me, so unexpected. He was speaking of strategies to break the back of segregated housing patterns in the suburbs, one of the most impenetrable obstacles to school desegregation; and he was speaking as if he believed that this was actually possible.

When the conversation shifted to the present educational debates about school governance and school reform approaches in the segregated schools themselves, he began to sound less optimistic for a time. "The problem," he said, is that "so many people who are caught up in these situations cannot step outside the box," by which he said he meant the inner-city teaching situation as it stands, "schools as they are, poor children *where* they are."

Virtually everything that's been presented as a useful strategy is "in this box, inside this school," he said. "It shows how thoroughly decontextualized the entire discussion about urban education has become since the beginning of the Reagan years. 'What do we do with kids like these, with demographics as they are, in buildings where they are and as they are?' Within this box, the only question that gets asked is, basically, the one we hear repeatedly: 'What works?' And now we're told, 'We've *seen* what works, so now we only need to scale it up' "—another term I also hear, somewhat obsessively, in talks with school officials and grant makers—"and people who won't do 'what works' and 'scale it up,' " he said with a satiric edge I hadn't noted in his voice before, "we fire you." Superintendents "have to promise that they know what 'works' to win these jobs to start with," he went on. "New superintendent: new plan for reform. Every district sees another way of 'doing *Plessy*.' Over the course of time, it doesn't work. It's still within that box. We need to break it out, to get outside. . . ."

Turning to the decade-long debate about school choice, which has sometimes been promoted as "a better way" to break down racial isolation than the more direct route of intentional desegregation, Orfield made an observation with which many of the ardent advocates for choice will not be pleased. "Choice, left to itself," he said, "will increase stratification. Nothing in the way choice systems actually work favors class or racial integration." Choice has had desegregative impact in some cities, Orfield said, only because there were strict guidelines in effect to make sure it would have this end result.

As for the current trend toward charter schools, which represent one form of choice, he noted that "most charter schools are more intensely segregated than the average public school, not less . . . ," and he argued firmly against charter schools and other programs of school choice that do not have specific stipulations that will lessen segregation rather than increase it. Among such stipulations, Orfield said, should be not only the provision of the costs and means of transportation for the students and a form of information access for the parents on a scale one rarely sees in school choice plans today but also "explicit policies" to guarantee a racially mixed student population and a prohibition against all requirements for entrance to a school that could exclude a child based on "disability, behavior, or low levels of achievement"—prohibitions that would be anathema to many advocates for choice and to most advocates for vouchers.

In reference to almost every other aspect of the intertwining issues of inequity in funding, concentrated poverty, and racial isolation, Orfield returned to his insistence on the need for mobilized political behavior and his faith that a determined movement reembodying a struggle left unfinished years before is not merely possible but ought to be a heightened focus of strategic thinking. I was reminded of the words in Jack White's essay in Time magazine. "Before we gave up on integration," he had said, "we should have tried it." White had spoken also of the price that we as a society might have to pay for a new round of turmoil to revitalize the struggle; but Orfield did not seem to view such turmoil with alarm. He spoke about the prospect of a movement-driven struggle almost joyfully.

The instances of school desegregation to which Orfield had alluded are more numerous and more successful than most people in our nation are aware. In the Milwaukee area, for instance, 22 suburban districts presently participate in a student-transfer program to promote school integration across district lines, which has been in operation now for nearly 30 years. Under the program, 4,200 students transfer between Milwaukee and its suburbs. In the middle-class suburb of Shorewood, for example, 11 percent of the student population comes into the district from Milwaukee. Including minority children who already live in Shorewood, says Jack Linehan, the recently retired superintendent, "our school district is about 19 percent black and Hispanic, and the community has a great comfort level with that. . . . I think parents got to know each other as friends. . . . I think that evaporated away a lot of the psychological resistance. . . ." Linehan also notes that starting integration in the elementary grades made it much easier for children "simply to be children with each other." Stereotypes fall away, he adds—"it's more difficult to conjure up 'the other'—when you're building sand castles together. . . ."

In St. Louis also, a suburban-urban interdistrict transfer program has been taking place for more than 20 years. The program, initiated under a court order in 1983, today enrolls about 10,000 children from the city, who represent nearly a quarter of the school-age population of black children in St. Louis, while about 500 children from the suburbs make the opposite commute. Although recent cutbacks in the funds provided by the state to underwrite these transfers have imposed a heavier financial burden on the 16 suburbs that participate, most of the education leaders in these suburbs have made clear their preference to continue with the program, even in the face of opposition from the state.

In the Louisville area, as well, school integration, initially carried out under court order, has now been in place without court order for a quarter-century. The sweep of the program, under which the city's schools and county schools have been combined into a single system in which more than 90,000 black, Hispanic, white, and Asian children are enrolled, has had the effect of rendering Kentucky's public schools the most desegregated in the nation. The typical black student in Kentucky now attends a school in which two thirds of the enrollment is Caucasian.

When a proposal was made in 1991 to terminate or cut back on the integration program, protests were voiced by community groups, the teachers union, the local press, the Human Relations Commission of Jefferson County, and the regional branch of the National Conference of Christians and Jews. A survey revealed that the number of black parents who believed their children's education had improved under the busing plan exceeded those who took the opposite position by a ratio of six to one. Less than two percent believed that education for their children would be better in resegregated schools. In spite of occasional recurrences of opposition from groups or individuals who represent small pockets of resistance, support for school desegregation in the Louisville community continues strong and unabated to the present day.

In Prince Edward County, Virginia, which shut down its public schools from 1959 to 1964 in opposition to the mandates of *Brown v. Board of Education,* "the same community that treated its black children like so much trash is now a model for the nation," as Newsday has noted. A virtually all-black system from 1965 to 1972—only 130 of its 1,850 students were Caucasian in that year—the district now enrolls 2,800 children, of whom 40 percent are white and 59 percent are African-American. After years in which the system was abandoned by white people, nearly 1,000 of whom sent their children to a private white academy, more than 90 percent of children in the county now attend the public system, as the superintendent of the district told me with considerable pride in 2004.

Public policy has largely turned its back upon the aspirations represented by these instances of school desegregation. "Even many black leaders," notes education analyst Richard Rothstein, weary of the struggle over mandatory busing programs to achieve desegregation, "have given up on integration," arguing, in his words, that "a black child does not need white classmates in order to learn." So education policies, instead, he says, "now aim to raise scores in [the] schools that black children attend."

"That effort," he writes, "will be flawed even if it succeeds." The 1954 decision, he reminds us, "was not about raising scores" for children of minorities "but about giving black children access to majority culture, so they could negotiate it more confidently. . . . For African-Americans to have equal opportunity, higher test scores will not suffice. It is foolhardy to think black children can be taught, no matter how well, in isolation and then have the skills and confidence as adults to succeed in a white world where they have no experience."

Drawing upon a book about the interdistrict integration program in the Boston area by the education writer Susan Eaton, Rothstein cites a black adult whose mother had her bused from Boston to suburban Lexington, one of the 32 districts that have welcomed inner-city students in one of the longest-lasting voluntary integration programs in the nation. In her suburban school, she says, "everyone talked about college," so she "just assumed" that she would go to college too. She had never before heard about Brown University, she says, but a student two years ahead of her had gone there—"I admired her"—so she decided she would go there too. By the time she got to college, she observes, "I had already sat next to white students. I had been on teams and in student politics with them. So at Brown I could deal with the academic part" and wasn't "stressed about the social part." She graduated from Brown in 1985, obtained a job with Procter & Gamble, and then went to graduate school to be a reading specialist. "None of that would have been possible, she says," as Rothstein notes, "if she had not gone to integrated schools."

Dozens of children I originally met when they were attending Boston's segregated schools and whose parents subsequently took advantage of the transfer program to suburban districts have related stories like this. Almost all these students went to college, retained the friendships they had made in school, and now most frequently lead social lives and have professional careers in racially mixed settings, even while many have returned to live, and some to take on leadership positions, in the city's black community.

It is self-evident that there are many parents who do not approve of sending children outside of their neighborhoods and who resist the interdistrict option for good reasons of their own. Still, the lengths of the waiting lists for programs like the one in Massachusetts ought to teach us something about preferences of kids and parents when the integration option actually exists. The Boston program, which is known as Metco, now enrolls 3,300 children. There are nearly 16,000 on the waiting list at any given time—an enormous number in a city that enrolls only about 47,000 black and Hispanic students in its public schools.

The continuing support this program has received from the participating suburbs is all the more impressive when one recognizes that the state of Massachusetts reimburses only about half of the expense the average district must incur in the per-pupil cost of education for the children it receives. The wealthiest suburbs pay more than $6,000 for each urban student they enroll. "I wish we could take in far more Metco children," said the principal of one of the elementary schools in the historically progressive town of Brookline, which immediately borders one of the more segregated neighborhoods of Boston. The primary barrier to an expansion of this program, he observed, is not attitudinal resistance on the part of local parents but the fiscal penalty these districts are obliged to pay for doing something they regard as ethical and also to the betterment of children in their own communities.

Programs like these are being threatened, however, in some sections of the nation. In Milwaukee, for example, legislation has been introduced three times since 1999 to do away with interdistrict transfers or substantially reduce them, much of the pressure coming from those who argue that the money spent for integrated education should be spent instead to upgrade schools within the city, the assumption being that the state cannot afford to make both of these purposes attainable. In the first two attempts, the legislation was defeated. When, on the third attempt, in 2003, the legislation was approved, it was vetoed by Wisconsin Governor Jim Doyle. There will be further legislative efforts like these in the future, says Jack Linehan, the former Shorewood superintendent—this, he notes, despite the fact that academic outcomes for the students in the transfer program are consistently far better than for students who remain within Milwaukee. The four-year graduation rate of inner-city students who have been attending school in the suburban districts is typically 95 percent or higher, Linehan observes, while the rate for students in Milwaukee's schools averages below 60 percent.

If the legislature should succeed in cutting funding for the interdistrict plan, says Linehan, suburban districts would be forced to raise their local levies up to 25 percent to keep on with the program. "The only other option is to send these children back, which I believe would be immoral. We cannot say, 'We didn't mean it, now there's no more money. . . .' "

In perhaps the most disheartening development, the

interdistrict program in St. Louis is facing the risk of termination in the next three years. A court-supervised phase-out of state funding for the program, while it does not prohibit integration, significantly discourages suburban districts from accepting students from St. Louis after the 2008–2009 academic year. The suburbs, for the most part, have wanted to continue; and, indeed, students in the affluent community of Clayton walked out of classes in 2004 to protest a possible withdrawal from the program, according to The St. Louis Post-Dispatch. The principal of Clayton High School told the paper he was "proud to be part of a community that values diversity in a metro area so segregated." But the state, beginning in September 2004, cut assistance to the district from the full per-pupil cost in excess of $13,000 to approximately half that sum, a loss in funding that has led the Clayton school board, against the wishes of its students, to vote to terminate the program and accept no further applicants after 2008.

Other St. Louis suburbs may be driven to the same decision. Already, as a result of the first stages of the phase-out, the number of city students going to suburban schools has dropped by about 3,000 from a peak of 13,000 in the 1990s, while the number of suburban children going to St. Louis schools has dropped to half the number who were making this commute during the 1990s. "The state government," as Orfield notes, "beginning under former Governor John Ashcroft, has fiercely opposed the integration program. It works, so it will be killed, unlike charter schools, which do not work and will be expanded."

As in Milwaukee, the success of students in the program has been documented thoroughly. Ninety percent of transfer students graduating from suburban high schools have pursued post-secondary education, most attending two- or four-year colleges, compared to only 47 percent of graduating seniors in St. Louis. And the volume of applications by minority parents to enroll their children in the program has continued strong and is, indeed, increasing. In 2004, 6,000 parents submitted applications for the 1,300 openings that were available.

Is it accurate, then, to say that most Americans, and black Americans especially, as we are told so frequently, have decided to give up on integrated education? National surveys, Orfield notes, do not support this misconception. Over two thirds of Americans believe "desegregation improves education for blacks," and "a growing population is convinced" it has a positive effect for whites as well. In surveys among young adults, 60 percent believe the federal government ought to make *sure* that public schools are integrated, while the same percentage of black respondents do not merely favor integrated education but believe that it is "absolutely essential" that the population of a school be racially diverse. (Only 8 percent of blacks and only 20 percent of whites say that this is not of much importance.) Opposition to desegregation among whites, Orfield pointedly observes, is highest among those who have no experience of integration.

Yes, as those who have participated in these programs rightly note, there are the multitude of challenges that transfer students often do confront; and these are not always minor problems, nor are they exclusively, as some may think, "the problems they bring with them." Many are created by insensitivity or insufficient care in prior planning on the part of the receiving districts, others by resilient racist suppositions on the part of educators or administrators even in some of the most selfconsciously progressive white communities. Still, oral histories of students who experience desegregation usually reveal that, even when the social adaptations may be difficult at first, the students consider the benefits they ultimately gain to be well worth the challenges they've faced. And despite the social tensions students in these interdistrict programs do sometimes encounter—and despite those famous "separate tables" in the cafeterias to which black students often gravitate, and in regard to which an awful lot of lamentation is devoted in the press—many of the white and nonwhite students get to know each other far too well not to be drawn to one another, finally, as friends.

In the program here in Massachusetts, parents tell me that their children often visit or stay over at each other's homes, spend time on holidays together, and, in several cases of which I've been told, have also chosen colleges together. No matter what the social obstacles that children, both minority and white, must learn to overcome, no matter what the necessary games that must be played and roles that must be filled in adolescent years (the emphasis on style differences, and music tastes, and all the rest of what may seem to separate them at the start), a strange phenomenon—normality, humanity—kicks in; and, not in every case, but far more often than a social order with our racial history has reason to expect, they do reach out across the structural divide time and again and we are better, as a nation, for the consequence.

Most parents of black and Hispanic students who have asked for my advice when they were trying to decide upon a school their children might attend have told me they have rarely thought about the pros and cons of trying to enroll their children in suburban schools or, indeed, in racially desegregated schools within their district, because they do not believe it possible that they would have the chance to exercise this option if they wanted to. Orfield believes that we can *make* it possible on a far broader scale for those who do elect this option and that we have, in any case, a moral obligation to devote ourselves to heightening that possibility in any way we can. In answer to those who say they share this goal but point to the obstacles presented by the current make-up of the federal courts and the lack of any apparent interest in advancing such a purpose on the part of national elected leaders or the leaders of state government, Orfield, a political scientist by training, gives a clear, unshakable response.

"The notion that apartheid in the South could be dismantled 50 years ago seemed wildly improbable as well," he noted when I pressed him on this point a final time. "Breaking down the barriers to interdistrict integration and reducing residential segregation in the suburbs have at least as good a chance of ultimate success. It will take a major political thrust in order to achieve this. We will certainly need some better people on the courts. But look at what Charles Hamilton Houston and DuBois and those who worked with them during the decades long before the *Brown* decision faced when they were looking at a system of apartheid in the South which nobody was seriously resisting and which neither political party was opposing. And they nonetheless were asking, 'How do you take this thing apart?' And they *did* it. They started a movement. They created the intellectual force to make it possible. This is what *we* need to do as well." And, in his unwavering refusal to accede to seemingly resistless circumstance, he said, "And when we *do* create that force, it will be successful also."

In the last moments of our conversation, Orfield made a cautioning suggestion that I ought not to allow myself to be restricted in my thinking on these issues by the situation of extreme apartheid I have witnessed for so many years in the South Bronx. "There's a saying, 'Hard cases make bad law.' If you start with the hardest cases in the country, you're not going to come up with the right answers. You don't *need* to desegregate New York in order to desegregate

Des Moines!"—and he spoke of other middle-sized and smaller urban districts, county districts, and suburban districts elsewhere in the nation "where the obstacles are of an order of far lesser magnitude," he said, and the resistance less intractable. "You've seen the heart of segregation in New York. But when you look for possible solutions, you have got to start by looking elsewhere."

I have continued to revisit schools in the South Bronx. P.S. 30, the school where Louis Bedrock works, is one to which I keep returning because I know children who attend the school and good things take place in their classes every day, no matter what the overarching obstacles their teachers face. But when it comes to contemplating strategies for breaking down the hypersegregation of our public schools, New York City and its metropolitan community do not provide the sense of possibility that is still discernible in other sections of the nation where the structural arrangements that perpetuate the isolation of black and Hispanic children do not seem so firmly set in stone or where, at least, some of the apertures between the stones that Orfield looks for may more easily be found.

There are integrated schools in New York City and its suburbs; and, in some districts near the city, multiracial education is defended strongly by communities of parents. But the overall scale of racial isolation in New York is so extreme that it is hard to build political optimism on these relatively few exceptions. In order to believe that we or those who follow after us can ever hope to build the force to "take this thing apart," in Orfield's words, I think he's right in saying that we need to start by looking elsewhere.

CHAPTER 10

A National Horror Hidden in Plain View: Why Not a National Response?

At the age of 73, Roger Wilkins is a tall and thoughtful man of slender build, with white-gray hair and deep and generous brown eyes. One of the most enduringly respected figures in the older generation of black intellectuals, Wilkins has served our nation in a number of distinguished roles. Assistant attorney general of the United States under Lyndon Johnson, a prize-winning editorial writer at The Washington Post, the first black editorial board member of The New York Times and, later, first black columnist for that newspaper, he is now a professor of history and American culture at George Mason University.

"Any serious effort to reopen the debate about desegregation," Wilkins told me when we met in Washington to talk about the current climate of opinion on this issue among those who have the power to affect the policies of government, "is going to be enormously more difficult than the dismantling of apartheid in the South. Apartheid of that era was so gross and open in its manifestations that it was unsustainable within the age that followed World War II. But just as legal segregation in the South was a huge national horror hidden in plain view, so too the massive desolation of the intellect and spirits and the human futures of these millions of young people in their neighborhoods of poverty is yet another national horror hidden in plain view; and it is so enormous and it has its ganglia implanted so profoundly in the culture as we know it that we're going to have to build another movement if we hope to make it visible."

Choosing his words deliberately, Wilkins spoke of what he termed "the small-minded triumphalism" of contemporary political leaders who grew up in "isolated worlds of white male privilege" and have, as a result, "inadequate education for the responsibilities they hold." He learned from his own experience, he said, "that integrated education creates better citizens for a democracy. In an increasingly diverse society and an increasingly connected world, it is more important than it ever was."

Wilkins himself, after beginning school in Missouri, then completing elementary school and the first year of junior high in Harlem, moved with his mother to Grand Rapids, Michigan, where he attended an almost totally white high school. In the beginning, he told me, he felt isolated socially—"it was, at first," he said, "excruciatingly hard." Then, however, "I started making friends" and "found that I was popular" among the other students and, in an interesting side note I have heard from others who have faced this situation, "I benefited from the stereotypes white teachers may have held about black students, the expectation that we were not very bright, by doing good work academically, surpassing what my teachers thought that I could do." He subsequently won admission to the University of Michigan and received his law degree at Michigan as well.

"The point is this: Yes, it was hard, but there was wonderful two-way learning going on between me and my classmates. I learned the greatest lesson of my life during those years: that whites were not 'a master race,' and not all devils either, but that they were ordinary people like myself. It gave me an ease around white people that made the rest of my life possible. . . .

"I'm still not completely at ease among white people," he went on. "When you walk into the centers of white dominance, no matter what you've done in life, you feel like an outsider. But what my high school education did successfully was to teach me to function effectively in that environment. I don't think I could possibly have done this if I had not had that kind of education."

Wilkins told me he had served for several years as a member of the Washington, D.C., Board of Education and recalled the anguish he had felt at graduation ceremonies when he recognized how few of those who had enrolled as freshmen in the city's schools were still enrolled as seniors and were qualified to win diplomas. "I used to feel sick at graduations when I saw how many of the ninth grade students had been lost in those four years. It was like seeing an army regiment returning from a war." Americans, he said, "look at these young black people who have fallen by the way and think, 'They're just not up to it. If they'd just pull up their socks, they could be Colin Powell too.' 'Why not?' they ask. 'We have a full-opportunity society today' and one, by the way, in which 'these blacks have extra opportunities. . . .' "

He said that when he speaks of the effects of racial isolation on these students, he commonly encounters a familiar answer from white people whom he meets in social situations. He quoted a woman in New York who said, "You know, we tried the integration thing, but it was just *so* difficult!"

In a conversation of more than two hours, Wilkins spoke of the immense complexity of trying to bring these issues back into the national attention. "Here's the thing that I believe," he said. "Racist beliefs are so profound and the supportive structures have now been in place so long that after an upheaval like the one we lived through 40 years ago, it leaves the nation morally exhausted" with "a huge desire not to be obliged to think of it again." And yet, he said, "the nation *must* be asked to think of it again" and, looking directly in my eyes, Wilkins went on, "I hope you won't allow yourself to be deflected from expressing this, or any other damn thing that you please in this regard, because these issues need to be raised forcefully. These things need to be said."

What stayed in my mind in the days that followed were his words about "the ganglia implanted so profoundly in the culture as we know it," as he had described "the massive desolation of the intellect and spirits . . . of these millions of young people"—"a national horror hidden in plain view," as he had said. If it was a national horror, whether hidden in plain view or, as others may believe, too obvious to be concealed but clearly seen yet somehow "disallowed" at the same time, why was there no national response?

Some, I suppose, would argue that the education bill enacted in the first years of the Bush administration, No Child Left Behind, with its emphasis on national accountability procedures, nationally authorized instructional techniques, and nationally standardized examinations constitutes "a national response" of sorts. But this was a response, as we have seen, that did not bring the power of the federal government to bear on lessening inequities in funding or in infrastructure between wealthier and more impoverished districts, nor did it even indirectly touch on the apparently forbidden question of intensifying racial isolation.

On the opposite side of the political divide, most of the struggles being carried out by advocates for children of low income, whether they addressed inequity alone or in rare cases spoke of racial isolation also, were specific to one state or district and did not address these issues on a scope that challenged and indicted our behavior and our policies as an entire nation. What Wilkins recognized to be a national calamity was being addressed instead as an injustice that was caused by the particulars of politics and funding practices at local levels, with the moral obligations of the nation as a whole almost entirely shunted out of view.

In order to understand the reasons why this has been so and why attorneys who try to defend the interests of low-income and minority children in the courts have stepped back from the national arena and have limited their efforts to the state and district levels, we may briefly look at a decisive episode of legal history that took place starting slightly more than 30 years ago. I have described some of this history in Savage Inequalities, published in 1991, but it may help to recapitulate one portion of it here.

The date that experts in school finance generally pinpoint is March 21, 1973, the day on which the U.S. Supreme Court overruled the judgment of a district court in Texas that had found the inequalities of education finance in that state to be unconstitutional. A class action suit had been filed five years earlier by a resident of San Antonio named Demetrio Rodriguez and by other parents on behalf of their own children, who were students in the city's Edgewood district, which was very poor and 96 percent nonwhite. Although Edgewood residents paid one of the highest property tax rates in the area, the district could raise only $37 for each pupil because of the low value of its property. Even with assistance granted by the state, Edgewood ended up with only $231 for each child. Alamo Heights, meanwhile, the richest section of the city but incorporated as a separate schooling district, was able to spend $543 on each pupil. Alamo Heights, then as now, was a predominantly white district.

Late in 1971, a three-judge federal district court in San Antonio had held that Texas was in violation of the equal protection clause of the U.S. Constitution. "Any mild equalizing effects" from state aid, said the court, "do not benefit the poorest districts."

It is this decision that was then appealed to the Supreme Court. The majority opinion of the high court, which reversed the lower court's decision, noted that, in order to bring to bear "strict scrutiny" upon the case, it must first establish that there had been "absolute deprivation" of a "fundamental interest" of the Edgewood children. Justice Lewis Powell wrote that education is not "a fundamental interest" inasmuch as education "is not among the rights afforded explicit protection under our Federal Constitution." Nor, he wrote, did he believe that "absolute deprivation" was at stake. "The argument here," he said, "is not that the children in districts having relatively low assessable property values are receiving no public education; rather, it is that they are receiving a poorer quality education than that available to children in districts having more assessable wealth." In cases where wealth is involved, he said, "the Equal Protection Clause does not require absolute equality. . . ."

Attorneys for Rodriguez and the other plaintiffs, Powell wrote, argued "that education is itself a fundamental personal right because it is essential to the exercise of First Amendment freedoms and to intelligent use of the right to vote. [They argued also] that the right to speak is meaningless unless the speaker is capable of articulating his thoughts intelligently and persuasively. . . . [A] similar line of reasoning is pursued with respect to the right to vote.

"Yet we have never presumed to possess either the ability or the authority to guarantee . . . the most *effective* speech or the most *informed* electoral choice." Even if it were conceded, he wrote, that "some identifiable quantum of education" is a prerequisite to exercise of speech and voting rights, "we have no indication . . . that the [Texas funding] system fails to provide each child with an opportunity to acquire the basic minimal skills necessary" to enjoy a "full participation in the political process."

In any case, said Justice Powell in a passage that anticipates much of the debate still taking place today, "experts are divided" on the question of the role of money in determining the quality of education. Indeed, he said, "one of the hottest sources of controversy concerns the extent to which there is a demonstrable correlation between educational expenditures and the quality of education."

Justice Thurgood Marshall, in his long dissent, challenged the notion that an interest, to be seen as "fundamental," had to be "explicitly or implicitly guaranteed" within the Constitution. Thus, he said, although the right to procreate, the right to vote, and the right to criminal appeal are not guaranteed, "these interests have nonetheless been afforded special judicial consideration . . . because they are, to some extent, interrelated with constitutional guarantees." Education, Marshall said, was also such a "related interest" because it "directly affects the ability of a child to exercise his First Amendment interests both as a source and as a receiver of information and ideas. . . ."

Marshall also challenged the distinction, made by Justice Powell, between "absolute" and "relative" degrees of deprivation, as well as Powell's judgment that the Texas funding scheme, because it had increased the funds available to local districts, now provided children in these districts with the "minimum" required. "The Equal Protection Clause is not addressed to . . . minimal sufficiency," said

Marshall, but to equity; and he cited the words of *Brown* to the effect that education, "where the State has undertaken to provide it, is a right which must be made available to all on equal terms."

On Justice Powell's observation that some experts questioned the connection between spending and the quality of education, Marshall answered almost with derision: It is, he said, "an inescapable fact that if one district has more funds available per pupil than another district," it "will have greater choice" in what it offers to its children. If "financing variations are so insignificant" to quality, he wrote, "it is difficult to understand why a number of our country's wealthiest school districts," which, he noted, had no obligation to support the Texas funding scheme, had "nevertheless zealously pursued its cause before this Court"—a reference to amicus briefs that affluent Bloomfield Hills, Grosse Point, and Beverly Hills had introduced in their support of the defendants.

Nonetheless, the court's majority turned down the suit—the vote was five to four—and in a single word, "reversed," Justice Powell ended any expectations that the children of the Edgewood schools would now be given the same quality of education as the children in more affluent school districts. From that point on, with few exceptions, legal efforts to reduce or to abolish inequalities in education were restricted to state levels.

Since that era, legal actions have been brought in 45 of the 50 states under the constitutions of those states. In 27 states, courts have ruled in favor of the plaintiffs. In 18 states, courts have ruled in favor of defendants. Even, however, in those cases in which victories were gained by plaintiffs, less than half these states have taken action in compliance with court orders or with court-mandated settlements that have brought sustained relief to children in poor districts. Under persistent pressure from attorneys, some of these states have brought a nearly level playing field to education finance; but the overall rate of progress has been fitful, and the victories often short-lived and generally incomplete, and even after all these years of litigation unacceptable inequities remain the norm in the majority of states.

According to the Education Trust, a politically moderate advocacy institute in Washington that has reviewed the recent trends in education finance, "the top 25 percent of school districts in terms of child poverty . . . receive less funding than the bottom 25 percent." In 31 states, districts with the highest percentage of minority children also receive less funding per pupil than do districts with the fewest minority children.

These, moreover, are what are known as "unadjusted numbers." In their calculation, no consideration has been given to the greater needs of children of low income. (The sole adjustments that the Education Trust has made in this case are for local differences in costs that districts must incur for purchasing supplies and services and for costs of educating children who have disabilities.) When we *do* make an adjustment for the extra costs of educating children of low income, using a standard cost-adjustment factor that the federal government has codified, the inequalities become still more apparent. Thirty-five out of 48 states spend less on students in school districts with the highest numbers of minority children than on students in the districts with the fewest children of minorities.* Nationwide, the average differential is about $1,100 for each child. In some states—New York,

*These numbers exclude the District of Columbia, Hawaii, and Tennessee, in the first two instances because they operate as single districts, in the third because minority data is not made available by Tennessee.

Texas, Illinois, and Kansas for example—the differential is considerably larger. In New York, the most unequal state for children of minorities, it is close to $2,200 for each child, and when New York City is compared to its immediately surrounding affluent white suburbs, as we've noted, the differential soars a great deal higher.

When children are shortchanged financially, of course, the individual per-pupil penalty that they incur is greatly magnified because a child is not educated individually but in a class of 20, 25, or 30 or more children. Using a classroom size of 25, the Education Trust observes, a typical class of children of low income in Virginia receives some $36,000 less than does a classroom in a district with the fewest numbers of poor children. In Arizona, a typical class of children of low income receives $29,000 less than does a class of nonpoor children, in Texas $23,000 less, in Pennsylvania $33,000 less, in Illinois nearly $62,000 less, in New York some $65,000 less. If we look at an entire school, rather than a single class, these differences are magnified again. A high-poverty elementary school that holds about 400 students in New York receives more than $1 million less per year than schools of the same size in districts with the fewest numbers of poor children.

In several states, moreover, the funding gap for children of color is a great deal larger than the gap for children of low income. "The minority funding gap in California, for example, is almost twice the size of the shortfall for low-income students," notes the Education Trust. Other states that have "a significantly larger funding gap for minority children" than for children of low income include Colorado, Kansas, Nebraska, Texas, and Wisconsin. "The minority funding gap in Wisconsin is almost three times larger" than the gap for children of low income.

"Knowledge of the funding gap and its fundamental unfairness is not new," the Education Trust observes, and the policies required to abolish this inequity "are relatively straightforward and well known." Despite this knowledge, however, "we've actually *lost* ground since the Education Trust began issuing this annual funding gap report." While many states have reduced their gap since 1997, "at the aggregate national level . . . the funding gap got worse."

The Education Trust also substantiates a further problem we have noted in the case of New York City. "The inequitable distribution of resources . . . between districts" is often equally "pervasive *within* districts." This is because most districts simply give their schools the money that they need to pay the teachers they are able to employ. "Since high-poverty . . . schools tend to employ a disproportionate number of inexperienced, low-paid teachers, these schools end up getting much less money per student" than do schools in wealthier communities of the same districts.

Inequitable support of public schools, notes Kevin Carey, author of the two most recent studies by the Education Trust, is such a persistent problem "that it has acquired an . . . air of inevitability. Politicians come and go, blue-ribbon commissions are formed and eventually disband, lawsuits are filed only to embark on a seemingly endless journey of decision and appeal. . . ." The problem "has gone on so long," says Carey, "that some states have come perilously close to accepting this as the natural order of things."

Even more troubling in some respects, attorneys in most of the states where cases are now pending have been forced, as a result of legal precedents and in order to subdue political resistance on the part of wealthy districts, to renounce the goal of fully equal education and to ask the courts to give poor children not the same high level of resources offered by the wealthiest white districts but merely "sufficient" funding to achieve the standards now demanded of them by the state. Michael Rebell, a brilliant legal strategist who is the director of the New York City–based Campaign for Fiscal Equity, has spoken with me at length about the logic of renouncing equity as an objective and, instead, pursuing what is now described as "adequate provision" and defining "adequacy" at a level corresponding to the various particulars of state accountability requirements. Since the standards now imposed by New York State are relatively high, an "adequate education" by this definition would, while not achieving equity, at least come a lot closer to that goal than what is now provided in the schools that children like Pineapple and Alliyah have attended.

The important victories that the Campaign for Fiscal Equity has won in court, although they have not yet been implemented by the state, appear to most observers in New York to vindicate this strategy. At the same time, Rebell is frank in recognizing what this strategy cannot achieve. "We really came to the decision that if we could get . . . an adequate education in every school—to get there is such a huge battle," he told The New York Times in 2004—"maybe in 20 years, if we ever get that, somebody else can say that they want to go for equity. But that's not our battle."

Rebell and his associates deal with reality as it exists, not as they wish that it might be. They are trying "to move society an inch," as one member of their legal team put it to me bluntly, "when it needs to be moved a mile." It may be that they will end up moving it a lot more than "an inch" if legislative leaders in New York should someday act in a responsible compliance with the rulings of the court. Every inch they gain, in any case, is worth the effort it requires to achieve it.

Still, the consequences of *Rodriguez* cast their shadow upon even the most valiant efforts that attorneys at state levels undertake. In part, this is because the wording of the educational provisions in state constitutions tends to vary greatly and compels attorneys in the several states to figure out a multiplicity of strategies in order to address these variations. Then, too, there is the sheer expenditure of time and energy required by the duplication of these efforts in state after state in which the ethical argument attorneys ultimately hope to make is basically the same. And, finally, no matter what the state in which a case takes place, the most important disadvantage advocates for equal education or for adequate education have to face is that attorneys are unable to incorporate within their pleadings legal claims deriving from the U.S. Constitution—the only constitution that has truly elevated moral standing in the eyes of most Americans—and cannot, as a consequence, defend the rights of children in these cases *as Americans.* But for a single vote by any one of the four Supreme Court justices appointed by President Richard Nixon in the years from 1969 to 1972, none of the subsequent cases brought in 45 state courts would have been necessary.

Efforts to return the focus of this struggle from the local courts and legislative bodies to the federal level, not through further litigation but through legislative processes, have been attempted in the past few years by several members of Congress. The leadership has come, in large part, from black members of the U.S. House of Representatives.

U.S. Representative Chaka Fattah, for example, who represents a Philadelphia district, introduced a bill four years ago that uses the language of accountability and standards for a purpose that the Bush administration certainly did not intend. If the federal government can hold a district or a state "accountable" for demonstrating high performance by its students on their standardized exams, according to the reasoning of Mr. Fattah, the federal government should also have the power to hold states accountable for making sure that children in all districts are provided with the resources they need to *meet* these high demands. Isolating several elements of "educational necessities"—among them, "safe facilities," "updated libraries," and "small classes"—the congressman's bill requires that the states provide "comparable educational services" to "all school districts" and comply with all court orders that may already exist to this effect or suffer the penalty of losing a portion of their federal funds. Where states fail to comply with these requirements, they would need to demonstrate that they are making "adequate yearly progress" toward the stipulations of the bill; and, if they fail to make such progress in a given period of time, the bill provides "a cause of action" in the federal courts "for students and parents aggrieved by violations of the bill."

Congressman Fattah's bill, which he reintroduced in 2003, and again in 2005, represents an almost precise reversal of the notion that our teachers, principals, and schools need to be held to certain state and federal standards and be made to suffer "sanctions" when those standards are not met. And it is a reversal, too, of the demand that principals show "adequate progress" in complying with those school improvement plans that we have seen, even when their classes may be packed with 30 or more students and their teachers lack sufficient textbooks or, at secondary levels, do not even have the science laboratories needed to teach courses on which students will be tested.

Establishing "a cause of action" in the federal courts is the item in the congressman's proposal that returns us to the questions raised, and obstacle created, in *Rodriguez.* If Congressman Fattah's bill, or a new incarnation of this bill, were ever to be approved by Congress and enacted into law, it would admittedly not force the federal government to spend more money to redress inequities within a given state but it would represent an instrument by which the power of the federal government could be employed to force a state to make more equitable distribution of the resources it presently commands. A nearly identical Senate version of this bill, introduced by Connecticut Senator Christopher Dodd in 2001 as an amendment to another legislative motion, received the votes of 42 members of the Senate, an intriguing and, to some of us, tantalizing bit of evidence that more than a few of our elected leaders are prepared to countenance the use of federal power to redress some of the consequences of *Rodriguez.*

In a considerably more sweeping effort to address the long-abiding consequences of the Texas case, Congressman Jesse Jackson Jr., who represents a district in Chicago, has proposed a constitutional amendment that would guarantee the right to public education "of an equally high quality" to every American child and has introduced a resolution in the U.S. House of Representatives to this effect. Jackson's amendment, introduced in March 2003, would establish education as "a fundamental human right" under the U.S. Constitution and, as he described its purpose to me, would essentially strike down *Rodriguez* and defend the education rights of children that are not defended by the high court's present readings of the equal protection clause of the Fourteenth Amendment. "Today," he said, "we have a 'states' rights education system'—50 states, 3,067 counties, 95,000 public schools in 15,000 locally controlled districts in which 50 million children go to separate and unequal public schools. We need the assistance of the Constitution to correct this. Until we have it, 'savage inequalities,' to use your words, will not be an aberration in the system—it will *be* 'the system' as it stands."

In spite of the complexity of reasons for the patchwork system of school funding that exists today, much of which derives from policies and practices devised nearly a century ago, Congressman Jackson is persuaded that our nation's racial history provides the clearest lens by which to understand why this archaic system has not been subjected to the radical revision that fair-mindedness would seemingly demand. Both race and class, in his belief, are at the heart of these inequities, but he is convinced that race, in the long run, is the commanding factor. In speaking of the perennial refusal of state legislative bodies to provide resources needed by low-income districts even when a legislature is so ordered by a court, Jackson evoked the words of Dr. King about "a promissory note" for which the payment keeps on coming back "marked 'insufficient funds,' " and he observed that "insufficient funds" is the familiar explanation heard from governors and legislative leaders when they fail to act on court decisions that would bring relief to overwhelmingly minority school districts.

"The entire present system in its structural irrationality needs to be rooted out"—" 'root *and* branch,' " he said, while walking around a wide mahogany table in the conference room in which we talked in order to stand directly over me as I wrote down his words—"and there is no way that this is going to be done but by the passage of a constitutional amendment."

The congressman observed, as well, that "if the nation ever *wants* to end the segregated status of our public schools, this amendment means it could, and can," because the amendment, in his belief, "would also strike down *Milliken,*" the 1974 decision that created massive obstacles to the enforced participation of the suburbs in desegregation orders. (This is a point on which some legal scholars disagree with Mr. Jackson, but Orfield argues that the congressman may be correct if it could be proven that "an equally high quality of education," Jackson's words in the proposed amendment, "cannot be achieved under conditions of apartheid," which, he says, "might introduce a legal basis for compelling the participation of the suburbs.") Although, in describing his amendment, Jackson spoke in terms of "human rights" for all our children, rather than of "civil rights" for black and Hispanic children in particular, the amendment nonetheless, he argued, "would advance both integration and equality"—"and *yes,*" the congressman continued, "if the parents of black students want their children to be educated in an integrated public school, society does have to make that option possible. . . ."

Congressman Jackson's resolution has been given only scant attention by observers in the world of education policy and in the mainstream press. "Unfortunately," notes William Taylor, one of the veteran lawyers who has litigated race and education cases through the years, "the state of our public and political discourse nowadays is such that anything like this tends to be ridiculed." This, he believes, is why a number of people he has spoken with in Washington "tend to view the resolution skeptically."

Other advocates and intellectuals, however, whether or not they support the resolution, do support the view that equal education ought to be regarded as a national entitlement and ought to be protected under federal law. Any notion that a child's education is essentially a state and local matter "is increasingly so out of line with the realities of our society as to be obsolete," as civil rights attorney Theodore Shaw expressed this to me in his office at the NAACP Legal Defense Fund in New York. "The whole idea of 'state and local control' has come to be a good deal less convincing in the past few years," he said, "now that the federal government has grown involved in public education at a level of specific stipulations it has never dared to touch upon before." In spite of the restrictive readings given to the Fourteenth Amendment in the decades since *Rodriguez*—"an historically ignorant decision," as he worded it—Shaw noted that most Americans are unaware that children have no constitutional protection where equality of education is at stake. The notion that education is not a protected right under the U.S. Constitution comes as a surprise to the majority of citizens, he said. "Most Americans believe that education is a fundamental right and when you tell them that it's not, they say, 'It *should* be.' "

The argument will certainly be made that it would take unusually courageous leadership, as well as a long period of years, if not of decades, to create a groundswell of informed opinion to support either a legislative act or an amendment that might finally create a clear-cut federal obligation to protect the interests of all children in receiving equally high qualities of education. And even if a constitutional amendment should someday be passed and ratified, the enforcement of its terms would still depend upon the disposition of the federal courts to implement it and of the states and local districts to comply with its demands. Yet winning even piecemeal vindication for low-income children through the courts at local levels has already proved to be a slow and grinding process and, in those cases where a victory is finally achieved, the courts too frequently seem powerless to cut through the resistance of executive and legislative branches of state governments.

It has taken over 30 years of litigation to achieve a genuinely substantial victory for children in poor districts of New Jersey. In Ohio, more than a decade since a suit was filed to achieve a similar objective, courts have now determined four times that the system of school finance is in violation of the constitution of that state, and still the governor and legislature have defied these rulings with impunity.

The victory in the New York City case, which was filed initially in 1993, took a decade to achieve and, even then, the court allowed the governor and legislative branch an additional year in which to remedy the constitutional violation it had found. A year later, in 2004, the state's deadline came and went without the governor and legislature taking action on this ruling. A panel of three distinguished jurists was subsequently appointed by the court to specify exactly how much added money New York State must spend to meet its obligations under the state's constitution, and the trial judge embodied these specific numbers in a new court order to the state, which set another deadline for compliance by June 2005. The state again ignored the deadline and has, for a second time, appealed the ruling to a higher court, which is unlikely to arrive at a decision before late 2005 or winter of 2006, after which there will be another level of appeal, which may well extend the case into the year 2007.

If New York should someday, at long last, be forced to live up to the constitutional requirements it has defied for all these years, a new generation of New York City children will receive a higher quality of education, but this cannot compensate the students who were children when this case was filed, since their years of childhood have since been taken from them and can never be restored. Even when courts decree, after long years of litigation, that an entire generation of low-income children in a state has been denied the education that the constitution of the state required all along, they do not grant the victims reparations.

In the California case, attorneys for the plaintiffs came to an agreement with the state in August 2004 that brings only a modest gain to children in poor districts. Some $140 million was assigned to buy instructional materials aligned with the state standards and $50 million to meet infrastructure needs. If the state keeps faith with this agreement, another $800 million will be spent between 2005 and 2009 for emergency repairs to public schools and to develop a "facilities inspection" program. The settlement also specifies that students now attending schools with shortened academic years, like Fremont High, will be provided with the 180 days of school that presently are given to the vast majority of children in the state, but not before the year 2012. The agreement does not mandate funds for the construction of new schools, raising the qualifications of instructors, or reducing class size in the schools as they now stand. It does, however, stipulate that every child from now on ought to be allowed to have a textbook and to be provided with a desk and chair.

The settlement, says Michael Kirst, a well-known education scholar and a former president of the California Board of Education, "gets them [that is, the students in low-funded schools] from the basement to the first floor, but there are two more floors to go. . . ." More skeptical observers who have noted the historic tendency of governmental leaders to retreat from minimal commitments to low-income children once a case like this is settled out of court are not as confident that students in the kinds of schools we've visited will likely even get out of that metaphoric basement in the years while they're still children.

Then too, apart from the delays that plaintiffs face in winning vindication through court actions in a given state, there is the question of the educational inequities *between* the separate states. If at some point in the future, children in all 50 states receive whatever version of an adequate education each state may determine to be suitable under its constitution, children in some states will still receive an education only "half as adequate" as children in another state with more resources. In Mississippi, at the present time, an equitable system merely at the level of the statewide average in per-pupil spending would provide all children with an education worth not quite $6,000 yearly. A comparably equitable system in Connecticut would give the children of the state an education worth more than $11,000. Even with adjustments made for differences in local costs of operations, local costs for teachers' salaries, and other factors that distinguish one state from another, this remains a hopelessly outdated and inherently unequal way to educate a nation.

In spite of all the reservations I have stated here, I have done my best for more than 15 years to rally the support of friends and colleagues for these statewide cases. Whether or not these cases are successful, or success is long delayed, the legal actions in themselves have sometimes had the positive effect of heightening the public's consciousness of the extreme inequities of which some citizens may have been unaware. In the New York City case, the act of filing the suit, the evidence presented in the trial stage, the affirmative decision of the trial judge, then its reversal, then its affirmation in 2003, the decision of the trial judge to intervene directly in enforcement of this ruling, and the subsequent obstructive tactics of the state have attracted a great deal of press attention, much of which has been supportive of the plaintiffs' claims. Attorneys in the case have also waged a strong campaign to generate political engagement in the issues that the suit has raised among broad sectors of the New York population.

Without such efforts, legal actions on their own, as attorney Theodore Shaw observes, cannot create the ferment needed for a serious political upheaval, for "a movement," for "a mobilization," in the terms that Orfield has described; and Shaw insists upon the need for activism outside of the legal process and *preceding* it. "In the Montgomery bus boycott," he notes, "litigation didn't lead the movement. It came afterwards and *served* it. . . . When lawyers think that they can lead a movement in their role as lawyers, they are doomed to failure, because courts themselves are socially reactionary institutions," and he said he meant "reactionary" in both of the common senses of that word. "Then, too, because the litigation process is so slow and so complex, it can turn activists into bystanders far too easily. Lawyers like Gandhi and Mandela can awaken and create a movement, but not in their role as lawyers. You need to create a climate of political momentum first. That, then, is the challenge."

Even when attorneys do try to reach out beyond the courts to build political support, it has been very hard to build a movement of dynamic national importance out of adequacy claims in a variety of separate states. "Adequacy" itself, as a political objective, is hardly a heart-stopping and exalted cry to battle. (One cannot imagine millions of young activists rising up in moral indignation in reaction to a banner asking "Adequacy Now!") And, although attorneys in these cases have established linkages with one another to develop strategies and advocate for common goals, most of this remains beneath the recognition of the public and has barely even percolated into the awareness of most of the liberals I meet in states in which these legal battles have been taking place.

Many progressives in these states have only the most general idea of what these cases are about, and in certain states in which these cases were, and are, most heatedly contested, even the teachers of the children in low-funded districts tend to have little or no knowledge of these legal actions and, even when they do have smatterings of knowledge, most of them evince no sense that great political determinations are at stake. Their level of affect is repeatedly, I find, far lower than that of the litigators in these cases. It is the same with parents of poor children in most of these states. We are a long way from Montgomery.

There is another aspect of these cases that cannot fail to remind us of how far the nation has retreated from the high ideals and purposes identified with *Brown*. As a result of the federal precedents that we have seen, as well as the combustible political realities in some of the most stridently divided metropolitan communities, lawyers for the plaintiffs rarely choose to speak at all of racial isolation. Indeed, the argument in almost all these cases rests implicitly upon the premise that the Warren Court was incorrect in its decision and that separate education can be rendered, if not equal, at least good enough to be sufficient for the children who attend school in a segregated system. If attorneys were to argue that the finding in *Brown v. Board of Education* was correct, it would be difficult to make the case that funding increments will bring sufficient gains to segregated children to be worth the court's consideration.

"I'm dealing with the de facto world of segregated schools," said Joseph Wayland, one of the two lead attorneys in the New York City case, during the course of an extremely candid conversation when I pressed him on this question. "Whatever damage segregation might or might not do, the premise of our case is that the state and city can provide sufficient resources so that students in a school, even if that school is segregated, can achieve a respectable level of success." Wayland made it clear that he regarded *Brown* with reverence and, indeed, he had alluded to it movingly in his initial statement to the court. "We stand before the court . . . ," he said, "because the effect of the constitutional wrong visited upon the children of New York City is no less insidious than the harm that the Supreme Court condemned in Brown against the Board of Education. . . . In 1999 we remain a house divided." Although "the line is no longer a line of state-sanctioned discrimination . . . ," he went on, it is nonetheless "a de facto line of color."

In reference to the termination of de jure segregation in the *Brown* decision, Wayland said, "The doors are open" now—in at least a legal sense—but they lead into schools where "far too many children" are denied necessities of education. "And so," he told the court, "a cruel hoax has been visited on our children."

Lawyers in similar cases elsewhere make allusions to *Brown v. Board of Education,* drawing a dotted line of sorts between the Warren Court's insistence on the damage done to children by their racial segregation and the contemporary emphasis on adequate provision for those segregated children. When they do this, they are paying homage to the morally commanding stature of that ruling while, in a sense, attempting to adapt its meanings, or at least its spirit, to the presentation of their cases. And yet the words of *Brown* defy such adaptation.

"We come then to the question presented," said the justices in *Brown* in words that bear repeating in this context. "Does segregation of children in public schools solely on the basis of race, even though the physical facilities and other 'tangible' factors may be equal, deprive the children of the minority group of equal education opportunities? We believe that it does. . . . In the field of public education, the doctrine of 'separate but equal' has no place." Yet separate but equal obviously *has* to have a place within these equity or adequacy cases. Given realities of politics and precedent, there is no other argument attorneys plausibly can make. Whether they ask for equal, adequate, high adequate, or basic minimal provision, they are asking for postmodern versions of the promise *Plessy* made and the next 60 years of history betrayed.

Like most advocates for children, I have celebrated the successes of these cases when the consequence of courtroom victories was to diminish even incrementally the inequalities faced by the children of poor districts. In the New Jersey case, far more than incremental gains have been achieved. Up until 1997, the funding gap between high-poverty and successful, affluent districts was more than $1,000 for each pupil. By 2004, per-pupil spending in high-poverty districts had increased to $11,000, the same amount that was being spent, on average, in the schools that served the children of the privileged; and the state has also made available an additional $2,000 for each pupil in the poorest districts to support "at risk" and supplemental programs. Meanwhile, the state has instituted full-day kindergarten and a full-day, full-year pre-K program for all three- and four-year-olds in the low-income districts and is spending an initial allocation of $6 billion to replace or to update school buildings in these districts.

Still, it has taken a third of a century to win these victories for children in New Jersey; and meanwhile there is Illinois, Ohio, Pennsylvania, Michigan, Louisiana, Arizona, Oklahoma, and Virginia, and those many, many other states in which inequities go on and on. Now, too, in Kentucky, in which plaintiffs won a landmark adequacy case in 1989, lawyers are back in court because the legislature has refused to meet its obligation to low-income districts, one consequence of which we have observed in the dilapidated Russell School I visited in Lexington. In Texas, where another major victory was won in 1993, a court has recently found the finance system now in place unconstitutional once more because, despite a law that forces wealthy districts to share revenue from property taxes with poor districts, a cap on property taxes has reduced these revenues to the degree that poor and minority districts cannot provide their students with the equal education that the court decision calls for.

In Kansas too, where a much-celebrated victory was won in 1991, a court has now been forced to find the system of school funding, as it has evolved since 1991, to be unconstitutional again. At this rate, and given the variety of ways in which state legislative bodies have been able to subvert and vitiate the consequences of these court decisions through the years, it might be another century before the promise made by *Plessy* may at last be realized in all 50 states.

These, then, are among the reasons why political initiatives that have any chance at all of redirecting policy discussion to the national dimensions of these questions seem to me to be deserving of more serious attention than they have received. As things stand today, the children in the schools we have examined in this book are not protected by their nation. Yet they are expected in school to perform at national standards, are graded on what are, in fact, no less than national exams that measure their success or failure according to nationally determined norms, are expected to vote someday in national elections, compete for earnings in a national job market and, because of their race and poverty, are far more likely than most other citizens to imperil their lives by serving in our nation's wars. The illegitimacy of the uneven social contract by which they are bound invites a more aggressive scrutiny than it can be accorded in the courts of separate states. These children are not citizens of Illinois, New York, or California. They are (most of them are, at least) the citizens of the United States; yet the flag that hangs above their classrooms and their schools does not defend their interest where it comes to preparation for adulthood in their nation, and the words of the pledge we ask them to recite can only mock their actual experience.

Many Americans, write Edwin Margolis and Stanley Moses in their book Elusive Quest, published in 1991, experience "a sense of shock and revulsion . . . when confronted with the reality that the American governmental system discriminates among the children of the wealthy and the poor in the provision of resources for public schooling. . . . There is something about this system that violates basic American standards of decency and fair play in a way that goes beyond ordinary political arrangements and compromises." Certainly, they note, "many, especially in the more affluent and suburban areas, benefit from this arrangement and will continue to resist attempts to change the status quo. But few will defend it as representing the better side of American democracy."

Whether the issue is inequity alone or deepening resegregation or the labyrinthine intertwining of the two, it is well past the time for us to start the work that it will take to change this. If it takes "new turmoil to bring that about," in *Time* writer Jack White's words, if it takes people marching in the streets and other forms of adamant disruption of the governing civilities, if it takes more than litigation, more than legislation, and much more than resolutions introduced by members of the Congress, these are prices we should be prepared to pay. "We do not have the things you have," the third grade child named Alliyah told me when she wrote to ask if I would come and visit at her school in the South Bronx. "Can you help us?" America owes that little girl and millions like her a more honorable answer than they have received.

CHAPTER 11

Deadly Lies

A sustained attack has now been under way for several years against those many teachers who do not ascribe to the beliefs and practices that are embodied in the federal law No Child Left Behind. President Bush accuses those who disagree with him about the wisdom of these practices of being the unconscious bearers of "soft bigotry," while one of the president's advisers overseeing federal education research has said that it is "racist nonsense" to reject the claim that school accountability alone will lead to equal outcomes for our children. Mr. Paige, the former education secretary, went so far a year ago as to call the National Education Association, our nation's largest teachers union, "a terrorist organization" because it criticized the White House for refusing to deliver on the funding that it promised at the time its education bill was shepherded through Congress.

Secretary Paige resigned from his position at the end

of January 2005. His successor, Margaret Spellings, was one of the authors of No Child Left Behind and, like Mr. Paige, came with the president from Texas, where she helped develop the accountability agenda in that state. The attack upon dissenting educators has become somewhat less strident in the months since her appointment, but the ideological certitude that drives these White House policies remains unchanged.

"ALL CHILDREN CAN LEARN!" the advocates for this agenda say hypnotically, as if the tireless reiteration of this slogan could deliver to low-income children the same clean and decent infrastructure and the amplitude of cultural provision by experienced instructors that we give the children of the privileged. If the officials who repeat this incantation honestly believe all kids can learn, why aren't they fighting to make sure these kids can learn in the same good schools their own children attend? To isolate the victim, and shortchange the victim, and then tell him he can "learn to his potential" if he and his teachers just try hard enough, is one of those bizarre political performances that's very much in fashion in our nation's capital today.

There is, moreover, a cynical message given to the relatively affluent when declamation takes the place of substantive delivery of educational necessities. Hortatory rhetoric costs nothing for society; giving the kids at Fremont High a dignified place in which to learn, cutting the number of students in their classes from the present impossible high of 40 to the typical class of 18 to 20 found in wealthier communities, while giving their younger siblings two or three exciting years of rich developmental preschool education, would extract a lot of money from the pockets of taxpayers.

Meanwhile, the Bush administration, as we've noted, has denied the Head Start program to one half the nation's eligible three- and four-year-olds, making it all the harder for these children to survive the high-stakes tests they will be taking once they enter public school. As for the efforts of school districts to reduce the size of classes or observe desegregation orders where they still are in effect, U.S. Department of Education officials have announced that these priorities will have to be subordinated to the stipulations of No Child Left Behind. With the president emboldened by his reelection to select another generation of conservative appointees to the federal courts, the few remaining school desegregation orders are, in any case, unlikely to survive intact for very long. Whether the consolidated districts and the voluntary interdistrict integration programs will prevail is anything but clear.

An expansive academic industry has now evolved around the elements of what is known generically as "standards-based reform." Graduate schools of education offer courses in accountability reform, not for future teachers but for future leaders in the world of education policy, which are often taught by people who have no experience in education but whose expertise lies in the world of systems management.

"There is no strong evidence linking additional resources to improved performance. . . . Stronger accountability will combat inequality, since schools will now face penalties if students do not meet expected goals," according to a bright young education analyst in summarizing what she termed the "ideologically consistent" message given to the students in a class on standards-based reform which she took two years ago at one of the more prestigious universities in Massachusetts. "Teachers will work harder, since there will be negative repercussions if they do not. . . . School segregation still exists, but it does not determine whether students receive greater opportunity than others. . . ."

State and federal education officers, by this point, have devoted so much time and effort to creating programs that respond to these beliefs—measurement systems, "intervention" programs, multiple items from the "what works" inventories, and the like—that it comes as an affront to many when the confidence they have invested in these principles and practices is seriously challenged. "We adhere, as though to a raft, to those ideas which represent our understanding . . . ," wrote John Kenneth Galbraith nearly 50 years ago. "For a vested interest in understanding is more preciously guarded than any other treasure. It is why men react, not infrequently with something akin to religious passion, to the defense of what they have so laboriously learned."

This may, in part, explain the fierceness with which Mr. Paige lashed out against the critics of his policies during his final months in office. It may also help explain why state officials often are so brisk in their dismissal of the discontent expressed by veteran educators such as Deborah Meier and so many of the younger teachers I have cited in this book, some of whom have since left public education out of their dismay at the impersonal and mechanistic practices mandated by the states. Few teachers, of whatever age, can take it as an evidence of even minimal respect for their intelligence to be provided with a "teacher-proof" curriculum. Yet the imposition of such practices, which are believed to guarantee the uniformity of "product," is defended stoutly by large numbers of administrators at the state and local levels.

The receptivity of many urban principals to these approaches is heightened, as we've noted, by the instability of staffing and the other factors of perceived emergency which they encounter when they are appointed to a school with a long history of failure. But these factors in themselves do not explain why a significant number of these principals do not merely seize upon directive practices that can restore decorum in chaotic situations, which any sensible administrator would be forced to do before real learning can take place, but have also turned their backs on almost every aspect of progressive thinking that is still regarded with respect, if moderated in its applications, in most of the better elementary schools that serve suburban children. There is at least one other reason why progressive values are rejected and, indeed, derided often by some of the tough, no-nonsense principals I meet. As painful as it is for educational progressives of my generation to concede, I don't think we can exempt ourselves from a substantial portion of responsibility.

In order to understand this, it may help to look at some of the unfortunate excesses of a naïve version of progressive education that were viewed noncritically by many intellectuals, most of whom were white and had had little prior contact with black children, but who came into the black community during the last years of the 1960s and the early 1970s in the belief that their ideas would be accepted in these neighborhoods. Veteran urban educators, to this day, recall with much unhappiness the "open education" movement of that era, in which "process" and "autonomy," and what was sometimes called "organic spontaneity of learning," were too frequently permitted to displace almost all elements of continuity and sequence in the process of instruction.

The parents with whom I was working here in Roxbury opposed this movement strongly at the time and were disturbed when highly privileged young people who had had the benefits of culturally strong, well-balanced, and successful education came into the neighborhood denouncing lesson plans and any concentrated emphasis on basic skills as "instruments of cultural oppression" and who spoke of "children's independent learning" as if it were incompatible somehow with grown-ups' conscientious teaching. An aversion to giving poor black children difficult work—real work at all, indeed—was one of the familiar attitudes that parents noted with dismay among some of these well-intending but unconsciously quite patronizing intellectuals.

"He's a beautiful child. When he's ready for books," or "when he senses his organic need," "he'll let us know. . . ." Parents whose nine-year-olds did not know how to read found this preposterous, and dangerous. I also worried that this movement, which was highly publicized, would lead a lot of absolutely reasonable people to reject progressive values altogether and would be exploited by educational conservatives to drive the nation's public schools as far as possible into the opposite direction. With the rise to power of some very angry and impatient education figures such as William Bennett in the middle and late 1980s, I believe these fears proved to be justified.

As a matter of reality, there were never more than a small number of what were described as "open schools" (or "free schools," as some people called them) in the urban districts, and not many in the suburbs either, even though the media attention they received conveyed the misimpression that this movement was pervasive almost everywhere. It is also a matter of reality that virtually no public schools like these exist today in either black or white communities. Even among progressive friends of mine who value a high degree of informality and unmanipulated self-discovery within the education of their children, very few dismiss the need for substance, thoroughness, completedness, and continuity. Most parents recognize that certain things that matter in a child's education do require hard work and well-organized sequential processes of learning and expect their children's teachers to provide the framework in which this is possible.

Nonetheless, and even to this day, the argument is sometimes heard that "middle-class education" (or "white education," as it's sometimes said by very conservative and ethnocentric urban educators) is essentially devoid of structure, lacking in substance, and bereft of serious intentionality, and that schooling more in line with military practices and "road-to-Rome" predictability now represents a necessary antidote for inner-city children who, it is argued, have too little discipline and order in their neighborhoods and homes. "If you do what I tell you to do, how I tell you to do it, when I tell you to do it," said the South Bronx principal I have cited earlier, "you'll get it right. If you don't, you'll get it wrong." This tough didacticism is the polar opposite of the romantic mantra of the 1960s counterculture—"do your own thing"—which had at least an indirect effect upon the open classroom movement, as ephemeral as that movement proved to be. Both are extremes, however; neither, in the opinion of most thoughtful educators, represents a wise or healthy way of educating children.

The notion that school systems have to choose between euphoric freedom as serene apotheosis for one class of children and mercantile delivery of product as a sad alternative for children of another class is unconvincing to the principals and teachers of most public schools in the United States. It is only in the most calamitous apartheid settings that school principals have often been stampeded into an acceptance of the second of these two extremes, and frequently because this is the only option that has been purveyed to them by their superiors.

As the distance widens and these protocols become encoded as the proven methods of instruction for the children of these neighborhoods, as increasing numbers of administrators are recruited to enforce these practices and more and more young teachers are indoctrinated to accept their premise and deliver their particulars, the logic of attempting to move children of their caste and color into racially desegregated settings is accordingly diminished. If the differentness of children of minorities is seen as so extreme as to require an entire inventory of "appropriate" approaches built around the proclamation of their absolute uniqueness from the other children of this nation, it begins to seem not only sensible but maybe even ethically acceptable to isolate them as completely as we can, either in the segregated schools they now attend or else in wholly separate tracks within those schools in which some mix of economic class and race may now and then prevail.

The insistence upon nothing less than a distinctive pedagogy for these children makes it easier, of course, for parents of the middle class and upper middle class to put away for good whatever inclinations some initially may have to see their children educated in the same schools as black and Hispanic children. Why, they understandably may ask, should they inflict upon their children a compendium of stick-and-carrot practices and strange salutes and silent signals and direct commands modeled upon military terminology when they have reason to believe their children can be educated well and wisely by instructional techniques that draw upon a child's *thirst* for learning rather than relying on the inculcation of docility and fear? Why should their children be denied exposure to the arts and music, history and science? Why should they also lose the healthy exercise of recess? Why, too, should all the virtues of the Eriksonian enlightenment in early-childhood instruction—the entire legacy identified with humanists like Erik Erikson, Robert Coles, Jerome Bruner, Fred Rogers, and Jean Piaget—be ripped away in order to accommodate what are alleged to be the strategies of preference for the children of subordinated people?

"No excuses!" say the architects of these determined

strategies. "No excuses!" say the government officials who inscribe these battle-cries in their political denunciations of resistant teachers. "No excuses!" says the thoroughly intimidated and, therefore, intimidating principal in exhortation to the students of her slogan-loaded school; but wise psychiatrists and thoughtful parents understand that there will *always* be "excuses"—good ones, too—for children to resist some of these all-controlling items of adult manipulation at some moments in their first 15 or 20 years of life and that those who give our children messages like these, no matter what the short-term gains they hope to get, are likely to exact a devastating price.

The longer this goes on, the further these two roads divide, the more severe and routinized these race-specific pedagogies may become, the harder it will be to find a place of common ground on which the children of the many ethnic groups and social classes in our nation's public schools will ever actually meet.

Some may see in this no loss for now. Those who are convinced that educational efficiency is better served by targeting one group of children with one method of instruction, and another with a very different method, may regard the racial separation of our children in their public schools, no matter how distasteful it would be to say this, as a matter of convenience and of simple practicality. Those who have invested their careers in the development of these distinct curricula may reassure us that the data that they have at hand confirm the benefits to be derived from serving wholly different kinds of pedagogic fare to children who, in their belief, have wholly different kinds of psychological and pedagogic needs. Municipal and business leaders, who are likely to be more concerned with the defense of civic equilibrium in their communities than with potentially incendiary efforts to revise the patterns by which children are assigned to school, may not be sad to see the racial status quo unshaken for another period of years. White educated people who believe in racial integration as an ultimate ideal, but long ago abandoned public schools in which they had a chance to make it real, will have their old recordings of the songs of freedom that they used to sing when they were young and they may dig them out and play them now and then when they're nostalgic for the days when everything seemed possible.

But something good will have been lost. It will be lost not for a brief time, but enduringly. Once these things are set in stone—and pedagogic malformation of the wish-creations, preference-holdings, concept-makings of a generation of young people is as hard as stone can be—they may prove impervious to change for decades yet to come.

"It is a hard thing," wrote W. E. B. DuBois more than a century ago, "to live haunted by the ghost of an untrue dream," to know that "something was vanquished that deserved to live.... All this is bitter hard." He spoke of his people as "the children of disappointment" and, exception being made for children of black and Hispanic people who have had the means to exit from the segregated schooling systems altogether and who often send their children to the schools attended by the children of their white co-workers and acquaintances, the masses of children of the black and brown within our urban schools are disappointed still.

"I would not go back to the old order," says attorney Theodore Shaw. "Yet here we are with the realities we face today. If schools are going to continue to be separate in most cities, then we have to ask if we can get at least the 'equal' part. Nothing in our history would lead us to believe that this is probable, but that's the box we're in. . . ."

Shaw was standing in his office just beside the battered-looking maple desk that Thurgood Marshall worked at in the years when he was litigating *Brown*. He grazed it gently with his hand as he went on. "The NAACP Legal Defense Fund has not given up on *Brown* and we do not intend to do so," he said firmly. At the same time, he recognized, the overwhelming numbers of black and Hispanic children will continue to go to school in the same segregated settings where their older brothers and sisters and most of their parents also have been educated. "What *can* be done *has* to be done," he said, "for children who are in those schools right now." Sorting out the most enlightened possibilities of change from those that simply widen the divide and deepen the inequities of education as they now exist, he said, "must be a part of this."

In this tension between ultimate objectives and the search for realistic avenues of hope, many educators point to the development of small and innovative public schools, sometimes in buildings of their own, more frequently as mini-schools within a larger building. "Smallness" in the more successful of these schools is not a matter solely of the relatively small size of the student population. A good small school, as Deborah Meier and some of the other early pioneers within this movement have conceived it, is defined not only by its size but also by its sense of mission, as a place, indeed, that *has* a sense of mission, with a teaching staff that truly wants to be there in the first place. The school that Mrs. Meier founded here in Boston, a multiracial public school named Mission Hill, is a superb example of the small school concept in a carefully developed form in which good teachers flourish and the students seem to thrive upon the sense of warmth and intimacy that the school makes possible. If I were a student, I would love to go there.

There is, however, much unevenness among the small schools now evolving in New York and other cities. When school boards seize upon this concept as a panacea for systemic problems and begin to stamp out small academies without the long preliminary groundwork that has taken place at schools like Mission Hill, they end up making little more than fashionably smaller versions of the unsuccessful large schools they're replacing. In the case of the school that Elio attended where I walked into a hallway fight within an hour of arriving, the designation "small academy" turned out to be simply a novel-sounding decoration for another inner-city holding tank for students who could not obtain admission to a better and more academic institution.

There is also the problem posed by what are basically elitist "niche academies" that tend to attract the children of more privileged white families, while a totally different set of niche academies has been developed with career affiliations that are clearly targeted at poor children of color. A number of the small schools, for example, that have been set up for children of minorities in recent years are explicitly indoctrinational academies established to recruit young people to the military services and funded partially with money from the Pentagon. Chicago has created eight of these small military schools. Philadelphia has already set up one, with two others in the planning stage. Districts in at least four other states are copying these practices. Whatever we may think about inducting children into military training when they're still in public school, no one is proposing niche academies like these in white and affluent communities.

Space constraints in overcrowded schools have also led to situations in which students at a small academy within a larger school are given what appears to other students to be preferential treatment: an entire floor or wing within a building for perhaps 200 or 300 students in the small academy, while several thousand other students are compacted into a reduced space as a consequence. Advocates for Children, a nonprofit group that keeps watch over public education in New York, has conducted a survey of 145 small high schools in the city, in which it examines this and other problems closely. Most of these schools, according to the survey, "must share space—often with chaotic schools. . . . The teachers and students of the large school sometimes ooze resentment at the small school starting up within their walls."

Then, too, many of these small academies are given themes that have no real connection to the course of study they provide but are mostly marketing devices that create false expectations in their students. At the former Monroe High School in the South Bronx, for example, a small school known as the Business and Law Academy was created in 1994 as part of a proposed solution to longstanding problems at the larger school, which was notorious in the early 1990s for its physical dangers and its failure rates. The Business and Law Academy, however, "offers no business or law courses, despite its name," as Advocates for Children notes, ". . . and suffers from rapid turnover of administrators." The 97 percent black and Hispanic school continues to be plagued with a colossal dropout rate. Out of a freshman class of about 250 students in 1999, only 45 survived to enter twelfth grade three years later.

"The small school initiative," says Advocates for Children, offers "the best hope" for providing high school students in New York with "an adequate education." But "without careful planning" small schools "may merely replicate the problems of the past." These impressions are close to my own, although I would argue that "the best hope" lies in small schools that are also making conscientious efforts to appeal to a diversity of students rather than permit themselves to reproduce or to intensify the preexisting isolation of their student populations. This has not always been the case.

In Seattle, for example, one of the most prestigious of the new small schools, known as the Center School, was started at the pressure of white families from the city's affluent Queen Anne and Magnolia neighborhoods who were also in the leadership of those who filed the successful lawsuit that prevents Seattle's schools from using race as a tie-breaker in determining admissions. The school, which is sited in a cultural complex known as the Seattle Center, offers an impressive academic program to prepare its graduates for college while it also provides a wide array of opportunities for students to participate in science projects, theatrical productions, music, ballet, and other cultural activities, because of its proximity to the Pacific Science Center, the Seattle Repertory Theater, the symphony hall and opera house, and several art museums.

The school attracted an 83 percent white enrollment when it opened in 2001, in a city where whites are only 40 percent of high school students districtwide. The black enrollment was a meager 6 percent, although black children represent nearly a quarter of enrollment in the district. Three years later, in October 2004, white students continued to make up more than four fifths of the enrollment while black enrollment had remained unchanged.

Civil rights leaders and black parents were disturbed by the creation of the Center School, which was perceived—"correctly," according to David Engle, the principal who resigned his job at Ballard High when the tie-breaker was abolished—as a way of giving "something that they wanted" to white parents who had not been able to enroll their kids at Ballard when the tie-breaker had still been in effect. Ultimately, Engle says, they won both their objectives, "so what I learned from this is that they got it all. . . ."

A school official, in defending the creation of the Center School, pointed to the $23 million that was spent to build a new school called the African-American Academy in another section of the city. At the African-American Academy, which is an elementary school and middle school, black students make up 93 percent of the enrollment, while only 3 percent are white. According to educators in Seattle, many black parents, while they take pride in the beautiful new building they were given, nonetheless suspect that few of their children will ever find their way into a high school that provides the level of education that the students at the Center School receive.

"The school, in a sense, represents a local version of 'your own Liberia,' " says Engle, "but even with the pride that people feel, it hasn't been successful. There is concern within the black community about the low performance of its pupils." According to John Morefield, a senior associate at the Center for Educational Leadership at the University of Washington and himself a former principal in the Seattle schools, the African-American Academy is using a highly directive method of instruction that, in some respects, resembles the approach used in Success For All. The method, he says, delivers "a short-term boost in scores," but "this disappears too quickly, as becomes apparent when the kids go into middle school." A newly appointed principal—a veteran black educator deeply immersed in civil rights, Morefield reports—has come out of retirement to try to make some major changes at the school within the next two years. "She says it breaks her heart to walk into these classrooms and see children's eyes so dulled. She knows it's not the only way to teach black children. . . ."

It is more than a decade now since the drill-based literacy methods that have been adopted at the African-American Academy, as well as the proto-military instruments of discipline, the "incentivizing" that relies on stimulating children's acquisitional desires, and the narrowing of subject matter to those areas that will be tested by the state have been established as the practices of choice in thousands of the schools that serve minority communities. It is three and a half years since the systems of assessment that determine the effectiveness of these and similar practices were codified in the federal legislation Mr. Bush signed into law in 2002. Since the enactment of this bill, the number of standardized exams children must take has more than doubled. It will likely increase again after the year 2006 when standardized tests, which are now required in grades three through eight, may be required in Head Start programs also and, as President Bush has now proposed, in ninth, tenth, and eleventh grades as well.

The elements of strict accountability, in short, are solidly in place; and, in many states in which the present federal policies are simply reinforcements of accountability requirements that were established long before the passage of the federal law, these practices have been in place since 1995 or even earlier. The "no excuses" partisans have had things very much their way for an extended period of time, and those who were convinced that they had ascertained "what works" in schools that serve the children of minorities have had an ample opportunity to prove that they were right.

What then, it is reasonable to ask, are the results?

The achievement gap between black and white children, which narrowed for three decades up until the late years of the 1980s—the period, as Orfield notes, in which school segregation steadily decreased—started to widen once more in the early 1990s. From that point on, the gap continued to widen or remained essentially unchanged, and while there was a seeming diminution of the gap for fourth grade children between 1999 and 2002, these gains dissolved when students entered middle school.

As a matter of civic boosterism, local media inevitably celebrate the periodic up-ticks that a set of scores may seem to indicate in one year or another in achievement levels of black and Hispanic children in their elementary schools. But if these up-ticks were not merely temporary "testing gains" achieved by test-prep programs or, as in Houston and some other Texas cities, by less honorable means, but were authentic *education gains,* they would carry over into middle school and high school. Children who know how to write and read—and read with comprehension—do not suddenly become nonreaders and hopelessly disabled writers when they enter secondary school. False gains evaporate; real gains endure.

Yet hundreds of thousands of children who have made what urban districts often claim to be dramatic gains in elementary schools where principals have readjusted their entire schooldays and school calendars, forfeiting recess, canceling or cutting back on all the so-called frills (art, music, even social sciences, as we have seen) in order to comply with state demands—those students, now in secondary school, are sitting in subject-matter classes where they cannot comprehend the texts and cannot set down their ideas in sentences expected of most fourth and fifth grade students in the suburbs.

If the gains in elementary school that had been promised by accountability proponents ten years earlier had turned out to be real, the performance levels of black and Hispanic high school students ought to have at least drawn closer to the levels of white high school students by this time. The truth, regrettably, according to the director of the Education Trust, is that the math and reading skills of black and Hispanic twelfth grade students, as measured by state examinations, are below the level of proficiency achieved, on average, by white children who are in the seventh grade. The achievement gap, she notes, has "widened . . . on our watch."

It is not surprising, as a consequence, that dropout

rates for students at our hypersegregated secondary schools remain so high. In 48 percent of high schools in the nation's 100 largest districts, which are those in which the highest concentrations of black and Hispanic students are enrolled, less than half the entering ninth graders graduate in four years. Nationwide, from 1993 to 2002, the number of high schools graduating less than half their ninth grade class in four years has increased by 75 percent.

"New York City and Chicago," notes Education Week, "which enroll 10 percent of the country's African-American male students, fail to graduate more than 70 percent of those students with their entering classmates." Statewide, in the 94 percent of districts in New York in which white children make up the majority, nearly 80 percent of students graduate from high school in four years. In the 6 percent of districts where black and Hispanic students make up the majority, only 40 percent do so. Still more alarming, in the typical large high schools of the Bronx, as a new study by the Gates Foundation has revealed, 45 percent of ninth grade students did not even have the basic skills to be promoted to the tenth grade in the past two years. The overwhelming number of these children, classic products of apartheid education at its very worst, will never graduate.

At the same time that graduation rates for black and Hispanic students remain frozen or have gone into decline, the enrollment of minority students at a number of our most prestigious public universities has dropped alarmingly. In 2004, The Washington Post has noted, only 350 African-American freshmen enrolled at the University of Michigan, out of an entering class of almost 6,000 students—the lowest number of African-Americans in 15 years, and a decline from nearly 500 three years earlier. Other major universities, according to The Post, where there have been precipitous declines in the admission of black students are Penn State University, the University of Minnesota, the University of North Carolina in Chapel Hill, the University of Georgia, Ohio State University, the University of Pennsylvania (a private university), the Urbana-Champaign campus of the University of Illinois, where black enrollment in the freshman class declined by 32 percent in 2004, and many campuses of the University of California.

Changes in affirmative action policies, required by a Supreme Court ruling in 2003, The Post observes, are one important explanation for the drop in black enrollment at some of these colleges and universities. Other explanations are increases in tuition costs and "a restricted applicant pool" of African-Americans because of very low scores on their SATs. (In 2003, The Post reports, only "1,877 African-American students nationwide scored higher than 1300 out of a possible 1600" on the SATs, "compared with nearly 150,000 students overall" who scored better than 1300 the same year.) The Post did not attempt to associate the stark decline in black enrollment with the catastrophic dropout rates in inner-city schools, which may not be thought to have direct effects upon the number of successful applications to these premier universities. But, certainly, the widening gulf in math and reading levels between minority high school students and their white contemporaries—a devastating *five-year gap* between the races, as the Education Trust observed—does not pose an optimistic prospect for admissions of black students to our four-year colleges and universities during the years ahead.

The promulgation of new and expanded lists of "what works" inventories, no matter the enthusiasm with which they're elaborated, is not going to change this. The use of hortatory slogans, as enlivening as they may sometimes be, is not going to change this. Desperate historical revisionism that romanticizes segregation of an older order (this is a common theme of many separatists today) is not going to change this. The "Production of a Narrative Procedure" will certainly not change this. Turning six-year-olds into examination soldiers will not change this. Denying eight-year-olds their time for play at recess will not change this. What these policies and practices *will* do, what they are doing now, is expand the vast divide between two separate worlds of future cognitive activity, political sagacity, social health and economic status, while they undermine the capability of children of minorities to thrive with confidence and satisfaction in the mainstream of American society.

"I went to Washington to challenge the soft bigotry of low expectations," the president said again in his campaign for reelection in September 2004. "It's working. It's making a difference." It is one of those deadly lies which, by sheer repetition, is at length accepted by large numbers of Americans as, perhaps, a rough approximation of the truth. But it is not the truth, and it is not an innocent misstatement of the facts. It is a devious appeasement of the heartache of the parents of the black and brown and poor and, if it is not forcefully resisted and denounced, it is going to lead our nation even further in a perilous direction.

CHAPTER 12

Treasured Places

The issues are big; children are small. Back in the classrooms of the elementary schools to which I have returned while I was working on this book, far from the legislative offices in Washington, far from the offices of scholars in the universities, far from the courts, far from the culture wars that fill the pages of the education press, there are the daily struggles of courageous principals and teachers who are able somehow to resist the new severity that has been introduced to much of urban education in the past ten years. Beneath the radar of efficiency technicians and the stern disciples of instructional approaches based on strict Skinnerian controls, one still may find humane and happy elementary schools, both large and small, within poor neighborhoods in which affectionate and confident and morally committed teachers do not view themselves as the floor managers for industry whose job it is to pump some "added value" into undervalued children but who come into this very special world of miniature joys and miniature griefs out of their fascination and delight with growing children and are thoroughly convinced that each and every one of them has an inherent value to begin with.

In these settings, teachers do not tend to let concerns about our nation's competition in the global marketplace intrude upon the more important needs of childhood, such as the right to find some happiness in *being* children. Students still enjoy a break for recess in these schools. At Halloween they do things that are fun with pumpkins, not the "multimodal" kind but pumpkins as the earth delivers them. Children's writings go up in the corridors as children wrote them and without the prior editing of grown-ups. The drawings of young children, whether neat and clean or charmingly imperfect and chaotic, are displayed along the walls without official numbers posted next to them.

Many of the young and idealistic teachers that I meet when they are in their final year of university or college, or after they've completed their degrees but prior to the time when they apply for their first job, make it a point of seeking out these kinds of schools. They look for principals—they hear about these principals from teachers in their colleges and universities, from older teachers, or from sympathetic school officials—who will not regard the liberal education they've received as disadvantages ("I call that basket-weaving," said the principal of one of the test-driven schools in the South Bronx) but will welcome teachers who have backgrounds in the social sciences or literary history, for instance, or in philosophy or anthropology or art, if they also have been well prepared to do the work of teaching.

Students in these schools still have to take the standardized exams that are required of all children in our public schools, and some of the anxieties associated with these tests and with the annual publication of the scores are present in these schools as well; but nobody tells the children that their test results define their worthiness or that these numbers measure their identities, or that the limited forms of learning that are tested by a standardized exam are more important than the ones to which a governmental number cannot be attached.

Schools like these do not appear "political" perhaps, not in the sense in which a new amendment to the Constitution would most certainly be looked on as political, not in the sense in which Professor Orfield's views and those of Roger Wilkins are explicitly political, but they are places of resistance. Teachers in these schools must work, and know that they must work, within "the box" of segregated demographics and extreme inequities that Orfield has described; but in their temperaments and in their moral disposition many also stand *outside* that box, because they are aware of its existence, and this sense of double-vision, being part of something and aware of what it is at the same time, regenerates the energy they bring with them each morning to the very little place (one room, one set of chairs) in which they use what gifts they have to make the schoolday good and whole and sometimes beautiful for children.

The P.S. 30 picnic takes place on a sunny 85-degree day in St. Mary's Park in the South Bronx. Hundreds of children are sitting with their teachers in the shade beneath the branches of the trees just parallel to Jackson Avenue.

A first-year teacher, 22 years old, gets up from the grass where she was sitting with her pupils, who are finishing their lunch, and tells me that we met last year the day she came to P.S. 30 for her interview. Small and slender, with her long hair parted in the middle and drawn back into a ponytail, she tells me she grew up right here on

Brook Avenue and went to P.S. 30—"Miss Rosa was my principal!" she says—then won a scholarship to a boarding school in Massachusetts, after which she went to Swarthmore College, where she studied politics and education, now returning to her mother's home, from which she walks to school each morning as she did when she was a young girl.

She looks even younger than she is and tells me she has been mistaken sometimes for a high school student and that the children see her in the street, and at the store, and at the Laundromat, and that she has to be quite careful about how she dresses when she goes out on a date, because these little children "have big eyes" and if she's dressed, for instance, to go dancing they will note exactly what she wore and will remember it on Monday.

She has had to learn, she says, to try to make "a very stern expression" when the children misbehave. If a child interrupts the class and says something she thinks is funny, she reminds herself, she says, "I mustn't laugh!" Sometimes they can tell that she's pretending, though, she says, "and smile at me even when I'm trying to look mad."

She has 18 students in her first grade class, which is a victory Miss Rosa had to fight for, and they surround us as we stand and talk here on the grass. One of them, who doesn't yet speak English, studies me with curiosity, reaches up to touch my face, and almost pokes me in the eye, then looks at her and asks in Spanish, "Is he your papa?"

In class, she says, if children see her in a conversation with a man, they usually ask if he's her boyfriend. "They notice everything! 'Teacher, I like the way you did your hair today!' 'Teacher, you have pretty earrings!' 'Teacher, you have nice new shoes!' They notice every little thing I change in my appearance," she says, fascinated by the children's fascination.

The years she spent at secondary school and college

have accorded her some intellectual and social opportunities that were denied to most of those with whom she grew up in the neighborhood; but her ties to the community are strong and there is not a hint of condescension in her references to other teachers, few of whom have had the kind of education she received, or in her references to people living in the area.

The children seem delighted by her stylish charm and effervescent playfulness; but it's apparent also that she's working hard to fill the grown-up role she's been assigned, and when the children standing near us start to get a little too rambunctious she cuts short our conversation and assembles them into a line, as other teachers now are doing with their students too, in order to prepare them for an orderly procession back across the park and for their safe return to class.

The understated pride she obviously feels in bringing back the skills she has acquired to the neighborhood where she was born should not, I tell myself, be turned into a grandiose and moralistic tale of solidarity and sacrifice. There is, for her, a seemingly quite effortless simplicity about the choice that she has made. Watching her lead the line of six-year olds across the grass, stopping to make a double-tie in somebody's disorderly and dangling shoelaces, placing her hand on overheated heads to steer the children in the right direction, halting her charges at the stoplight before crossing St. Ann's Avenue, one gets the sense that she is where she needs to be and doing what she ought to do for now. How long she will choose to stay here after Aida Rosa leaves (Miss Rosa, who is 66 years old, has told me once a year for nearly ten years that the next school-year would be her last) is hard to know. Today at least, there is the sunshine and the greenness and the chatter of the children, and the pile-up of bodies at the stoplight, and the final lesson of the day yet to be taught.

I stay behind instead of crossing with them at the stoplight, so that I can say hello to Mr. Bedrock, who is coming down the hill behind us with his fifth grade children and looks hot but sporty in a striped Italian jersey and is in a buoyant mood and asks his students if he should invite me to their class. Some, to be perverse, say no; but Mr. Bedrock exercises veto power in my favor.

"I have a wonderful class this year," he says, to which one of the little girls makes clear her own reaction of deflating skepticism by the tilting of her head and goofy rolling of her eyes.

"Except for this one," Mr. Bedrock says, allowing her the pretense of a reprimand that she is willfully inviting, after which she scampers back in line to walk with other children.

"Her name is Serafina," he says softly as we come to St. Ann's Avenue. "An absolutely brilliant child. . . . Talk with her," he urges.

I step a few feet back in line to walk beside her. As often happens in my conversations with the children that I meet in public schools, an idle question that comes up while we are walking leads the child to reveal something to me that alters instantly the way that I would otherwise perceive her. One of the other girls, whose name is Jennifer, tells me that when she is grown up she would like to be "a poet or a dancer," to which Serafina volunteers that when she is a grown-up she would like to be a nurse. When I ask if there is any special reason why she has been drawn to this idea, she answers, "Since my mother had to leave. . . ."

In the heat of the afternoon, as we are crossing St. Ann's Avenue, I somehow miss the meaning of the child's words and ask, "Where did your mother go?"

"I don't think you want to know," says Serafina.

Mr. Bedrock later says, when we are back in class, that Serafina's mother died four months ago of AIDS.

The child, who, he says, is the best reader in the class, already reading eighth grade books, has an exquisite chiseled face, with dark brown skin and dark brown eyes, her hair drawn back into long braids but with a few strands left in front to stray across her eyes. She sits at a table close to Mr. Bedrock's desk with Jennifer and two other children who, it seems, are academic leaders in the class and, as I gather later from their teacher, have accepted gracefully the role of allies in the child's struggle for emotional survival.

"I don't know how I am going to survive this," Mr. Bedrock says she told him in the week after her mother died. "You know, I'm just eleven."

The statement sounded so mature that Mr. Bedrock had felt oddly reassured that Serafina would somehow prevail over her loss, believing, as he did, that her realistic recognition of the challenge she was facing might provide a platform of self-observation and stability on which she could assemble the ingredients of understanding, if not of acceptance.

If I had not known what Serafina had inferred in answering my question and what Mr. Bedrock had confirmed, I would not have guessed that there was any secret sadness in this child's heart. She does not seem somber but perhaps, at most, the slightest bit subdued. Like the other children who are sitting at her table next to Mr. Bedrock's desk, she keeps on getting up and hovering about him in this next-to-final day of school, as if she doesn't want the camaraderie to end.

At one point, another child, who has a Russian-sounding name, Nobrishka, even though she is Latina, plunks an orange plastic ring over her head, a Frisbee ring without a center, and gets up and dances right across the room singing a song, "You drive me crazy . . . ," with the Frisbee looking like a neon halo from pop culture.

Mr. Bedrock never loses sight of the diversionary

forays of these children from their chairs, which he allows them only now in the last half-hour of the day; and when he directs a suddenly admonitory glance at the adventurous Nobrishka, she removes her orange halo and subsides into her chair.

Mr. Bedrock spends the last few minutes of the schoolday opening a box of books the class has ordered from Scholastic and examining the order forms the children have filled out a week or two before. Then, as he calls their names, they come up to his desk, receive their books, and go back to their tables to examine and exchange with one another their new acquisitions, poring over one another's books and whispering about them with each other, and becoming so absorbed in this, indeed, that when their teacher has to leave the room to talk with someone in the hallway briefly, none of the children leave their chairs and nothing but the quiet hum of whispers fills the air.

"He's getting old," Nobrishka says of Mr. Bedrock, as he stands there just beyond the doorway, "but we love him anyway."

"He has these icky white things on his head," says Serafina.

"He's 56," Nobrishka says.

"That's not so old," another student says.

"It's old!" says Nobrishka.

Mr. Bedrock comes back to the room and, standing at his desk, starts to dismiss the class, table by table, to retrieve their backpacks from the closet and upend their chairs and take their places in a line beside the door. Serafina lingers in the room while Mr. Bedrock leads the others to the stairs. She will be heading off to one of the large middle schools in the South Bronx next year: a more anonymous and less protective setting than the one that Mr. Bedrock has created for her here. It's understandable that she would look for any little opportunity there still remains to have a few more minutes in his company.

On almost every visit that I've made to Mr. Bedrock's class during the past ten years, there has been some unexpected revelation of a child's joy, a child's loss, a child's power of transcendence over pain. This is true of other classes in the school that I slip into quietly when I am in the neighborhood—several teachers in the building have permitted me to stop by in their classrooms without needing to arrange these visits in advance—but I am drawn especially to Mr. Bedrock's class because I like to watch the way the children grow engaged with his unusual and somewhat undefended personality.

He puts in a long day at school, rising at four o'clock each morning and arriving here a little before six. Two mornings a week he runs a basketball program with another teacher in the gym. Twenty-five to 30 kids arrive, he says, as early as six-thirty. The regular schoolday starts at eight. He seldom gets back to his home before five-thirty. He tells me that he's usually asleep by eight. "My weariness sometimes amazes me," he says, stealing his lamentation from Bob Dylan.

He is not one of those "super-teachers" who are subject to idolatry in movies and in books from time to time. (There aren't too many teachers like that in the real world, to be truthful.) He has bad days when he gets cranky or the children, for some reason, temporarily go spinning out of his control. His personal life has ups and downs; he gets bad colds; he gets the flu; he comes into the classroom looking awful on some mornings, and his students tell him so.

He can be grouchy on occasion too. One day when the phone beside the door begins to ring during the last part of a lesson about reading "pie charts" he's been teaching, he gives it a pernicious look, then, as the children watch, he strides across the room and grabs it off the hook and flings it into the wastebasket.

"I'm not sure you should have done that," says a boy named Alejandro.

Mr. Bedrock looks at Alejandro, strokes his forehead, reconsiders his intemperate behavior, reaches down into the basket to retrieve the phone, and puts it on the hook. As soon as he does, it rings again. "I shouldn't have returned it," he says gloomily; but this time he picks it up and answers a few questions from the office.

The class, again, is good at governing itself while he is temporarily distracted. When someone talks too loud while Mr. Bedrock's on the phone, innumerable fingers rise to lips and velvet sounds of "shhhh . . ." converge into a single softness that restores the silence. There is a healthy feeling in this classroom; the children try to behave themselves not because they're scared of Mr. Bedrock but because they like him and don't want to make things hard for him.

In a rapid drill about his pie-chart lesson, Mr. Bedrock asks a dozen questions about reading charts and graphs.

"Okay, Ashley! Get it right!"

Before she can answer, he walks over to her desk. "If you mess it up, I'll have to punish Alejandro."

"Hey!" says Alejandro.

"That's not fair," says Serafina. "If someone messes up, you have to punish *her,* not someone else."

"Unfair to Alejandro!" several children say.

"Poor me!" says Alejandro, but he knows the teacher's ins and outs of personality so well by now that he does not appear to be concerned.

The New York Board of Education has provided Mr. Bedrock's children with an antiquated social studies text: Ronald Reagan is the nation's president. Other textbooks are in short supply and must be shared by several classes. Mr. Bedrock is often forced to photocopy pages for his lessons. His students are seldom able to take textbooks home with them to do assignments.

He vents his feelings on these matters frequently in talking with Miss Rosa. She gets impatient with him sometimes; but she likes him and she knows he's a good teacher, and she always tries to hear him out. "What can I say?" she asked me once. "The man is an eccentric. He talks about Noam Chomsky! He could teach in college if he wanted. But he's chosen to stay here at P.S. 30 so that he can drive me crazy. Why does he stay? One reason: He loves children."

It's not surprising that she puts up with his eccentricities so willingly, because she has some likably eccentric virtues of her own. I walked into her office once when one of the kids I knew was sitting with her at the table where she worked, which occupied about a quarter of the room. His teacher, who was generally very strict, was letting her second graders watch a movie, which he had already seen, so he had asked permission to come down and visit with Miss Rosa. They were having a tea party. The child was sipping tea with milk out of a coffee mug. Miss Rosa was drinking coffee from a Styrofoam container. There was a plate of cookies on the table.

Miss Rosa's office was notoriously untidy. The table was often piled high with food that parents from the neighborhood brought in. Other parents, who were facing tough financial crises (rental subsidies and children's food allowances were often cut off arbitrarily), might come to school and tell Miss Rosa that they had no food at home. Her office table functioned somewhat like a casual food pantry.

Teachers also came into the office to ask her advice on

problems they were facing, and not only classroom problems, those within their private lives as well. She was a good listener. Teachers who needed time alone with her knew that she would be there for long hours after school. I have stopped by at the school as late as eight p.m. and found her working in the office. Miss Rosa put her heart and soul into that school. There are many others like her.

"The position of principal" in a public system, according to John Chubb and Terry Moe, two of the well-known advocates for market-driven education, "is a bureaucratic office" in a hierarchy. "People who desire advancement in the educational system begin as teachers—the lowliest of bureaucrats—then advance up the ladder to assistant principal, then principal, then into the district office. . . . They are on a career track, and the principalship is one step along the way. . . ."

That is one way of looking at the aspirations of schoolteachers and their principals. Some do, no doubt, perceive the pleasure that they take in children only as a temporary compensation for an economically unsatisfying job and move as quickly as they can into more lucrative positions in administration; but this is hardly the main story about principals and teachers.

What, we may ask, is missing from this purely economic explanation of the motives that bring thousands of unselfish men and women into public schools each year and lead many to remain within these schools and classrooms during the full course of their career? One thing it lacks is any recognition of the role of altruistic and protective feelings, empathetic fascination, love of children, love of learning in itself, with all the mysteries and all the miracles and all the moments of transcendence. Teachers often cry on the last day of school. Is this because their paychecks are so small? Is it because they think themselves to be "the lowliest of bureaucrats" in Mr. Chubb and Mr. Moe's unfortunately chosen words? Or is it because they know that they will miss those children terribly? Sometimes a class of children and their teacher come to be so beautifully connected to each other that the teacher asks if he or she can "loop" with them, to be their teacher for another year or more, and sometimes principals permit this. Longings of the heart, not merely mercenary motivations, are at stake in this career.

Virtually all the truly human elements of teacher motivation have been locked out of the market misperceptions that control so much of education policy today; but when we go back to the schools in which these market ideologies have been most valiantly resisted, we are reminded of a set of satisfactions and devotions that are very different from the ones that dominate the present discourse about urban education. The debates on education would be very different if they had been driven not by economic theorists or the hard-nosed and acidic critics who have managed to demean the work of teachers and, increasingly, the worth of public education altogether but by those, like Aida Rosa, who have spent their whole lives in the company of children.

I developed a deep attachment to Miss Rosa and her teachers through the years, but they would be uncomfortable if I were to leave the misimpression that their school did not have all the normal problems other public schools must face, or that there aren't many other schools in New York City and in other urban districts in which thorough and effective teaching of essential skills is carried out without the sacrifice of all those elements of warmth and playfulness and informality and cheerful camaraderie among the teachers and their children that infuse most good suburban schools as well.

In a second grade class in Durham, North Carolina, which I visited in 2004, I sat for a while studying a brightly colored poster that the teacher had tacked up across one wall. "How to Be an Artist" was the heading. "Stay loose, learn to watch snails, plant impossible gardens . . . , make friends with freedom and uncertainty, look forward to dreams. . . ."

A group of children were working on a project about worms. One of the children, a squirmy boy named Oliver, showed a paper he had written to the other children at his table. "We have worms in our class. They don't like light and they don't have eyes. Their bodies are both male and female. Their eggs are *really* tinee!"

The other children looked over his writing, and a student named Alicia placed her finger on the final word.

"What's that letter at the end of the word that sounds like an 'e' but isn't an 'e'?" the teacher asked.

Oliver looked at the letters that Alicia pointed to and finally said, "Y."

He didn't seem embarrassed to have been corrected. This was the way the children worked with one another. They were obviously very interested in their classroom worms. They also had to learn their vowel sounds. Worms and phonics coexisted with each other nicely in this classroom, it appeared.

At one moment in the morning, two of the children got into a quarrel with each other. The teacher had a quick solution to this problem. She had reserved a special place, a carpeted section of the room approximately three or four feet square, where children who had disagreements were allowed a time-out to sit down and "talk and think it out" with one another.

The two boys sat in stubborn silence for a while. Little by little, they began to talk. Then, as I was watching, they shook hands with one another and came back to tell the teacher that their argument had been resolved. She put her arms around them both and peered down at their faces to be sure that this was so.

"That wasn't even hard!" the taller of the two boys said. He wriggled away from her and went back to his chair. The other boy, who was very small and seemed more vulnerable and shy, reached his arms around the teacher's waist and pressed his cheek against her skirt and then peeked up to see her looking down at him with an adoring smile that she quickly tried to hide beneath a look of customary firmness.

"I have very high expectations for my students," said the teacher. "I tell them, 'I expect you to do yourself proud.' " When she felt that they had let her down, she knew how to make that clear to children without uttering a word. ("One of my students calls me the Evil Barnacle," she said. "He told his mother, 'With one look she can freeze you!' ") At the same time, she said it was important to her to do certain things with children for no other reason than to make the classroom happy. "With the pressure coming down to ratchet up the scores, you have to struggle to protect that part—the sense of joy inside *yourself.* If not, you can't create it for the students."

Teachers and principals should not permit the beautiful profession they have chosen to be redefined by those who know far less than they about the hearts of children. When they do this, as in schools in which the principals adopt the borrowed lexicons of building managers or CEOs, they come out sounding inauthentic, self-diminished, and they end up by diminishing the human qualities of teachers. Schools can probably survive quite well without their rubric charts and numbered standards-listings plastering the walls. They can't survive without good teachers and, no matter what curriculum may be in place, whether it's approved by state officials or by Washington or not, they are no good at all if teachers are unable to enjoy the work they do and be invigorated by its unpredictables.

The schools where children and their teachers still are given opportunities to poke at worms, and poke around into the satisfactions of uncertainty, need to be defended from the unenlightened interventions of the overconfident. These are the schools I call "the treasured places." They remind us always of the possible.

Epilogue

Three years have passed since the events described in Mr. Bedrock's class in the preceding pages. Miss Rosa has at last retired from her post as principal of P.S. 30.

There was a period of instability—a series of principals tried unsuccessfully to take the helm—during the first 12 months after she left. Test scores plummeted and the school was placed in one of those state-labeled categories of strict scrutiny that have their parallels in every state, as now required under federal law. A capable new principal has been appointed since and, although the school is still on notice that it's being closely watched, Mr. Bedrock, who is sometimes tough to please, likes and admires his new principal tremendously. She has a hard, unenviable task before her now; but she has a strong, supportive faculty behind her.

Other schools described within this book have undergone substantial changes too. Two of the most troubled middle schools in the South Bronx—the dangerous school that Anthony and Elio attended and the ersatz "medical" academy to which Pineapple's older sister and so many other kids from P.S. 65 had been unwisely steered—have finally been closed. Meanwhile, a number of the South Bronx high schools have been reconfigured into smaller schools, some of which are said to be more orderly and academically successful than the larger schools from which they have been carved, although the record on these small academies, as I have noted, is uneven.

The Martin Luther King School in Manhattan has been broken up into four small academies. One of them, which is called Arts and Technology High School, was designed collectively by several of its teachers. The energy these teachers bring into their classrooms leaves me envious of their vitality each time that I am there. In a tenth grade history class about "the multiple causations for the fall of the Roman republic," a dynamic teacher named Ms. Dingledy sat me down to work with students on their essays while she raced from desk to desk to answer questions and to coax a few of the reluctant students into doing the assignment she had just explained. She was pretty near wiped out when classes ended in the afternoon but stayed an hour longer to sit down and talk with a young man whose personal life was in a state of crisis and who'd been withdrawn and anxious during class.

In a government class one afternoon, there was a knockdown conversation about racial segregation in New York. A veteran teacher who was standing in the back part of the room did not hesitate to voice her own opinions when the subject of the affluence and whiteness of the neighborhood around the school came up during the course of the discussion. "If I'm teaching in a school named Martin Luther King," she said to me in the hallway after class, "I'm not going to come in and sugar-coat the things that he believed in. This is exactly the kind of institution he regarded as a moral wrong. Students who come here have a right to know this."

The principal of Arts and Tech was blunt about this matter too. "Come here," she said while we were in the downstairs cafeteria. "I want you to meet one of my six white students." She introduced me to a tall blond boy named Max from Eastern Europe who told me that he "couldn't get into the other five schools that I tried" so he had found the telephone number for the principal of Arts and Tech. "I just called 411," he said with a big good-natured smile. "That's how I got in here!"

"Here we are in this segregated school right next to Lincoln Center," said the principal, "and we have to hunt around to find our six white students! I've had white families call me who were interested in our school, until they came and saw our kids. 'I could not send my child to your school when I discovered that it was minority,' one of the parents said. 'Would you send *your* children to your school?' "

As at Fremont High School in Los Angeles, the writing skills of students at Arts and Technology were very low; but this could not be reasonably blamed on any insufficiency of dedication on the part of teachers working here. The school today, as in the past, receives primarily students who have gone to unsuccessful elementary schools and middle schools (one of the kids I've met there twice went to the same middle school where Anthony learned nothing for three years), and many have been rejected from the other high schools they selected. "Our entering ninth graders typically are Level Ones and Level Twos," the principal told me recently. "My honors students are my higher Level Twos. This is the brutal truth. . . ."

The reflex of the government, as we have noted, is to blame persistently low test scores in such schools upon an absence of high expectations on the part of teachers; but no responsible person with a sense of fairness visiting classes here at Arts and Tech would be inclined, I think, to castigate these teachers for the low performance levels of young people who, before they had arrived here, were so badly damaged by the inequalities that some in Washington believe to be inconsequential.

At P.S. 65, there have been changes too. A new principal has been appointed. A new curriculum is now in use. In recent visits to the school, I noted that the hand-held timers and the scripted lesson plans were gone. Writings by children, as the children wrote them, were displayed in corridors and on the classroom walls.

Children gathered around the principal as we were walking through the building. In a second grade class, she sat down on the floor and chatted with a Haitian boy who barely spoke a word of English, helping him to count from one to ten in French, which he appeared to understand, then trying it in English too. A pensive girl whose name was Madeline looked out the window (it was snowing heavily that morning), squeezed her hands together, tossed her braids, and said with much emotion, "I just *love* it when it snows!" The teacher continued with the lesson she was teaching and did not seem disconcerted by the presence of two extra grown-ups in her room.

The principal, whose name is Fern Cruz, told me that she grew up in the Bronx, attended Lehman College where she did her undergraduate degree, after which she entered the doctoral program in philosophy at New York's City University, where she studied social ethics and political philosophy and later concentrated in the work of Wittgenstein, an unusual background for an elementary principal and one that may have helped to nurture the high emphasis she placed on teaching children to think critically and ask more questions than had been the practice here before.

In discussing conditions at the school when she had first arrived, she spoke with empathy of the administrative pressures that had been imposed upon her predecessor but described the atmosphere within the building as "a very cold environment for children. . . . It was like martial law. You couldn't talk at lunch. You couldn't play at recess." Drilling children for their tests "was almost all they did," she said, "because of the demand they felt to raise the scores." The scripted program did improve the phonics skills of children at the lowest levels, she conceded. "Children learned how to decode phonetically, and you could closely monitor the progress that they made," so in these two respects, she said, it did bring short-term gains, although in combination with the constant emphasis upon test-taking strategies, it ruled out almost all of what she termed "authentic learning," "natural learning," "learning from reality."

"What stultified the atmosphere of education more than anything," she said, was "not the scripted reading method in itself" but the effect on teachers of relying almost solely on external measurements. "What happens after a time is that the teachers start to judge their own performance solely by these scores, so they subordinate their own perceptions of their students to these numbers," which reminded me of Deborah Meier's observation that the teachers lose respect for their own judgment and begin to feel they cannot trust their own impressions of their pupils.

"Most insidious is the effect this has upon new teachers," said the principal. "Instead of teaching them to function with autonomy and creativity, it teaches them dependency. This 'thing' prevents real thinking. They subjugate themselves to this. It's as if they're being treated as a patient, for an illness!"—the "illness" in this case, she said, being "their consciousness," "their critical capacities."

The loss of autonomy in teachers, she believes, translates into a denial of autonomy to children. "Children are herded through the schoolday, herded through the corridors, herded even in the playground. They lose the opportunity to interact with one another in the normal ways. Children need to *learn* from play. If they can't play safely in the streets and in their neighborhood, I want them to have a chance to play here at their school—and play in their school playground!"

Hearing an inner-city principal praising the worth of "play" within an age when many systems have abolished recess altogether struck me as refreshingly subversive. I was also struck by the honesty with which she spoke of problems that persisted in the school. She made no effort to conceal these things or to disguise her discontent when we encountered classroom situations that she viewed as unacceptable.

"She shouldn't be here," she said briskly after we had left the classroom of a teacher whom she said she had "inherited" and wanted to remove as soon as possible. "A bad teacher. She doesn't like our children. She should not be teaching in this school."

In front of a bulletin board of children's writings which, unlike most of the children's writings on display within the school, were virtually identical in content, she made clear her disapproval. "These are cookie-cutter writings. They were written in response to prompts. There's no uniqueness here. This is a 'carry-over . . . ,' " she said as we moved along the hallway.

The building itself had been transformed. Classrooms had been renovated, and the hallways had been painted in all colors of the rainbow. "I wanted to create a magical non-institutional appearance," said the principal. The dilapidated desks that children had to use when Pineapple was there had been replaced by up-to-date work tables and new chairs, and all the rooms had now been given brand-new carpets. New bookshelves had to be created for the classrooms to accommodate a vast profusion of good children's literature—"every manner of big and little book," the principal said proudly—since genuine literary works, the old classics and the new ones, and some not-so-literary books that simply hold high interest for young children, had replaced those nearly plotless phonics readers which had been required by the old Skinnerian curriculum.

The new curriculum for teaching reading now in place at P.S. 65 is known as "balanced literacy," a shift in methodology that is the consequence of a decision by the city's chancellor which has been implemented in the past two years throughout most of the New York City system. The chancellor has been criticized for this decision by the advocates of scripted teaching systems. The balanced literacy method is, in their view, soft and fuzzy—"too progressive." (The modified phonics program by which it's accompanied "totally disregards the scientific evidence," according to a writer in The New York Post who favors "the true scripted phonics program" that has been replaced.) But the chancellor has stood his ground up to this point; and for the moment children in most schools in the South Bronx are learning how to read and write by methods that are not unlike the ones that teachers generally use in public schools that serve white children in America.

The ordering regime, unhappily, continues to be used in thousands of the elementary schools in other urban districts. SFA itself is used in 1,300 schools serving as many as 800,000 children. Other rote-and-drill approaches, although few quite so explicitly Skinnerian, are used with several million other poor children of color. Some superintendents who dislike these methods tell me they continue to accede to them because of the pressures brought to bear by Washington and by state boards of education. And principals of schools now under various forms of state review are hesitant to risk a drop in test scores, which is commonly the case at first when a tight system of authoritarian control is punctured suddenly and teachers have to start all over learning how to trust their own intelligence. Then, too, the very large sums of money that these schools have spent to purchase scripted programs, and to train their teachers in the ways that they must use them, also serve as a deterrent to a change in course, particularly at a time when many districts have been subject to the sharpest cutbacks in resources they have faced since World War II.

With the continuing effects of economic turndown undercutting state assistance to the local districts, even some of the less impoverished systems have been forced to such extremes as locking down their libraries for lack of funds with which to pay librarians. Full-day kindergarten in one low-to-middle-income district near my home has recently been cancelled. The only children in the district who receive full days of kindergarten now are those whose parents can afford to pay for it with private funds—this *within* a public system. The same undemocratic practice has been introduced in schools in Washington State, Colorado, Arizona, Indiana, Oregon, and elsewhere.

"We've got [the] money in place to fund the measurement systems," President Bush announced as school began two years ago. Even this was not entirely true. Many inner-city districts have been cutting back on buying educational supplies because they are diverting funds to purchase test materials and test-preparation programs. Others have been forced to spend large sums of money to support a virtually new profession of "test-checking" personnel to guard against the widespread cheating that has taken place, in Texas for example. But even if it were, in part, the truth that Mr. Bush had allocated all the money it will cost to measure every boy and girl in the United States and correctly calibrate their scores, it was a bleak confession of a president's priorities.

Meanwhile, the president has stalwartly refused to speak out with conviction on the racial segregation of schoolchildren, even as it has increased during the years while he has been in office. "Rather than fight school segregation," as The New York Times observes, "the Bush administration has been happy to exploit it." Members of the administration claim that "they would like to see increased diversity in education," notes The Times. "If that is indeed their goal, they should begin by coming up with a plan to reverse the present trend. . . ." Instead, the administration has been "telling minority parents that their child's best chance of attending a good college" is to be found in segregated public schools—with the alleged improvements, as administration leaders claim, that will result from research-based instructional approaches and the like—a misuse of the presidential bully-pulpit that The Times calls "cynical and wrong."

The silence on this question on the part of civic and religious leaders, the latter of whom tend to favor charitable efforts—"service programs," as they're called—rather than confronting structural injustices in ways that might make charity unneeded, makes it all the harder to reopen the discussion of apartheid education on a scale and with an unembarrassed honesty that can ignite a badly needed national debate. And, despite the polls which demonstrate that large majorities of black Americans believe in integrated education and that only 20 percent of white Americans do *not* think it to be of serious importance, the drumbeat of opinions that are cited in much of the non-print media (virtually no integrationists are ever invited to express their viewpoints on this subject on TV) give many citizens who favor integration the impression that their own beliefs must be archaic or unique.

There is, moreover, a familiar pattern of internal dissonance even in the more progressive sectors of the press, which tend to favor integration as a national ideal but, when it comes to the decisions being made within their own immediate communities, support those policies ("the neighborhood school," the niche academies, the non-inclusive charter schools) that cannot fail to have the opposite effect. So that, while they rightly castigate the views and actions of the president, they frequently end up defending local practices that reinforce the racial isolation they condemn.

In the end, I go back to those long-enduring figures in America's black leadership who were the inspiration to young people of my generation at the time when I began to teach. Congressman John Lewis was born in 1940 to a family of sharecroppers in Pike County, Alabama, where he went to segregated public schools, after which he studied for the ministry at a theological institute in Nashville, Tennessee, where he remained to study religion and philosophy at Fisk University. As a student at Fisk, he organized sit-in demonstrations at the segregated lunch counters of Nashville.

In 1961, when he was 21 years old, he became a Freedom Rider in the struggle to desegregate bus transportation in the South. During that year and those to come, he was arrested more than 40 times and was repeatedly attacked by mobs and beaten badly. At the age of 23, Lewis became the chairman of the Student Nonviolent Coordinating Committee, which led the student mobilizations in the South during the most intense years of the civil rights campaigns.

Today, Lewis represents the Fifth Congressional District of Georgia in the U.S. House of Representatives. Elected in 1986, he is serving his tenth term.

"I remember 1954," he said as we began our conversation. "I was fourteen years old at the time." When he heard about the *Brown* decision, he recalled that he felt almost jubilant. "I actually believed that we would *have* school integration before long. I was so hopeful and so optimistic. . . .

"Now segregation seems almost to be the order of the day. We don't have many people who believe that integration's even possible or worth attempting anymore, not in the government at least. You don't hear it from the president or other leaders here in Washington. You don't hear it being mentioned in political campaigns. We've made a mockery of the decision of the court in 1954 and yet we continue to commemorate its anniversaries.

"What is it that we are commemorating then?" he asked. "We commemorate the decision in itself. We commemorate the individuals who fought for it. We commemorate the bravery of students who risked life and limb to act upon it after it had been decided. But in terms of making real that promise in the years that have gone by since then, I think we know it's been betrayed. I don't believe that this is something we can hide under the rug. I don't think we can sweep it into a dark corner. As long as this continues we will be divided as a nation. It's in our national interest to address this and confront it openly. I don't think that we can be at peace within ourselves as a society until we do.

"I visit schools wherever I can," he said. "I was in New York some time ago, not in the city but in a smaller district on Long Island. I was invited to speak at an assembly of eighth graders. This was at a middle school. The children were black. The principal was black. I didn't see a single white child in the building. This was not in New York City. This was in a suburb. . . ."

A small man physically, of stocky build, almost completely bald with only a few patches of gray hair behind his head and just above his ears, Congressman Lewis spoke with understanding but with sadness of the inner-city principals who have, it seems, resigned themselves to segregation as it stands. I told him of the somewhat awkward look—uneasiness, impatience certainly—that I have seen within the eyes of certain urban principals when questions about racial demographics come up in our conversations. The congressman nodded quickly. "I sometimes say, 'They've had an executive session with themselves.' They've sort of decided, 'It's not gonna happen. I've *given*. I don't have the strength or energy to fight it anymore. I can't *give* anymore.' " Saying this, he clenched his fingers into fists, but with his index fingers out, and seemed to stab the air.

Separatist agendas that extol the benefits of segregated schools for children of black people stirred a passionate reaction from the congressman; and he rejected flatly the idea, heard with a surprising frequency in recent years, that segregated schools in olden days in the Deep South were something to be recollected with nostalgia. "That's nonsense," he replied. " 'Yes, in the 1930s and the 1940s we had good black segregated schools with no white children, no white teachers, in the South.' This is nonsense," he repeated. "Most of them were not good schools, and most of them are not good schools today."

He spoke of a high school in Atlanta which he told me Dr. King attended for a time and which is now a 99 percent black school from which approximately half the entering ninth graders disappear from the enrollment of their class by senior year. "Hardly a white teacher in that school today—maybe a handful, maybe some white TFAs," a reference to a program called Teach for America, which places uncredentialized but often talented young people in these low-performing schools. "President Bush went there to visit not so long ago," he added unenthusiastically.

"Don't listen to that. It's nonsense," he repeated. "White teachers and black and Hispanic teachers need to teach *together.* White children and black and Hispanic children need to *learn* together. You have to start it when they're very young, in elementary school, in kindergarten, when they're learning innocence," he said.

In a book of memoirs, titled Walking with the Wind, Lewis speaks about the national retreat from integration and equality. "What is happening right now in the poorest communities of America—which are largely black communities—," he writes, "is the worst situation black America has faced since slavery." There is "a mistaken assumption among many that the struggle for civil rights is finished," that "the problems of segregation" have been "solved," and that the only obstacles black people face today are mainly economic. "This is preposterous. . . . We need look no further than our schools and . . . neighborhoods to see that segregation still exists," and "on a massive scale." During the 1990s, he observes, there had been "a rising wave . . . of backlash" against principles that formed the basis of the civil rights campaigns. The dismantling of court-ordered integration and the recent movement toward school vouchers were, he writes, leading us to "turn away from one another" by retreating "into separate tribes," destroying much of the hope and structure of belief that hold "the most tenuous parts of our society together."

Conservative leaders have arisen in the black community, he notes, "who mock beliefs like mine" and who, "when you talk about integration" nowadays, "dismiss it as old-fashioned and out-of-date." This attitude is "an affront," he says, "to the struggle of hundreds and thousands of people, black and white, who devoted and in many cases sacrificed their lives for the principles it is now so fashionable to dismiss."

I told Congressman Lewis of the very similar reaction I encounter from some of the people that I meet in public policy positions and the characteristically dismissive attitude that any affirmation of the worth of integrated education usually invites unless it's rather vague and general and not specific to the city I am in or to the present point in time. "It's the same in Washington," he said. "Desegregation's not a part of the agenda anymore. I talked with the education secretary not so long ago"—a reference to former Secretary Paige—"and I didn't see it there. I talk with members of Congress. I don't see it here. They're talking of 'programs.' They're not talking of our nation's future. They're not looking ten or fifteen years ahead. . . .

"You hear them talk of 'standards'—'national standards'—in the White House now, but when it comes to *where* our children go to school and how we're supposed to pay for them to have an education, it's 'a local issue.' It's 'states' rights.' " For the first time in our conversation, there was bitterness in his voice.

A mixture of hope and wistfulness returned as he described his conversations with young people. "I go back to the people and I feel a discontent, not only among the young black people but among young white folks too. Something's stirring. Something's seething. I don't know how long it's going to take before it comes up to the surface. I tell them, 'You look too quiet! You got to push! You got to pull!' I tell them we need something more than people cheering in the stadiums. We need young people who will *act* on their beliefs."

Then, in a very gentle voice, this memory: "When I was a boy, they took us out of school to send us to the fields. I used to hide under the house. When I'd hear the school bus coming, I'd run out and climb onto that bus. And sometimes the buses were so ragged they would break down on the road or run into the ditch. These were small roads, dirt roads mostly, country roads. . . . I got on that bus anyway. I hid under the house until it came.

"You see, Jonathan, the high schools for black children in those days were known as 'training schools.' My high school was Pike County Training School. The full name was Pike County Training School for Coloreds, but we left out 'coloreds'—we said 'training school.' The bus would take us 20 miles, past the white school, to the training school. White children went to 'high school.' Their school was called Pike County High. Next door to us was Bullock County Training School. Then there was Macon County Training School for Coloreds. That's the way it was. . . .

"Sometimes I think, 'We've come a long way from those days.' But other times I think we're standing still or falling back. I hear about black students being trained in school for cooking jobs, for kitchen jobs, for other jobs like that. I think, 'This is the same thing that they did to *us* back there in Alabama in the 1940s and the 1950s.' This is a step backward. . . .

"Well, it seems that there's a lot of stepping backward now, not only in the schools. Still in America we are two separate worlds. Black kids in Atlanta, in Las Vegas, in New York, in Paterson, New Jersey, here in Washington, D.C., they grow up in a separate world and do not know white children.

"How long will it be," he asked, "before America will be an integrated nation, a 'beloved community' at last? How long will it be before our politicians and our other leaders even dare to speak of this again? I don't think that either of us knows the answer, but I do know it will take another struggle first. Of that, I'm very sure. . . ."

The note of only cautious hope that could be heard in these and other of the congressman's remarks reminded me of Roger Wilkins's observation that the struggle for integration in the 1950s and the 1960s left the nation "morally exhausted" with "a huge desire not to be obliged to think of it again." Yet there was no sound of ethical exhaustion in the words the congressman spoke next. "Sometimes," he said, "you have to ask for something that you know you may not get. And still you have to ask for it. It's still worth fighting for and, even if you don't believe that you will see it in your lifetime, you have got to hold it up so that the generation that comes next will take it from your hands and, in their own time, see it as a goal worth fighting for again.

"A segregated education in America is unacceptable," he said. "Integration is, it still remains, the goal worth fighting for. *You* should be fighting for it. *We* should be fighting for it. It is something that is good unto itself, apart from all the other arguments that can be made. This nation needs to be a family, and a family sits down for its dinner at a table, and we all deserve a place together at that table. And our children deserve to have a place together in their schools and classrooms, and they need to have that opportunity while they're still children, while they're in those years of innocence.

"You cannot deviate from this. You have to say, 'Some things are good and right *unto themselves,*' " he said again. "No matter what the present mood in Washington is like, no matter what the people who are setting policy today believe, or want us to believe, no matter what the sense of temporary hopelessness that many of us often feel, we cannot give up on the struggle we began and on the dream that brought us here.

"You cannot give it up. We cannot give it up. As a nation, as a people, I don't think that we have any choice but to reject this acquiescence, to reject defeat."

APPENDIX

Per-Pupil Spending in Public Schools of Six Metropolitan Areas

On Curriculum: A Note to Teachers

Updates and Acknowledgments

Per-Pupil Spending in Public Schools of Six Metropolitan Areas

High school (HS) districts and K–8 districts are so indicated. All other districts are K–12; spending levels indicated for these districts represent the average of all grades. *B, H, W,* and *O* refer to "black," "Hispanic," "white," and "others." Low-income numbers are based on eligibility for free or reduced price lunch.

SCHOOL FUNDING IN CHICAGO AREA, 2002–2003

DISTRICT	SPENDING PER PUPIL	% STUDENT POPULATION BY RACE	% LOW INCOME
Highland Park and Deerfield (HS)	$17,291	B+H: 10 W+O: 90	8
New Trier (HS)	$14,909	B+H: 2 W+O: 98	1
Lake Forest (HS)	$14,563	B+H: 1 W+O: 99	3
Palatine Township (HS)	$12,841	B+H: 15 W+O: 85	9
Lake Forest (K–8)	$10,301	B+H: 2 W+O: 98	0
Winnetka (K–8)	$10,627	B+H: 1 W+O: 99	0
Glencoe (K–8)	$10,935	B+H: 2 W+O: 98	1
Chicago	$8,482	B+H: 87 W+O: 13	85

SCHOOL FUNDING IN PHILADELPHIA AREA, 2002–2003

DISTRICT	SPENDING PER PUPIL	% STUDENT POPULATION BY RACE	% LOW INCOME
Lower Merion	$17,261	B+H: 9 W+O: 91	4
New Hope–Solebury	$14,865	B+H: 1 W+O: 99	1
Wallingford–Swarthmore	$12,107	B+H: 8 W+O: 92	5
Council Rock	$11,325	B+H: 1 W+O: 99	1
Hatboro–Horsham	$11,124	B+H: 6 W+O: 94	4
West Chester	$11,104	B+H: 11 W+O: 89	6
Philadelphia	$9,299	B+H: 79 W+O: 21	71

SCHOOL FUNDING IN DETROIT AREA, 2002–2003

DISTRICT	SPENDING PER PUPIL	% STUDENT POPULATION BY RACE	% LOW INCOME
Bloomfield Hills	$12,825	B+H: 8 W+O: 92	2
Birmingham	$11,798	B+H: 7 W+O: 93	3
Grosse Pointe	$10,131	B+H: 7 W+O: 93	3
Ann Arbor	$9,567	B+H: 19 W+O: 81	16
Detroit	$9,576	B+H: 95 W+O: 5	59

SCHOOL FUNDING IN **MILWAUKEE** AREA, 2002–2003

DISTRICT	SPENDING PER PUPIL	% STUDENT POPULATION BY RACE	% LOW INCOME
Maple Dale–Indian Hill (K–8)	$13,955	B+H: 20 W+O: 80	7
Nicolet (HS)	$13,698	B+H: 21 W+O: 79	6
Glendale–River Hills (K–8)	$11,561	B+H: 31 W+O: 69	22
Elmbrook	$11,214	B+H: 6 W+O: 94	5
Milwaukee	$10,874	B+H: 77 W+O: 23	76

SCHOOL FUNDING IN **BOSTON** AREA, 2002–2003

DISTRICT	SPENDING PER PUPIL	% STUDENT POPULATION BY RACE	% LOW INCOME
Lincoln (K–8)	$12,775	B+H: 19 W+O: 81	11
Dover–Sherborn (6–12)	$12,275	B+H: 3 W+O: 97	0
Lincoln–Sudbury (HS)	$11,480	B+H: 8 W+O: 92	5
Weston	$11,404	B+H: 8 W+O: 92	3
Newton	$11,140	B+H: 8 W+O: 92	5
Brookline	$10,578	B+H: 15 W+O: 85	10
Boston	$10,057	B+H: 77 W+O: 23	74
Chelsea	$8,291	B+H: 79 W+O: 21	80
Lawrence	$7,904	B+H: 86 W+O: 14	69

SCHOOL FUNDING IN NEW YORK CITY AREA, 2002–2003

DISTRICT	SPENDING PER PUPIL	% STUDENT POPULATION BY RACE	% LOW INCOME
Manhasset	$22,311	B+H: 9 W+O: 91	5
Jericho	$19,113	B+H: 3 W+O: 97	1
Great Neck	$19,705	B+H: 11 W+O: 89	11
Bronxville	$18,788	B+H: 1 W+O: 99	0
Rye	$16,132	B+H: 5 W+O: 95	1
Roosevelt	$12,834	B+H: 100 W+O: 0	92
New York City	$11,627	B+H: 72 W+O: 28	83

NEW YORK CITY AREA PER-PUPIL SPENDING: CHANGES OVER 16 YEARS

DISTRICT	1986–1987	2002–2003
Manhasset	$11,372	$22,311
Jericho	$11,325	$19,113
Great Neck	$11,265	$19,705
Bronxville	$10,113	$18,788
Rye	$9,092	$16,132
Roosevelt	$6,339	$12,834
New York City	$5,585	$11,627

ILLINOIS DATA: Interactive Illinois Report Card created at Northern Illinois University with support from the Illinois State Board of Education. See the following tables: District Financial Information, Expenditure Rates, Operational Expenditure Per Pupil, 2003; Student Demographics and Characteristics—Race/Ethnicity, 2003; Student Demographics and Characteristics—Educational Environment, Percent Low Income, 2003.

PENNSYLVANIA PER-PUPIL SPENDING: Financial Data Elements, Selected Data with Rankings, Expenditures Per Average Daily Membership, Pennsylvania Department of Education, 2002–2003.

PENNSYLVANIA AND MICHIGAN RACIAL DEMOGRAPHICS: Public School District Data, Table by District, Students by Race, Common Core of Data, National Center for Education Statistics, U.S. Department of Education, 2002–2003.

PENNSYLVANIA PERCENT LOW INCOME: K–12 Schools Statistics, Percent of Enrollment from Low-Income Families by Local Education Agency, Pennsylvania Department of Education, 2002–2003.

MICHIGAN PER-PUPIL SPENDING: Michigan Public Schools Ranked by Select Financial Information, Total General Fund Expenditures Per Pupil, Michigan Department of Education, 2002–2003.

WISCONSIN DATA: WINSS Data Analysis, Enrollment by Race/Ethnicity, Enrollment by Economic Status, Wisconsin Department of Public Instruction, 2002–2003.

MASSACHUSETTS PER-PUPIL SPENDING: Statistical Comparisons, Per-Pupil Expenditures by District, Massachusetts Department of Education, 2002–2003.

MASSACHUSETTS RACIAL DEMOGRAPHICS: Student Information Management System Report, Student Enrollment Data Files, Enrollment by Race, Massachusetts Department of Education, 2002–2003.

MASSACHUSETTS AND MICHIGAN PERCENT LOW INCOME: Public School District Data, Students in Special Programs, Free and Reduced Price Lunch Eligibility by District, Common Core of Data, National Center for Education Statistics, U.S. Department of Education, 2002–2003.

NEW YORK 2002–2003 DATA: Report to the Governor and the Legislature on the Educational Status of the State's Schools, New York State Education Department, 2002–2003.

NEW YORK 1986–1987 DATA: Statistical Profiles of School Districts, New York State Education Department, 1986–1987.

On Curriculum: A Note to Teachers

Educators who have read parts of this book in preparation have observed that certain of the highly formalized vocabularies that accompany the programs I've described, as well as the various lists and charts that break down cognitive activities into unusually tiny units that seemed arbitrary and bizarre to me, have their origins in academic work on learning theory on the part of scholars who would not be likely to approve of the constricting ways in which their work has often been applied.

During one of my visits to P.S. 65, for instance, Mr. Endicott directed my attention to a poster on the wall, headed by the three words "Understanding by Design," which broke down the act of understanding into several elements that teachers were to emphasize in a specific sequence. ("Explanation," "Application," and "Empathy" were three of them. There were six in all, but I did not have time to write the others.) I remember thinking it was odd to be so confident about our knowledge of one of the greatest mysteries of life as to believe that we can subdivide the act of understanding into six established categories and then post these on the wall as a reminder to the students. I still think it's odd. The notion that there really are "six elements of understanding" does not seem believable to me.

I mentioned this once during a seminar with educators and was told that this idea had been developed by a highly admired specialist in curriculum design who had described these elements as "the Six Facets of Understanding." I was cautioned not to be dismissive of a concept that is seen by teacher-educators as a helpful way of giving future teachers a schematic tool for thinking about education in the elementary grades. I felt reproved; I didn't like the feeling that I'd inadvertently been disrespectful of a scholar who, they told me, would not like to be identified with the rigidity and absoluteness that this classroom seemed to typify.

The problem for me, I realized later, wasn't the theory as a framework for reflection among teachers but the way this theory had been concretized into six items posted on a wall, as if they were as scientific as the items on a periodic table. It struck me as a way of locking-down a child's capability for thinking rather than an aperture to understanding.

On the wall of a fifth grade class in Seattle's Thurgood Marshall School the year that I first visited, there was a list of 44 sentences describing the proficiencies in language arts that children must achieve to be considered Level Threes. "I am proficient," according to one of these sentences, "in considering the six traits of writing so I can improve my work before I share it."

Intrigued to find the number six appearing once again, I asked the teacher, "What are the 'six traits'?"

She said she had them written down and could find them for me but could not remember all six at the time.

I asked, "Why do you teach this?"

The teacher answered that it was required for a writing test the class would have to take. When I later was provided with the list, I thought that most of the items it contained made reasonable sense ("good organization," "correct conventions," and "sound ideas" were three of them), although I couldn't help but notice that no credit would be given to a child for original ideas or for originality of style. The list was practical, and probably innocuous, but calling these "the six traits"—rather than six items someone had selected for convenience out of an innumerable number of such traits—was obviously arbitrary. The numbers made it possible for state examiners to judge a child's offerings empirically and not to have to look at other attributes, like charm or humor or sincerity or, on the reverse side, dutiful banality, which is unhappily the usual result of this kind of instruction.

The value of providing teachers with clear, overarching guidelines for the lessons that they teach, and for the best use of the time they have with children, is not questioned here. "We do want teachers to know they're being entrusted with the most precious thing a child has, which is time," as Lucy Calkins counseled me during one of our recent conversations. I hope that I have made it clear, in speaking of the countercultural excesses of the early 1970s ("when he's ready to read, he'll let us know"), that I wholeheartedly agree with her. But when the guidelines we give teachers are transmuted into lists of state-mandated jargon that are given an iconic status in the classroom, I don't think we're saving time for good instruction. I think we're *stealing* time from anything that actually contributes to a child's education.

In another instance of this process of congealment, teachers in some schools I've visited have been inducted into a reductionist technique by which to discipline their students' way of thinking about books or stories they may read. Literary works, according to this discipline, consist in every case of two specific elements: "a problem," "a solution." Teachers are told to post these words so children won't forget them; and the papers children write about a book or story will be judged, at least in part, by their proficiency in sleuthing out these two essential elements and stating what they are.

The trouble with this is that most books and stories, those at least that have much literary value, do not start out as "problems" and do not, in fact, *consist* primarily of "problems" to which answers or solutions finally are found; and even in those books in which the plot may pose some kind of problem that will later be resolved (Pooh and Piglet trying to find Eyore's house, to give a memorable example), the essence of the work is not this "what's the answer? can we find it?" factor, but the magical and incandescent way in which it all evolves.

"Does every book and every story that your students read have problems and solutions?" I inquired of a teacher who had written both these terms across the chalkboard in her room.

She smiled at my question and replied, "Not actually, now that I think of it. . . . But this is what we're supposed to look for. They'll be asked this on exams."

When she said, "Not actually, now that I think of it," I was surprised that she had never thought of it before; but, in the kind of school in which she worked, teachers were not asked to think about the things they had been told to do. That kind of thinking was, indeed, strongly discouraged.

Professor Calkins makes a clear distinction between "good ideas" and the unthinking misuse of a good idea within a situation in which teachers are inhibited from using common sense in adaptation of a concept to the situation and age-level and vocabulary-level of their students. Enlightened practices, when carried out on a large scale and not reflectively, "do run the risk of being ossified," she notes, and "these formal words and categories that surround the children" in the schools that I described to her "can get in the way of using language for authentic purposes." As with "Meaningful Sentences," "Accountable Talk," "Authentic Writing," and the other slogans posted at Pineapple's former school, it is the reification of a notion that initially might have some value into a schematic absolute which, in the context of fear-motivated education, too frequently becomes totalitarian.

There is, of course, the additional problem that most of these heavily promoted protocols pass quickly in and out of favor among educational officials. Five years later, there will almost surely be a different set of numbered "principles" and formal phrases to be posted on the wall. So teachers will be asked to shift allegiance to another set of Requisite Words in uppercase before too long. These shifts would not be so destabilizing if these rapidly evolving and then just as rapidly evaporating trends and concepts had been treated as ideas, and *only* as ideas, rather than, as Mr. Endicott described them, as "doxologies."

Many good teachers make use of these principles and concepts, but they do so with an artful flexibility and a degree of sensible irreverence that enable them to gain some benefits from what appears to be a good and innovative notion without letting it become another orthodoxy that defeats the purposes for which it was intended. In the second grade class I visited in Durham, for example—see the description of this classroom in the Epilogue—the teacher, whose name is Robin Franklin, was making use of balanced literacy, the writing and reading program that has been adopted in the New York City schools as well. In some schools where balanced literacy is being used, children are encouraged to select the books they want to read out of little bins or baskets that are color-coded, or otherwise identified, to indicate the level of proficiency a child needs to understand them. Teachers using this approach, which is known as "leveled reading," are usually assisted by a guidebook that categorizes children's literature according to its difficulty.

When I asked Ms. Franklin if I was correct in thinking she was using "leveled books," however, she said, "No—or not exclusively. Only *some* of the time." One problem with leveled reading, she explained, is that when children later sit together at their tables to discuss their books, they'll be doing so only with other children at their level of proficiency. "I'm a believer in letting children of different reading levels work together. So maybe we'll do leveled reading for two weeks, then mix it up by letting children pick their books by topics that appeal to them, books on worms, books on weather, for example. I like to mix it up!"

"Mixing it up," whether in a literacy program or in any other aspect of instruction, obviously poses problems for administrators in large urban systems when they introduce a previously unfamiliar method of instruction and need to be assured that it is being carried out with some degree of continuity. Ms. Franklin, moreover, a luminously gifted educator who had already been teaching for 11 years, had clearly won the confidence of those who supervised her work. Even for beginning teachers, nonetheless, a willingness to mix things up a little—or a lot, depending on the situation—is a healthy antidote to the sclerosis that sets in so commonly whenever a new curricular bandwagon has been set in motion.

One wishes that those state officials who, sometimes unconsciously, permit a set of new and useful innovations to be hardened into cold concrete of absolutes and certitudes would listen more to teachers like Ms. Franklin and those many others whose good common sense and independent spirits predispose them to resist some of the trends we have examined in this book. The opinions of teachers are not frequently solicited by those who set the policies that govern public education. Teachers may have to raise their voices louder if they want their own ideas about these matters to be heard. There are some signs that this is happening already. We may hope that it will happen on a wider scale in years to come.

Updates and Acknowledgments

As this writing goes to press in June 2005, there is cause for cautious optimism in the long-embattled Roosevelt district on Long Island. The newly appointed superintendent, Ronald Ross, has made the decision to reject the SFA curriculum. "Are you kidding?" he asked me recently. "I don't believe in turning a school around with canned remedial materials. Our students need acceleration, not remediation." He has also rejected a related program known as Project GRAD ("consistency management manager applications," as we've noted in Columbus), which was also brought to Roosevelt by his predecessor.

Defenders of Project GRAD and SFA have mounted an attack on Ross for these decisions. "They have some good PR," he said. "They've rounded up support from politicians." But the district's department of evaluation has discerned no gains in reading skills for children in the period in which Success For All was used—"in fact," says Ross, "we've noted a regression"—and, despite the claims of Project GRAD, which is intended to raise graduation rates, Roosevelt's graduation rate remains one of the lowest on Long Island. "Only a quarter of our ninth grade students graduate in four years," Ross observes, an even lower number than state documents imply, and only 16 percent of that one quarter, approximately four percent of the original ninth grade, received the now-required state diploma in 2004.

Ross nonetheless expresses guarded optimism, based in part upon the fact that a $200 million building program has begun. Both the elementary schools I visited will be replaced within the next three years, and Ross intends to do away with the vocational program I observed at Roosevelt's junior high. "I'm requesting a waiver from this program," Ross informed me when I questioned him about the sewing class I visited. "I'm just not having it," he said.

Ross, who came out of retirement at the age of 60 in order to assume his present role in Roosevelt's schools, is a veteran administrator who comes to this task with that sense of earned authority that does not rely upon the quick-fix answers that are commonly expected of a new appointee to a district with a troubled past. I'm grateful to him for sharing with me the plans for change that he envisions, as well as the daunting challenges he faces.

Among the many other people who have helped to educate me in the day-to-day realities of life and work within our public schools are dozens of teachers, principals, and school officials, some of whom I've had the privilege to know for a long period of years. I am indebted especially to Aida Rosa, Fern Cruz, Roxann Marks, Anne Geiger, Sara Dingledy, Belinda Munoz, Nina de Fels, Sarah Knopp, Brian Gibbs, Rebecca Constantino, Beatrice Goodwin, Cami Carter, Angela Gallombardo, Christina Young, Audrey Bullard, Sandra Wilson, Arturo Delgado, Daniel Arellano, Lillian Watson, Robin Franklin, Casie Baddeley, Sandra Hailey, Wes Christianson, Dana Lyman, Phil Cunningham, Judith Weiss, William Librera, David Summergrad, John Dempsey, Melissa Tonachel, John Walker, Richard Korb, Cheryl Foster, David Hornbeck, Megan DeMott-Quigley, Pamela Appleton, Harold Levy, Rudy Crew, David Engle, Gerald Brookhart, Duncan Pritchett, Thomas Payzant, and Sandra Mitchell-Woods.

I am also indebted to Adam Urbanski at the American Federation of Teachers affiliate in Rochester, New York;

Susan Amlung at the United Federation of Teachers in New York City; Wendy Stack at the Chicago Teachers Center; John Morehouse at the Center for Educational Leadership in Seattle; Walter Haney at the Center for the Study of Testing at Boston College; Thomas Sobol at Teachers College; Jean McGuire and Thelma Burns at Metco; Diana Coleman, a parent leader and community organizer in Roosevelt; Catherine Lhamon at the ACLU in Los Angeles; Donald Shaffer, Arthur Eisenberg, and Barbara Bernstein at the NYCLU in New York City and Long Island; William Phillis at the Coalition for Equity and Adequacy in Ohio; Debbie Phillips at the Ohio Fair Schools Campaign; Al Kauffman at the Civil Rights Project at Harvard University; David Sciarra at the Education Law Center in Newark; Michael Rebell, Molly Hunter, and Samira Ahmed at the Campaign for Fiscal Equity in New York City; Samuel Meisels at the Erikson Institute in Chicago; Monty Neill at FairTest in Cambridge; Theodore Shaw at the NAACP Legal Defense and Educational Fund; Kevin Carey at the Education Trust; Jill Chaifetz, Clara Hemphill, and Rachel Kravitz at Advocates for Children; Bethany Little at the Children's Defense Fund; U.S. Representatives Chaka Fattah, Jesse Jackson Jr., John Conyers, and Bobby Scott; and the late Senator Paul Wellstone, who encouraged me to begin this book during the months preceding the congressional debates about No Child Left Behind and in the year that followed its enactment.

A number of authors have influenced my thinking in the years in which this book was in gestation. I owe a particular debt to Peter Irons, David Berliner, Gerald Bracey, Elliot Eisner, Deborah Meier, Maxine Greene, Peter Sacks, Susan Eaton, Michelle Fine, Linda Darling-Hammond, Asa Hilliard, Michael Eric Dyson, John Hope Franklin, Lisa Delpit, Amy Stuart Wells, Susan Ohanian, Bill Bigelow, Stan Karp, Douglas Massey and Nancy Denton, and—perhaps the most relentless and perceptive critic of the present testing movement in our nation—Alfie Kohn. My debt to Gary Orfield is apparent in the text. I cannot adequately thank him for the many conversations in which he has helped me understand the forces that have led to the dismantling of *Brown* and to the present deepening of racial isolation in so many of the schools I have described.

In the writing of this book, I have relied on the advice of many trusted friends. I thank especially Robert Bonazzi, Kate Berndtson, Sam Graham-Felser, Bob Peterson, Barbara Miner, and my longtime colleagues Tisha Graham and Cassie Schwerner, who have assisted me with multiple revisions of this writing. Georgetown University law professor Peter Edelman and Michael Casserly, executive director of the Council of Great City Schools, also reviewed this work in manuscript and helped me in my understanding of the federal policies, and consequences of those policies, that are addressed in several sections of this book. Both were candid in expressing disagreement with me on occasion. Casserly believes more progress has been made in raising the achievement levels of black and Hispanic students in our urban districts than the data I've examined and my own experience in visiting the schools within so many of these districts would support. Edelman has a far more comprehensive understanding of the project known as "school-to-work" than I and sees more justification than I do for the emphasis on industry-embedded secondary education in the schools that serve low-income children. In the end, I have relied upon my firsthand observations of the schools in which I've seen this emphasis applied and, especially, upon the words of students in such schools as Fremont High; but I am grateful for the challenges both Edelman and Casserly have posed and for the many years of personal encouragement they've given me.

I owe a special debt of gratitude to Lucy Calkins of Teachers College for expanding my understanding of the principles underlying balanced literacy, as well as to a number of teachers in the public schools of Boston, Brookline, and Ipswich, Massachusetts, for the opportunity to spend long periods of time in classrooms modeled on Ms. Calkins's principles. I would like to thank in particular a remarkable young teacher named Jane Ehrenfeld who allowed me to visit in her first grade class in Boston on innumerable occasions during the writing of this book and frequently inducted me into participating in the children's lessons and their other class activities. Ms. Ehrenfeld's class is one of those treasured places in which serious and successful teaching coexists with a true sense of happiness and mystery and fascination in the act of learning. I am deeply grateful to Ms. Ehrenfeld for the sense of hopeful possibilities her class repeatedly restored in me.

Finally, my thanks to those who have assisted me in the demanding task of researching this book. I am indebted to Rachel Becker, who has greatly helped me in the final 12 months of this work; to Elizabeth Gish, who did a heroic job of ferreting out the documentary sources for much of this writing in the course of two years of painstaking research while she was a graduate student at the Divinity School of Harvard University; and especially to Amy Ehntholt, who has been my chief researcher and assistant from the time that I began this book five years ago and has continued in this role up to the present time, working with selflessness and generosity of spirit and enormous stamina and patience and sheer kindness without which I do not believe I could have brought this project to completion. To all of these people, and to my faithful friend and editor Doug Pepper, I offer my deep thanks.

NOTES

Page **INTRODUCTION**

1 MY FIRST YEAR OF TEACHING: I described this school in *Death at an Early Age* (Boston: Houghton Mifflin, 1967).

6 *BROWN V. BOARD OF EDUCATION OF TOPEKA:* See note for p. 29.

7 SCHOOL VISITS LATE 1980S: These schools are described in my book *Savage Inequalities* (New York: Crown Publishers, 1991).

8 RACIAL BREAKDOWN OF STUDENTS IN CHICAGO AND OTHER CITIES CITED: "Characteristics of the 100 Largest Public Elementary and Secondary Districts in the United States" and Common Core of Data, Table by District, both from the National Center for Education Statistics, U.S. Department of Education, 2000–2001.

9 RACIAL BREAKDOWN OF STUDENTS IN BRONX HIGH SCHOOLS: Annual School Reports, New York City Public Schools, 2000–2001.

RACIAL BREAKDOWN IN DISTRICT THAT INCLUDES P.S. 65: The statistics for what was then known as Bronx District 7 are provided in *Keeping Track of New York City's Children,* Citizen's Committee for Children of New York, 1997.

10 THOMAS MERTON CITED: *No Man Is an Island* (New York: Harcourt Brace, 1955).

JUSTICE CLARENCE THOMAS CITED: *Brown v. Board of Education: A Civil Rights Milestone and Its Troubled Legacy,* by James Patterson (New York: Oxford University Press, 2001).

CHAPTER 1: DISHONORING THE DEAD

13 PINEAPPLE: I have described conditions in Pineapple's school in *Ordinary Resurrections* (New York: Crown Publishers, 2000).

14, 15 PINEAPPLE'S TEACHERS IN FOURTH GRADE: "The 4 teacher Class 410 Pass Thougth," an illuminating little essay Pineapple wrote in the summer of 1998.

15 DEMOGRAPHICS OF P.S. 65: At the time of my conversation with Pineapple, black and Hispanic students made up 99.3 percent of the enrollment at her school. One tenth of 1 percent (one student) was white.

18, 19 GARY ORFIELD AND COLLEAGUES CITED: "A Multiracial Society with Segregated Schools: Are We Losing the Dream," by Erica Frankenberg, Chungmei Lee, and Gary Orfield, the Civil Rights Project, Harvard University, January 2003; and "*Brown* at 50: King's Dream or *Plessy*'s Nightmare," by Gary Orfield and Chungmei Lee, the Civil Rights Project, Harvard University, January 2004.

IN CALIFORNIA AND NEW YORK, ONLY ONE BLACK STUDENT IN SEVEN ATTENDS A PREDOMINANTLY WHITE SCHOOL: Gary Orfield, correspondence with author, May 2005.

20 "TO GIVE UP ON INTEGRATION, WHILE AWARE OF ITS BENEFITS": Gary Orfield and Susan Eaton are cited from "The Most Unequal System," *Newsday,* September 9, 2001.

RACIAL ISOLATION AND CONCENTRATED POVERTY: "*Brown* at 50," cited above. In Massachusetts, according to *The Boston Globe* (April 21, 2004), "97 percent of intensely segregated minority schools have a majority of students eligible for free or reduced price lunch," while in the state's "intensely segregated white schools," only 1 percent are "similarly poor."

"SO DEEP IS OUR RESISTANCE": Orfield is cited from *Dismantling Desegregation,* by Gary Orfield and Susan Eaton (New York: New Press, 1996), and "Schools More Separate," the Civil Rights Project, Harvard University, July 2001.

21, 22 CHILDREN FROM "DIVERSE BACKGROUNDS" IN KANSAS CITY: Message from the school administration to the parents, J. S. Chick Elementary School, Kansas City, Missouri. School demographics: "Annual Public Reporting of Information by School Districts," Missouri Department of Elementary and Secondary Education, 2004. In the course of conversation with Audrey Bullard, the principal of the school, which I visited in October 2004, she spoke of the persistence of segregated education in these words: "There's so much denial. There's so many things no one can say—because, supposedly, we have come such a long, long way. . . . I still believe in *Brown* and the dream of Dr. King, and I believe another generation will pursue it. But I don't believe that you and I will see it."

"RICH VARIATIONS OF ETHNIC BACKGROUNDS": See notes on Roosevelt (New York) public schools in Chapter 6.

MISUSE OF THE TERM "DIVERSITY": On his first day in office, according to *Newsday* (August 20, 2002), New York City Schools Chancellor Joel Klein selected a school district to visit in Brooklyn because "this district represents the rich diversity of New York. . . ." As *Newsday* noted, the district had a student population 97 percent black and Hispanic and less than 1 percent white.

22ff. DEMOGRAPHICS OF THURGOOD MARSHALL SCHOOL, SEATTLE: *Seattle Post-Intelligencer,* September 24, 2001; *Washington Post,* May 14, 2002; Annual Report for Thurgood Marshall Elementary School, Seattle Public Schools, 2001–2002. The principal, Ben Wright, told me that approximately 55 percent of families in the area were white.

INTERVIEWS AT THURGOOD MARSHALL SCHOOL: I visited the school initially in March 2002 and revisited the school in November 2002.

24 SCHOOLS NAMED FOR DR. MARTIN LUTHER KING JR., AND OTHERS: "Racial Characteristics, Enrollment by Race/Ethnicity," Common Core of Data, National Center for Education Statistics, U.S. Department of Education, 2002–2003. Graduation rate for Cleveland's Martin Luther King High School: School Year Report Card for Martin Luther King Law and Public Service High School, Ohio Department of Education, 2002–2003.

24, 25 NEW YORK CITY SCHOOLS NAMED FOR INTEGRATIONISTS: Annual School Reports for Langston Hughes, Jackie Robinson, Fannie Lou Hamer, and Thurgood Marshall Schools, New York City Public Schools, 2003–2004.

25 MARTIN LUTHER KING HIGH SCHOOL IN NEW YORK CITY "WAS SEEN AS A PROMISING EFFORT TO INTEGRATE WHITE, BLACK, AND HISPANIC STUDENTS": *New York Times,* January 17, 2002.

26 DEMOGRAPHICS OF MARTIN LUTHER KING HIGH SCHOOL: Annual School Report, New York City Public Schools, 2001–2002 (numbers for 2000–2001).

MARTIN LUTHER KING PRINCIPAL RONALD WELLS CITED: My first visit to the school was in October 2000.

26, 27 HISTORY OF VIOLENCE AT MARTIN LUTHER KING AND SHOOTING ON BIRTHDAY OF DR. KING: *Newsday,* January 16, 2002; *New York Times,* January 16 and 17, 2002; *New York Post,* January 19, 2002; *New York Daily News,* January 31, 2002.

MAYOR OF NEW YORK CITY NOTES IRONY OF TIMING: *New York Daily News,* January 16, 2002; *New York Amsterdam News,* January 17, 2002.

SPECULATIONS ON CAUSES OF VIOLENCE: *New York Times,* January 17, 2002; *Newsday,* January 17, 2002.

28, 29 "IT'S LIKE WE'RE BEING HIDDEN": The students in Harlem are cited from my book *Amazing Grace* (New York: Crown Publishers, 1995).

29 *BROWN V. BOARD OF EDUCATION OF TOPEKA:* The complete text of the decision is found in *Simple Justice,* by Richard Kluger (New York: Vintage, 1977).

30, 31 "WELL-ORGANIZED PARENT GROUPS": *New York Times,* October 11, 2000.

31 NEW YORK SCHOOLS "LOST THEIR DISTINCT NEIGHBORHOOD CHARACTER" AS A RESULT OF DESEGREGATION EFFORTS AND "PRODUCED LACKLUSTER RESULTS": *New York Times,* October 11, 2000.

WHITE PARENTS SAY THEY ARE "SEARCHING FOR AN OLD-FASHIONED SENSE OF COMMUNITY": *New York Times,* September 28, 1997.

32 "HOW DID NEW YORK . . . BECOME THE EPICENTER OF SEGREGATED PUBLIC EDUCATION?": Orfield and Eaton, "The Most Unequal System," *Newsday,* September 29, 2001. A study by the federal Department of Housing and Urban Development in 2002 "found that New York had the highest rate of discrimination against prospective Hispanic home buyers among 20 cities, and the fifth highest against African-Americans." (*New York Times,* June 14, 2004.)

32, 33 ROOSEVELT HIGH SCHOOL DEMOGRAPHICS: New York State Comprehensive Information Report for Roosevelt High School, State Education Department, 2002–2003.

PLAINVIEW HIGH SCHOOL DEMOGRAPHICS: New York State Comprehensive Information Report for Plainview-Old Bethpage High School, State Education Department, 2002–2003.

33 "WE CANNOT BE SATISFIED": Dr. Martin Luther King Jr.'s words are cited from his speech "I Have a Dream," delivered in Washington, D.C., on August 28, 1963.

34 *PLESSY V. FERGUSON:* "The 1896 *Plessy v. Ferguson* decision," notes Gary Orfield, "formalized the abandonment of equality and integration by making 'separate but equal' a fundamental principle of our constitutional law. Today, historians and legal scholars view *Plessy* as a historic catastrophe . . . , even as we repeat its mistakes by adopting its logic." (*Dismantling Desegregation,* cited above.)

35 AUTHOR ELLIS COSE CITED: *Newsweek,* August 30, 1993.

CHAPTER 2: HITTING THEM HARDEST WHEN THEY'RE SMALL

39, 40 "DEAR MR. KOZOL": Letters from students at P.S. 28 in the South Bronx, November 1997.

40ff. CONDITIONS IN SCHOOLS IN BRONX AND HARLEM, LOSS OF SCHOOL LIBRARIES: See *Savage Inequalities* and *Ordinary Resurrections,* cited above.

42 REMOVAL OF SCHOOL PHYSICIANS, PEDIATRIC ASTHMA, WASTE INCINERATOR: See *Amazing Grace,* cited above.

43 NOREEN CONNELL CITED: Interview with Ms. Connell, May 2002.

THOMAS SOBOL CITED: Interview with Dr. Sobol, December 2003.

WINDOWS OF BRONX SCHOOL FALLING OUT OF THEIR FRAMES: *New York Times,* February 2, 1998.

44, 45 PER-PUPIL FUNDING IN NEW YORK CITY AND SUBURBS 1997–1998: See *Ordinary Resurrections,* cited above.

45 TEACHER IN AFFLUENT SUBURB LIKELY TO BE PAID $30,000 MORE: A Report to the Governor and the Legislature on the Educational Status of the State's Schools, Statistical Profiles of Public School Districts, New York State Education Department, April 1999 (numbers for 1997–1998). In all later citations, this document is identified as Report to the Governor and the Legislature.

PRESENT FUNDING LEVELS NEW YORK CITY AND MANHASSET: Report to the Governor and the Legislature, New York State Education Department, June 2004 (numbers for 2002–2003).

PER-PUPIL FUNDING IN MANHASSET IN 1986–1987: *Savage Inequalities,* cited above.

MEDIAN SALARIES IN ALLIYAH'S NEIGHBORHOOD (BRONX DISTRICT 9), RYE, MANHASSET, SCARSDALE, IN 1997: Report to the Governor and the Legislature, April 1999, cited above.

45, 46 INCREASES IN SALARY SCALE FOR NEW YORK CITY TEACHERS IN JUNE 2002: "Even with the raises . . . , New York City's teacher salaries will be on a par with the lowest-paying districts in the city's suburbs." (*Education Week,* June 19, 2002.) See also *New York Daily News,* June 11, 2002, and *New York Times,* June 11, 2002.

46 MEDIAN SALARIES IN NEW YORK CITY (CITYWIDE), MANHASSET, SCARSDALE, IN 2002–2003: Report to the Governor and the Legislature, June 2004, cited above.

DIFFERENCES IN MEDIAN SALARIES BETWEEN PINEAPPLE'S SCHOOL DISTRICT (THEN KNOWN AS BRONX DISTRICT 7) AND WEALTHIER NEW YORK CITY DISTRICTS IN 2002–2003: According to the State Education Department's Report to the Governor and the Legislature, June 2004 (numbers for 2002–2003), median teacher salary was $45,500 in Bronx District 7; $59,300 in Manhattan District 1; $64,000 in Queens Districts 25 and 26.

46, 47 PARENTS RAISE EXTRA MONEY PRIVATELY FOR PUBLIC SCHOOL (P.S. 41) IN GREENWICH VILLAGE: *New York Times,* September 20, 23, 24, 26, and 28, 1997.

47 CHILDREN IN POVERTY AT P.S. 41: The *New York Times* (September 28, 1997), using statistics from the previous year (1996), says that 22 percent of the students came from families of low income. The correct number for 1997 (Annual School Report for P.S. 41, New York City Public Schools, 1997–1998) was 18.5 percent.

CHILDREN IN POVERTY AT PINEAPPLE'S SCHOOL, P.S. 65: Annual School Report for P.S. 65, New York City Public Schools, 1997–1998. ("Poor" and "low-income" children here, as elsewhere in this book, are identified by their eligibility for free or reduced price meals.)

NEW YORK CITY CHANCELLOR INITIALLY REJECTS PRIVATE FUNDS, BUT DISTRICT LATER PROVIDES THE MONEY FOR THE EXTRA TEACHER: *New York Times,* September 23, 26, and 28, 1997.

PRIVATE FUNDS RAISED AT SCHOOLS ON UPPER WEST SIDE AND IN PARK SLOPE: *New York Times,* June 17, 1996, and September 24, 1997.

"MORE THAN $1 MILLION RAISED, MOSTLY FOR ENRICHMENT PROGRAMS": *New York Times,* July 23, 1995.

48 FUNDS RAISED AT P.S. 6 COMPARED TO THOSE RAISED AT LOW-INCOME SCHOOL WITH IMMIGRANT POPULATION: *New York Times,* July 23, 1995.

OTHER EXAMPLES OF PRIVATE FUNDING: *City Limits,* June 2002. For examples of the same trends nationally and in Massachusetts, see *Boston Globe,* June 1 and September 5, 2004.

"YOU ALMOST EXPECT A NOTICE . . . SAYING THERE'S GOING TO BE TUITION": *New York Times,* July 23, 1995.

"A QUESTION OF HAVES AND HAVE-NOTS": *New York Times,* July 23, 1995.

48, 49 "INEQUALITY IS NOT AN INTENTIONAL THING": *New York Times,* June 17, 1996.

49 "CHEAP CHILDREN" AND "EXPENSIVE CHILDREN": *Into the Dangerous World,* by Marina Warner (London: Chatto and Windus, 1989).

50 "BABY IVIES," COSTS, COMPETITION, PRIVATE COUNSELORS: *New*

York Times, October 25, 2000. In 2003, the West Side Montessori School cost $17,884 for full-day pre-K for children ages three to five (*New York Times,* January 12, 2003), while pre-K classes for four-year-olds at New York City's Horace Mann School cost $22,500. (The Horace Mann School, Tuition Schedule 2003–2004.) Also see *New York Times,* July 31, 2002, and May 28, 2003.

51 ESTIMATES OF PRE-K ENROLLMENT IN THE DISTRICT THAT INCLUDED P.S. 65 IN FALL 2002: District 7 Superintendent Myrta Rivera in conversation with author, October 2002.

UNIVERSAL PRE-K IN NEW YORK STATE: *New York Times,* February 2, 2003; *Education Week,* April 9, 2003. The principal of Pineapple's school, P.S. 65, told me in November 2003 that only 36 children in her school had been enrolled in Universal Pre-K—less than one third of her first grade enrollment of 110 pupils.

51, 52 HEAD START, NATIONAL FIGURES AND AVAILABILITY IN NEW YORK CITY: Interviews with Bethany Little, director of government relations, Children's Defense Fund, November 2004 and February 2005. In New York City in 2001, Head Start served 11,000 three-year-olds, 12,600 four-year-olds, and 1,100 five-year-olds; but as many as 6,000 of the four-to-five-year-olds were in programs that combine funding from Head Start and Universal Pre-K, so as few as 8,000 four-to-five-year-olds were being served in free-standing Head Start programs at the time.

52 PRE-K IN MILWAUKEE: According to Milwaukee Superintendent of Schools William Andrekopoulos (conversation with author, June 2004), 92 percent of Milwaukee's four-year-olds are enrolled in all-day early kindergarten programs.

PRE-K IN NEW JERSEY: Interview with Assistant Commissioner Judith Weiss, New Jersey State Department of Education, March 2005. See also *New York Times,* November 21, 2001.

EXCLUSION OF LOW-INCOME CHILDREN FROM PRE-K OPPORTUNITIES: According to "The State of Preschool," National Institute for Early Education Research, November 22, 2004, only one in ten three- and four-year-olds in the United States were enrolled in state-supported pre-K programs in 2002.

54, 55 PAY-FOR-PRE-K IN CHICAGO: *Chicago Sun-Times,* September 12 and 18, 2000, and June 10, 2002; *Chicago Tribune,* September 13 and 27 and December 15, 2000, and February 13, 2001; *New York Times,* June 15, 2001. According to Amy Hendrickson of the Chicago Teacher Center (correspondence with author, February 2005), there were 15 pay-for-pre-K programs operating in Chicago in the academic year 2004–2005.

7,000 LOW-INCOME CHILDREN WERE ON WAITING-LISTS: *Chicago Tribune,* September 13, 2000. A spokesman for Chicago Mayor Richard Daley estimated two years later that "between 10,000 and 20,000" children "could take advantage" of pre-K programs if they were available and parents were informed of this, according to the *Chicago Tribune,* September 3, 2002. "Chicago is setting up tuition programs for middle-class children when it is unable to meet the needs of children at risk . . . ," said the executive director of Parents United for Responsible Education. (Letter to *New York Times,* June 22, 2001.)

56 BLACK PHYSICIAN IN BRONX CITED: See *Savage Inequalities,* cited above.

57 TUITION AT NEW YORK CITY PRIVATE SCHOOLS: At the highly regarded Dalton, Brearley, and Collegiate schools, for example, tuition ranges from $22,000 to $25,000, according to the websites for these schools and *The Manhattan Family Guide to Private Schools,* by Victoria Goldman and Catherine Hausman (New York: Soho Press, 2001).

TUITION AT NEW ENGLAND BOARDING SCHOOLS: Tuition and boarding at Andover, Exeter, and Groton ranged from $31,000 to $36,000 in 2004–2005, according to the admissions offices of these schools in September 2004.

58, 59 PRESIDENT GEORGE W. BUSH CITED: *New York Times,* August 2, 2001.

59 DEBORAH MEIER CITED: *In Schools We Trust,* by Deborah Meier (Boston: Beacon Press, 2002).

60 DIFFERENTIAL IN PER-PUPIL SPENDING BETWEEN HIGHEST-MINORITY AND LOWEST-MINORITY SCHOOLS. "The Funding Gap 2004," by Kevin Carey, the Education Trust, Washington, D.C., October 2004. (See additional data on spending differentials from the Education Trust in Chapter 10.)

CHAPTER 3: THE ORDERING REGIME

64 SOUTH BRONX PRINCIPAL, INFLUENCE OF IDEAS OF B. F. SKINNER: *New York Times,* August 26, 1995, and June 6, 2001.

65 SILENT LUNCH, SILENT RECESS, CHAOS IN BRIANA'S ROOM: Conversations with former P.S. 65 teacher Christina Young and other P.S. 65 teachers, 2001, 2002, and 2004.

"SUCCESS FOR ALL": SFA is a literacy program generally used in an uninterrupted 90-minute "literacy bloc" at the beginning of the day. But the program's Skinnerian ethos, silent signals, and "faultless communication" are intended to govern the entire schoolday, and the three-word slogan tends to dominate the corridors and classrooms of the schools in which it's used.

66 MR. ENDICOTT'S FOURTH GRADE CLASSROOM: Mr. Endicott (not his real name) entered public education under a program called the Chancellor's Fellows, which recruits highly motivated people without teacher preparation to work in New York City's low-performing schools while taking education courses in the evenings or during the summer break.

"ZERO NOISE" SALUTE: The severity with which the gesture is performed appears to depend upon the sensibilities of teachers or directives of a supervisor. Materials provided to me by SFA in 2005 illustrate the signal being given with elbow bent, but a South Bronx principal who has observed its use described it to me recently in these words: "Stiff arm. Hand up. Flat palm." SFA is no longer used in the New York public schools. (See Epilogue.)

69 "AUTHENTIC WRITING," "ACTIVE LISTENING," "ACCOUNTABLE TALK": See further discussion of these and similar phrases in the Appendix.

73 "THE SCHOOL, ADMITTEDLY, IS NOT A MELLOW PLACE": A memorable exception to this pattern at the time I visited was a kindergarten program in the classroom of a teacher named Yolanda Smith, who somehow managed to create an island of real warmth and tenderness within a school in which these qualities were hard to find. Ms. Smith is still at P.S. 65 under a new administration that has brought dramatic changes to the school. (See Epilogue.)

"LEVEL FOURS, PLEASE RAISE YOUR HANDS": This was reported to me by teacher Christina Young, cited above.

74, 75 RACIAL DEMOGRAPHICS OF UNNAMED ELEMENTARY SCHOOL IN HARTFORD, CONNECTICUT: Common Core of Data, National Center for Education Statistics, U.S. Department of Education, 2001–2002. I visited the school in winter of that year.

78 "THERE'S SOMETHING CRYSTAL CLEAR ABOUT A NUMBER": Tracy Locklin, former chief counsel to the U.S. Senate Committee on Health, Education, Labor, and Pensions, in conversation with Jacob Ludes, executive director of the New England Association of Schools and Colleges, in 2002. (Author's interview with Mr. Ludes, December 2004.)

"I WANT TO CHANGE THE FACE OF READING INSTRUCTION": Susan B. Neuman, assistant secretary of education for elementary and secondary education, U.S. Department of Education, cited in *New York Times,* January 9, 2002.

79 "RUBRIC FOR FILING": The teacher who provided me a copy of this document and the district in which the teacher works are unnamed at the teacher's request.

80 "THE MULTIMODAL PUMPKIN" AND OBSERVATIONS OF UNIVERSITY FACULTY MEMBER: California State University, Sacramento, October 2002.

81 "FIVE ELEMENTS OF A GOOD BULLETIN BOARD": *New York Times,* June 18, 2002.

82 "I'M SO TORN UP . . . I'M THINKING ABOUT LAW SCHOOL": P.S. 65 teacher Christina Young, cited above. Another teacher, the only African-American among the 15 young recruits at P.S. 65 the year I visited, told me he refused to falsify his students' writings for the hall displays. "You're a great teacher, but we need that bulletin board," the principal informed him. "I write wonderful letters for teachers. . . ."

83, 84 STUDENTS TRY TO EXPLAIN "MEANINGFUL SENTENCES" AND "WORD MASTERY": Inner-city school unnamed to protect privacy of teacher.

85, 86 MR. ENDICOTT'S EMPATHY WITH PRINCIPAL AND CANDID OBSERVATIONS ON THE SFA CURRICULUM: Written correspondence from Mr. Endicott, May 2001. For a similarly candid revelation of a teacher's reactions to her first exposure to SFA at another New York City school, see "A View from the Trenches," by Jacqueline

Goldwin Kingon, *Education Life,* a Sunday supplement to *The New York Times,* April 8, 2001.

86 "ONLY ABOUT ONE PERCENT" OF CHILDREN IN NEW YORK CITY SCHOOLS USING SCRIPTED TEACHING METHODS ARE WHITE: *New York Times,* January 19, 2003.

87 LUCY CALKINS CITED: *New York Times,* January 19, 2003. Ms. Calkins is Professor of Curriculum and Teaching at Teachers College, Columbia University, and the director of the Teachers College Reading and Writing Project.

CHAPTER 4: PREPARING MINDS FOR MARKETS

89ff. UNNAMED ELEMENTARY SCHOOLS IN COLUMBUS, OHIO: I visited these schools in November 2002, following a preliminary visit in October 2001.

POVERTY AND RACIAL DATA FOR BOTH SCHOOLS DESCRIBED: School Year Report Cards, Columbus City School District, 2003–2004 (race and poverty data from 2002–2003).

"CONSISTENCY MANAGEMENT MANAGER APPLICATION": This document, part of a self-described "comprehensive classroom management program" known as "Consistency Management and Cooperative Discipline," is published by Project Grad USA, based in Houston, Texas.

94 "WE MUST START THINKING OF CHILDREN AS WORKERS": Albert Shanker, American Federation of Teachers, cited in *Fortune,* November 7, 1988.

95 ERIK ERIKSON CITED: *Young Man Luther,* by Erik Erikson (New York: Norton, 1962).

95, 96 "FAULTY PRODUCTS," "THE BUSINESS OF DEVELOPING MINDS," "MANUFACTURING BUICKS": *Wall Street Journal,* February 9, 1990.

97, 98 "THESE ROBOTS ARE GOING TO BE PRODUCING TAXES": "Learning in America," a MacNeil/Lehrer Production, PBS, April 3, 1989.

101 DROPOUT NUMBERS AND RACIAL DEMOGRAPHICS OF HEALTH OPPORTUNITIES SCHOOL: Of 294 ninth graders in the fall of 1999, only 60 remained as twelfth graders in 2003. White students made up 1.6 percent of the school's enrollment of 665. (Annual School Report for Health Opportunities High School, New York City Public Schools, 2002–2003; Common Core of Data, National Center for Education Statistics, U.S. Department of Education, 1999–2000 and 2002–2003.)

OTHER CAREER-EMBEDDED SCHOOLS IN NEW YORK CITY: Clara Barton High School for Health Professionals (95 percent black and Hispanic) had 633 ninth graders and 301 twelfth graders in 2002–2003). Graphic Arts Communications High School (94 percent black and Hispanic) had 1,096 ninth graders and 199 twelfth graders. Metropolitan Corporate Academy (98 percent black and Hispanic) had 90 ninth graders and 55 twelfth graders, of whom 34 graduated in 2003. Metropolitan Corporate Academy was conceived as a partnership with the financial firm Goldman Sachs, which provided mentors and internships for students. A school's reliance on resources from the private sector carries risks of instability, however. After serious layoffs at Goldman Sachs in 2002, according to Insideschools, an online service of Advocates for Children, "the number of mentors was cut in half." (Annual School Reports for all three schools, New York City Public Schools, 2002–2003 and 2003–2004; Insideschools 2002.)

102 "BUSINESS HAS TAKEN OWNERSHIP OF SCHOOL-TO-WORK": Tim Barnicle, director of the Workforce Development Program at the National Center on Education and the Economy, Washington, D.C., in a letter to *Education Week,* February 3, 1999. "The most viable school-to-work partnerships," Mr. Barnicle writes, are "tied to high academic standards . . . , supported by business and industry partners that provide students with technical skills needed to succeed in a job. . . ." He concedes that "too often school-to-work" has not been "viewed as being connected to higher academic performance in the classroom," but nonetheless believes that career-embedded schools, if properly conceived, can improve retention and increase "access to postsecondary education."

CULINARY ARTS PROGRAM IN CHICAGO: The program is sited at the Roberto Clemente High School. For racial demographics, see Illinois School Report Card for Roberto Clemente Community High School, 2002, and Roberto Clemente Community High School Profile 2003–2004, Chicago Public Schools, 2004.

102, 103 TEACHER'S DESCRIPTION OF HER STUDENT AND EXPLANATION OF THE WORKINGS OF THE PROGRAM: Interview with teacher (unnamed for privacy concerns), July 2003, and subsequent correspondence in 2004 and 2005.

IMPLEMENTATION OF CULINARY ARTS AT ROBERTO CLEMENTE HIGH SCHOOL IN AFFILIATION WITH HYATT HOTELS: "Project Profile, Roberto Clemente Community Academy," Executive Service Corps of Chicago, 2002–2003. An early evaluation of the program is provided in "The Millennium Breach, the American Dilemma, Richer and Poorer," a report by the Milton S. Eisenhower Foundation and the Corporation for What Works, Washington, D.C., 1998.

104, 105 CHARLES MURRAY CITED: Op-ed essay, *New York Times,* January 8, 1993.

CHAPTER 5: THE ROAD TO ROME

110, 111 "IF THE ROAD DOES NOT LEAD TO ROME": The summer test-preparation program in Chicago was described in *Education Week,* August 6, 1997.

111 NATIONAL GUARD TRAINING MANUALS: Former Chicago schools CEO Paul Vallas, cited in *The New York Times,* November 26, 1999. "Some critics out there will say, 'Oh my God, you're lobot-

omizing teachers,' " Mr. Vallas said. "No, what we're saying is, 'What every major successful corporation is doing, what the military is doing, is giving teachers a model of quality instruction and curriculum. . . .' "

111, 112 "TEST BEST" WORKBOOK IN CHICAGO'S SUMMER SESSION: *Education Week,* August 6, 1997.

112 PINEAPPLE'S MATHEMATICS WORKBOOK: *Bridging the Test Gap* (North Billerica, Mass.: Curriculum Associates, 1994). Angela Gallombardo, a teacher at P.S. 65 when Pineapple was in third grade, tells me she had "boxes full of this stuff" and similar test-preparation materials, which she refused to use with her own students. (Visits to Ms. Gallombardo's class and subsequent conversations, 1996, 1997, 1998, 2004.)

112, 113 PEORIA, ILLINOIS: Interviews with principal and school system superintendent and classroom visits at Tyng Primary School in October 2001, and Annual Report Card for Tyng Primary School, Illinois State Board of Education, 2001–2002.

113 SACRIFICE OF TEACHING TIME TO TEST-PREPARATION, CHILD THROWS UP AND CAN'T TAKE HER EXAM: Former fifth grade teacher Christina Young, cited above, and other teachers at P.S. 65.

113, 114 STANDARDIZED TESTS FOR KINDERGARTEN CHILDREN IN SANTA PAULA, CALIFORNIA: "In Santa Paula, Kindergartners Put to the Test," a description of the extremes to which high-stakes testing appears to be leading us, by Jenifer Ragland, *Los Angeles Times,* October 6, 2001.

114 DEMOGRAPHICS SANTA PAULA PUBLIC SCHOOLS: School and District Profiles for Santa Paula Elementary School District, Education Data Partnership, Palo Alto, California, 2000–2001.

115 "FRONT-LOADING CHILDREN": I was first introduced to this term by Gloria Flaherty, a professor of education at Wilmington College, Wilmington, Ohio, in 2003. Dr. Flaherty, who supervises student-teachers in the public schools, explained that the term refers specifically to delivering, as early as in kindergarten, "testable proficiencies" that, in the past, would not have been introduced until first grade or later. "Front-loading" is also used in reference to the new test-driven practice of placing emphasis, during the months before exams, only on those basic skills that will be tested and postponing other basic skills until after the exams. See, for example, "Building Level Academic Intervention Programs. . . . Skill-of-the-Week Program to begin in October 2002 by 'front-loading' basic skills through January in preparation for the ELA [English Language Arts] exam. . . . The other basic skills to follow." ("Building Action Plan," VanWyck Junior High School, Wappingers Falls, New York, 2002–2003.)

"KINDERGARTEN IS NOT LIKE IT USED TO BE": "Schools Drop Nap Time for Testing Preparation," *Atlanta Journal-Constitution,* October 3, 2003.

LONG DELAYS BETWEEN ADMINISTRATION OF EXAMS AND RECEIPT OF SCORES: For a characteristic example in a district on Long

Island in New York, see columnist Michael Winerip, *New York Times,* September 17, 2003. According to *USA Today* (October 12, 2004), "New federal requirements say tests given in the spring must be processed before students return in the fall. . . ."

115, 116 "INTERIM ASSESSMENTS": In New York City, for example, Schools Chancellor Joel Klein initiated a series of interim tests, the results of which, the chancellor said, "will help teachers identify problems during the school year so that they can effectively intervene. . . ." (*New York Post,* July 17, 2003). In Texas, according to *Newsday* (May 5, 2003), the Texas Education Agency claims "that test results are given back to schools and students . . . usually . . . within ten days." If true, this is an unusual exception to the pattern elsewhere. In 2004, then Education Secretary Rod Paige told an audience in St. Louis that because "children are now being tested regularly in math and reading . . . , teachers can use this new information to tailor instruction to meet every child's needs." He conceded later in his speech, however, that "the best feedback is real-time feedback." With online tests, he said, results might someday be available "within 24 hours." (Speech to Technology Summit, St. Louis, Missouri, text released by U.S. Department of Education, March 10, 2004.)

116 ONE SUCH DIAGNOSTIC TEST: The ECLAS, which stands for Early Childhood Literacy Assessment System, is typically used in kindergarten through second or third grade and takes about 45 minutes to an hour to administer. Most of the test is given individually, although some sections are administered in small groups.

117, 118 "WE CANNOT TRUST SUCH TESTS": *In Schools We Trust,* by Deborah Meier, cited above.

ODDS OF DROPPING OUT FOR CHILDREN WHO REPEAT GRADES: See *Raising Standards or Raising Barriers,* edited by Gary Orfield and Mindy Kornhaber (New York: The Century Foundation Press, 2001); *Dropouts in America,* edited by Gary Orfield (Cambridge, Mass.: Harvard Education Press, 2004); *Texas Observer,* August 30, 2002.

118, 119 HISTORY AND GEOGRAPHY MARGINALIZED OR ABSENT FROM CURRICULUM IN MANY HEAVILY TEST-DRIVEN SCHOOLS: Teachers throughout the nation's inner-city schools have described this pattern to me in the past ten years. My conversation with the children who had gone to P.S. 65, or were still enrolled there, took place in June 2000. For a survey of the impact testing pressures have had in limiting the teaching of the social sciences, especially in low-performing schools, see "State and Federal Mandates Making History of Social Studies," *Education Week,* March 16, 2005.

120 BANISHMENT OF RECESS: "Major school districts across the country, like Orlando and Atlanta, have cut recess out of the schoolday altogether," noted National Public Radio, "Here and Now," December 1, 2004. In Chicago, according to *Technos* (Winter 2001), "80 percent of the schools . . . have decided there's no time for recess. . . ." According to the *Chicago Reporter* (June 1999), "Schools

with the lowest percent of poor children are the most likely to still get recess," according to a survey of 485 Chicago schools. "Thirty of the 59 schools with a student enrollment at least 30 percent white still have recess, compared to only 40 of the 318 schools that are less than 5 percent white." See also *Chicago Tribune,* September 27, 2001, September 29, 2002, and April 26, 2004; *Education Reporter,* October 20, 2001; *Atlanta Journal-Constitution,* March 11 and 13 and December 26, 2004; *Las Vegas Sun,* March 10, 2004; *New York Times,* November 11, 2004; *Christian Science Monitor,* November 16, 2004.

FORMER ATLANTA SCHOOL SUPERINTENDENT CITED: *What Happened to Recess and Why Are Our Children Struggling in Kindergarten,* by Susan Ohanion (New York: McGraw-Hill, 2002).

121 SUMMER SCHOOL FOR PRE-TEST PREPARATION: See, for example, "Can Pupils Learn in One Hot Month What They Didn't Learn in Nine?" in *The New York Times,* June 16, 2003. Also see *Education Week* on Chicago summer session, cited in notes for Chapter 3.

121, 122 DISTORTION OF SCHOOL CALENDAR BY TEST SCORE CONCERNS: See, for example, "Parents Push School Date Start," Associated Press, February 19, 2004; "In Heat of Midsummer, It's Schooltime for Many," *New York Times,* August 6, 2004; "District Considers Starting School Year in August. . . . Would Help with Standardized Exams," *Anchorage Daily News,* November 17, 2004.

122 "HALLS OF SHAME . . . THE WORST OF THE WORST": *New York Post,* October 14, 2002.

CASH REWARDS FOR PRINCIPALS: New York City elementary school principals can receive a bonus of up to $15,000 based on the rate of improvement in their students' test scores, which is technically known as the "performance change index." For high school principals, the criteria are a weighted combination of test scores, dropout rates, and diploma rates. (Maisie McAdoo, senior research associate, United Federation of Teachers, New York, in correspondence with author, April 2004.)

CASH REWARDS FOR TEACHERS: *St. Petersburg Times,* August 31, 2002, and September 12, 2003; *Tampa Tribune,* January 25, 2003; *Atlanta Journal-Constitution,* October 16, 2003; *Denver Post,* August 28, 2003; *Akron Beacon Journal,* March 8, 2002; *Times-Picayune,* June 7, 2003; *New York Times,* January 24, 2001; National Center on Teacher Quality, overview of merit pay practices, citing media and school system sources, 2002; Susan Ohanian, *What Happened to Recess,* cited above. In California, where rewards "in the form of $25,000, $10,000, or $5,000 checks" (*Los Angeles Times,* October 16, 2001) went to teachers and other school professionals in fall 2001, scoring errors by Harcourt, one of the nation's leading producers of standardized exams, led to the awarding of $750,000 to teachers, principals, and schools that turned out to be ineligible to receive them—part of a total $100 million to be awarded that year (*Los Angeles Times,* September 28 and October 10, 2001; *Education Week,* October 10, 2001; *FairTest Examiner,* Fall 2002).

123, 124 SCHOOL EXPERIENCES DECLINE IN TEST SCORES AFTER ADMITTING CHILDREN FROM SCHOOLS THAT HAVE BEEN CLOSED: Interview with Aida Rosa, principal of P.S. 30, July 2002.

126 HERBERT KOHL CITED: *I Won't Learn from You,* by Herbert Kohl (New York: New Press, 1994).

127ff. "WHENEVER I WENT INTO THOSE BUBBLE-TESTS, I KNEW THAT I WAS DONE FOR": Anthony's years in middle school are recounted in my book *Amazing Grace,* cited above. His subsequent experiences in secondary school and college are drawn from my visits with him in the Bronx and at his school and repeated meetings and conversations between 1997 and 2005.

BOOK THAT PROMPTS ANTHONY'S QUESTION: *Ruby Bridges,* by Robert Coles (New York: Scholastic, 1995).

131ff. THOMAS SOBOL ON TESTS AND STANDARDS: The former New York State commissioner of education, now professor of education at Teachers College, is cited from his unpublished lecture delivered to the School Law Institute, Teachers College, Columbia University, July 10, 2001.

133 CONCERN THAT DROPOUT RATES WILL RISE AS A CONSEQUENCE OF NONPROMOTION POLICIES: See notes for Chapter 11.

CHAPTER 6: A HARDENING OF LINES

136, 137 PRACTICES THAT FAVOR "SAVVY" PARENTS IN ADMISSIONS TO THE BETTER NEW YORK CITY PUBLIC ELEMENTARY SCHOOLS: Katha Pollitt, *New York Times* (op-ed), November 25, 2002. Parents write letters, Pollitt notes, to affirm that they subscribe to a school's "educational philosophy" and "prep their kids for IQ tests and for interviews masked as classroom visits." Among the upscale catchment areas with excellent zoned schools, Pollitt identifies the Upper East Side, the West Side, and Greenwich Village.

137 GUIDEBOOKS FOR THE BEST PUBLIC SCHOOLS: *Public Middle Schools: New York City's Best,* by Clara Hemphill (New York: Soho Press, 1999); *New York City's Best Public Schools,* by Clara Hemphill (New York: Teachers College Press, 2001); *New York City's Best Public Elementary Schools,* by Clara Hemphill with Pamela Wheaton (New York: Teachers College Press, 2002).

138, 139 DESCRIPTION AND DEMOGRAPHICS OF HUNTER COLLEGE ELEMENTARY SCHOOL: According to Hemphill (cited above), black children make up 25 percent of the enrollment, but less than 1 percent of the student body qualifies for free or reduced price lunch. According to the Annual School Reports for New York City's elementary schools (New York City Public Schools, 2002–2003), 75 percent of students citywide qualify by poverty for free or reduced price lunch. See also Report to the Governor and the Legislature, New York State Education Department, June 2002.

$165 FOR IQ TEST: *New York City's Best Public Elementary Schools,* cited above.

"A LITTLE WIGGLE ROOM": *Public Middle Schools: New York City's Best,* cited above.

FAKING AN ADDRESS: *New York City's Best Elementary Schools,* cited above.

139, 140 $150 MILLION BUILDING FOR STUYVESANT HIGH SCHOOL, MOST EXPENSIVE HIGH SCHOOL EVER BUILT IN NEW YORK CITY: *New York Times,* September 8 and 10, 1992, and April 29, 1996; *Technos,* Fall 1993. See also *Amazing Grace,* cited above. The newest high schools to have been built for students in the Bronx were Truman High School and Lehman High School, both built in 1972. (James Lonergan, executive director, Division of School Facilities, New York City Public Schools, in response to a Freedom of Information request, May 27, 2004.)

140 STUYVESANT DEMOGRAPHICS AND DECLINE IN BLACK ENROLLMENT: Blacks made up 12.9 percent, and Hispanics 4.3 percent, of Stuyvesant's enrollment in 1979 (*New York Times,* March 18 and August 4, 1995). According to the school's 2003–2004 Annual School Report, blacks made up 2.7 percent, and Hispanics 3.2 percent, of Stuyvesant's enrollment as of spring 2004. See also "Secret Apartheid II," by the New York ACORN Schools Office, New York City, May 5, 1997, one of a series of reports from ACORN documenting patterns of racial discrimination or exclusion in the city's public schools.

PROGRAMS INTENDED TO INCREASE MINORITY ENROLLMENT AT STUYVESANT: "For Poor but Talented, a Shot at Opportunity," *New York Times,* August 4, 1995.

"WE'RE SUPPOSED TO BE THE BEST KIDS": *New York Times,* September 10, 1992.

141 PERCENTAGE OF LOW-INCOME CHILDREN IN STUYVESANT ENROLLMENT: Annual School Report for Stuyvesant High School, New York City Public Schools, 2003–2004.

"NEW YORK IS A 'TALE OF TWO CITIES' ": David Dinkins, letter to *New York Times,* July 17, 1986.

142ff. MIDDLE SCHOOL IN HARLEM: The Academy for Community Education and Service had "an average class size of 30 students" and most teachers were "new and very young," according to Insideschools, February 2003. Orlando Ramos, the principal of ACES when I visited in November 2002, has since left the New York City schools.

PROVISIONAL TEACHERS: The formal term for such teachers was "PPT's"—"Preparatory Provisional Teachers"—which refers to individuals who have not yet qualified for either provisional or permanent certification but are working on a temporary license. According to Susan Amlung, director of Policy Research, United Federation of Teachers, New York City (interview with author, August 2004), teachers with only temporary licenses are seldom, if ever, allowed to teach any longer in the city's public schools. Approximately 5,000 New York City teachers, however, work with what is called "alternative certification" granted after a single summer's preparation in the Chancellor's Fellows program (see notes for Chapter 3) or in a similar national program called Teach for America.

I MEET ELIO: See my book *Ordinary Resurrections,* cited above. Alexander Burger, Elio's former middle school, was closed in June 2002.

145ff. WALTON HIGH SCHOOL: My visit to the school in November 2002 was made possible by Cami Carter, who had previously taught there, and by Walton High School science teacher Beatrice Goodwin.

OVERCROWDING OF BUILDING: According to Walton High School's Annual School Report (New York City Public Schools, 2002–2003), the enrollment at Walton High exceeded the building's capacity by 71.3 percent, but the report listed only 3,134 students, apparently not including students in two small academies in the same building. Insideschools (September 2003) placed the enrollment at nearly 3,600. Teachers and students at the school placed the number at about 4,000. On the basis of the lower enrollment number (3,134) from which the New York City Public Schools calculated an overutilization rate of 173 percent, the number of students the building was intended to hold (what the school's annual report terms its "capacity") is about 1,800.

RACIAL DEMOGRAPHICS OF WALTON HIGH SCHOOL: Annual School Report 2002–2003.

148 "YOU ARE NO LONGER STUDENTS—YOU ARE EMPLOYEES": "Welcome to Virtual Enterprises, International," Virtual Enterprise Center, Board of Education of the City of New York, 2001.

149, 150 CLASS SIZE: "Classes with 39 students" were reported by a Walton student to Insideschools (September 2003). Cami Carter, who had taught music at the school, told me she had 40–50 students in each class. I observed no classes holding more than 34.

150 ATTRITION AND GRADUATION RATES: Annual School Reports for 1999–2000 and 2002–2003. According to the 1999–2000 Annual School Report, there were 1,275 ninth graders in fall 1999, of whom more than half appear to have been held back from promotion at least once. According to the 2002–2003 Annual School Report, 188 of these students graduated in 2003, of whom only seven percent received the New York State Regents diploma.

NUMBER OF RECENT IMMIGRANTS AT WALTON HIGH SCHOOL: Annual School Report, 2002–2003.

150, 151 ROOSEVELT PUBLIC SCHOOLS: I visited two elementary schools, the middle school, and the high school (the latter two are housed in the same building) in November 2002.

SIZE AND STUDENT DEMOGRAPHICS OF DISTRICT: "The Roosevelt UFSD 21st Century Community Learning Centers Program," Roosevelt Public Schools, provided by school officials to the New York Civil Liberties Union's Nassau County chapter, January 2002. "The diversity of the population," according to this document, "is in the rich variations of ethnic backgrounds found in its 99.7 percent minority population." But, according to the Annual School Report for the Roosevelt district, 85 percent of students in the district were black and 15 percent Hispanic in 2002–2003. There were three white students and one Native American or Asian student in the total K–12 population.

151 HIGH TAX RATES, WHITE FLIGHT, LOSS OF PROPERTY VALUE: *New York Times* (editorial), November 30, 2001. "The community," said the *Times,* "has struggled since the late 1960s, when county welfare officials damaged its fortunes by dumping welfare clients into the area, depressing property values and driving away upper-income white and blacks alike." Arthur Eisenberg's colleague at the NYCLU, attorney Donald Shaffer, notes that despite a recent reduction in Roosevelt's tax rate, it remains one of the highest in New York State and Nassau County. (Correspondence with author, February 2004.)

ROOSEVELT LOWEST-SPENDING DISTRICT IN NASSAU COUNTY: *Newsday,* April 21, 2002. The Nassau County district of Manhasset, according to *Newsday* (June 13, 2004), has "20 times more property and income wealth" than Roosevelt for each pupil in its system, spends "nearly twice as much in the classroom," but has "less than half the proportional tax burden per homeowner."

PER-PUPIL SPENDING IN ROOSEVELT, GREAT NECK, MINEOLA, NASSAU COUNTY: Report to the Governor and the Legislature, New York State Education Department, July 2003 (including numbers for 2001–2002).

"ROOSEVELT IS NEW YORK'S SOWETO": Roosevelt school official cited is unnamed at official's request.

152 NUMBER OF ROOSEVELT CHILDREN WHO RECEIVE PRESCHOOL EDUCATION: According to *Newsday* (June 17, 2004), half the children eligible for pre K in the district remained on a waiting list more than a year and a half after my visit.

152, 153 FIRST SCHOOL VISITED: Washington Rose Elementary School. According to the New York State School Report for Washington Rose (New York State Education Department, 2002–2003), 79.4 percent of students at the school were black and 20.3 percent were Hispanic. There was one white child in the student body of 472. Every child in the school was eligible for free lunch.

RESPIRATORY DANGER TO STUDENTS: Onyekachi Akoma, director of facilities and grounds for Roosevelt's schools at the time of my visit. He has since left the Roosevelt system.

CONSTRUCTION OF A NEW SCHOOL: The first of several new schools in the Roosevelt district is scheduled to open in fall 2005. (*Newsday,* October 7, 2004.) See update on construction plans in Updates and Acknowledgments.

153–154 SECOND SCHOOL VISITED: Ulysses Byas Elementary School. According to the New York State School Report for Ulysses Byas (New York State Education Department, 2002–2003), 79 percent of students at the school were black and 21 percent were Hispanic. There was 1 white child in the student body of 473. Every child in the school was eligible for free lunch.

PRINCIPAL DESCRIBES EVACUATION, SUBSEQUENT DOUBLING UP OF CLASSES, AND PHYSICAL CONDITIONS OF SCHOOL: The principal of the Ulysses Byas School is Lillian Watson.

155 ROOSEVELT JUNIOR-SENIOR HIGH SCHOOL: The principal, according to *Newsday* (October 27, 2002), had been hired only two weeks before the start of school.

156 SCHOOL OFFICIAL CORRECTS TEACHER'S STATEMENT THAT TWO YEARS OF SEWING ARE REQUIRED: Newly appointed Roosevelt Superintendent Ronald Ross. See note for pp. 159, 160.

ALL BUT TEN EIGHTH GRADERS HAD FAILED ENGLISH LANGUAGE LITERACY EXAM IN THE PREVIOUS YEAR: The principal, who has since departed the Roosevelt system, told this to me and Mr. Eisenberg during our visit. According to the New York State School Report for the Roosevelt Junior-Senior High (New York State Education Department, 2001–2002), 16 out of 213 eighth graders had passed this exam.

NO BOYS IN TWELFTH GRADE HAD RECEIVED REGENTS DIPLOMA IN THE PRECEDING YEAR: According to *Newsday* (October 27, 2002), a total of five seniors had received Regents diplomas in June 2002. In 2001, according to *The New York Times* (November 30, 2001), "only 6 percent of Roosevelt's students received Regents diplomas, as compared with an average of about 60 percent for the adjacent districts. . . ."

ATTRITION RATE IN SENIOR HIGH SCHOOL: According to a series of New York State School Reports for Roosevelt High School, recording enrollment figures over a four-year span, there were 178 ninth graders in fall 1999, 157 tenth graders in 2000, 151 eleventh graders in fall 2001, and 80 twelfth graders in fall 2002.

157, 158 DISSOLUTION OF ROOSEVELT DISTRICT SUGGESTED: *Newsday,* July 14, 2000, December 19, 2001, February 13, 2002. "More than 3,000 children are languishing right now in schools that are killing their futures," said *The New York Times* (November 30, 2001). "To save them, the state should dissolve the district. . . ."

"DUMPING WELFARE CLIENTS" IN ROOSEVELT: *New York Times* (November 30, 2001).

REACTION WAS "SHEER TERROR": New York State Commissioner of Education Richard Mills, in conversation with author at a conference sponsored by the New York State United Teachers and the New York State Education Department, November 2002.

VIRULENT RESISTANCE IN EAST MEADOW: "Keep Roosevelt Students Out of East Meadow," flyer distributed in 2002, according to Barbara Bernstein, executive director, New York Civil Liberties Union, Nassau chapter, who provided me a copy of the document. East Meadow Superintendent Robert Dillon confirmed the wide dissemination of such materials in East Meadow when we met in September 2004.

159 STATE TAKEOVER OF ROOSEVELT DISTRICT: *New York Times,* May 10, 2002.

"CONSISTENCY MANAGEMENT MANAGER APPLICATIONS": The "consistency management" program is one element of Project GRAD ("Graduation Really Achieves Dreams"), the Texas-based regimen which is also used in the Columbus, Ohio, schools, as described in Chapter 4. ("The Roosevelt UFSD 21st Century Community Learning Centers Program," cited above.)

"NO CIVIC OR POLITICAL VOICES CAME TO OUR SUPPORT": New York Civil Liberties Union attorney Donald Shaffer (conversation with author, December 2003). *Newsday,* on the other hand, has taken a consistently strong and progressive stand on this issue. "They are the shame of the suburbs," the paper wrote in an editorial (June 13, 2004), "these poor and isolated islands of exception to the educational excellence that defines Long Island. . . . In the nation's most segregated collection of suburban school systems, they represent nothing less than academic apartheid."

159, 160 RECENT CHANGES IN THE ROOSEVELT DISTRICT: The new superintendent, Ronald Ross, discussed these changes with me in a meeting in September 2004 and in correspondence in March and April 2005. (See Updates and Acknowledgments.)

CHAPTER 7: EXCLUDING BEAUTY

161, 162 MY FOURTH GRADE STUDENTS' WRITINGS: *Death at an Early Age,* cited above.

163, 164 OKLAHOMA CITY SCHOOLS, DESEGREGATION AND RESEGREGATION: *Dismantling Desegregation,* by Gary Orfield and Susan Eaton, cited above. The decisive ruling, which was made by the U.S. Supreme Court (*Oklahoma City v. Dowell,* 1991), "allowed school districts to declare themselves 'unitary,' end their desegregation plans, and return to neighborhood schools . . . ," according to "*Brown* at 50," Harvard Civil Rights Project, cited above. "The Rehnquist Court's position in 1991," according to the report, "was that years of compliance with a court order and a judicial determination that the district had done what was feasible to eliminate any remaining effects of the prior discrimination, whether or not it had actually overcome the history of discrimination," justify the conclusion that a school system is "unitary." I visited the Columbus Enterprise School in Oklahoma City in October 2002.

164 OVERCROWDING OF SCHOOL, CONDITION OF BUILDINGS, DEMOGRAPHICS, SALARIES, TEACHERS' YEARS OF EXPERIENCE: School Report Cards for Columbus Enterprise School, Office of Accountability, Oklahoma City Public Schools, 2000–2001, 2001–2002, 2002–2003; Statistical Profiles, Oklahoma City Public Schools, 2002–2003; interview with principal Phillip Cunningham at time of my visit and follow-up interviews and correspondence, 2003 and 2004.

164, 165 "BARRACKS CLASSROOMS": These conditions had been noted in the press for many years. The *Daily Oklahoman* (September 29, 1997) described "students crowded into barrackslike annexes" but cited the assurance of the vice chairman of Kerr-McGee that, with the corporation's involvement, "we would not be a month into the school year with the problem unaddressed."

166 KINDERGARTEN LITERACY PROGRAM: The lesson I observed was based upon a program known as "Sing-Spell-Read-and-Write" (Pearson), which was supplemented by a program called "The Letter People" (Abrams). The school "deliberately chooses" to use this material in kindergarten "because it does offer wide latitude for teacher and student . . . to create total language experiences rather than drill and practice," according to the principal. In kindergarten and first grade, he adds, the school also uses "a computer-based early literacy program focused on letters and sounds."

167 LEXINGTON, KENTUCKY: I visited the Russell Elementary School in October 2002.

"COLORED SCHOOL NUMBER 1": "History of Russell School," part of an informational packet provided to me by the principal.

THE PRESENT BUILDING OPENED IN JANUARY 1954 AND WAS TO BE DEDICATED ON APRIL 4, 1954: *Lexington Leader,* January 8, 1954.

168 THE RUSSELL BECAME A "MAGNET FOR INTEGRATED ARTS THROUGH MULTIPLE INTELLIGENCES" BEGINNING IN 1997–1998: School Report Card for Russell Elementary School, Fayette County Public Schools, Lexington, Kentucky, 2001–2002. See also *Multiple Intelligences,* by Howard Gardner (New York: Basic Books, 1993).

SCHOOL DEMOGRAPHICS: According to the Common Core of Data, National Center for Education Statistics, U.S. Department of Education, white children made up 29 percent of students at the Russell School in 2001–2002; but, according to the principal, the number had declined to approximately 20 percent a year later when I visited. The school was closed in June 2003 because the Fayette County School Board decided it "was not cost-effective to spend the estimated $3 million needed to renovate the 49-year-old building" (*Lexington Herald-Leader,* June 10, 2003), whose 229 students were "among the least affluent in the city" (*Lexington Herald-Leader,* March 24, 2003).

169 SCHOOLS VISITED IN CALIFORNIA: Monterey Elementary School in San Bernardino; Woodworth Elementary School in Inglewood; 75th Street Elementary School, Roosevelt High School, and Fremont High School in Los Angeles.

FORMER GOVERNOR GRAY DAVIS CITED ON OVERCROWDING IN CALIFORNIA SCHOOLS: "Letter from Governor Davis to Fellow Democrats," April 20, 2000, cited in "Statewide Picture of Conditions Addressed in *Williams v. State of California,* provided by American Civil Liberties Union attorney Catherine Lhamon (see note for p. 171).

NEARLY 1,000 SCHOOLS ON YEAR-ROUND CALENDARS: "Statewide Picture of Conditions . . . ," California ACLU, cited above.

SAN BERNARDINO: My visit to the Monterey Elementary School took place in October 2001.

DUAL CALENDAR: The "San Bernardino Unified School District, 2001–2002 Continuous Year-Round and Traditional School Calendars" was provided to me by Superintendent Arturo Valdez. The dual calendar ceased to be necessary since 2003–2004, when all schools in the district moved to the 12-month calendar.

170 CLASS SIZE, TEACHER QUALIFICATIONS, AND STUDENT DEMOGRAPHICS: School Accountability Report Card for Monterey Elementary School, San Bernardino Unified School District, 2001–2002. See also Common Core of Data, National Center for Education Statistics, U.S. Department of Education, 2002–2003.

LACK OF PRE-K AVAILABILITY, STANDARDIZED EXAMS BEGINNING IN FIRST GRADE: Interview with principal Daniel Arellano and conversations with kindergarten and first grade teachers at the time of my visit.

"IMMEDIATE INTERVENTION PLAN" CALLS FOR SPECIFIC LEVELS OF IMPROVEMENT: "Immediate Intervention/Underperforming Schools Program, California Department of Education. . . . Dates of Project Duration: July 21, 2001, to June 30, 2003." The school was classified as no longer underperforming in 2002 and has apparently been relieved since of the provisions in this document.

171 LEGAL ACTION BY AMERICAN CIVIL LIBERTIES UNION: *Williams v. State of California* was filed in May 2000, with an "Amended Complaint" filed in August 2000 and additional motions (including depositions of students and teachers) filed in 2001 and 2002. (Attorney Catherine Lhamon, American Civil Liberties Union of Southern California, interview in Los Angeles, April 2003, subsequent correspondence, and follow-up interview January 2005.)

DEPOSITIONS, NUMBER OF STUDENTS AND SCHOOLS: "More than 60 students at 18 schools were named as plaintiffs in the suit, which was filed on the 46th anniversary of . . . *Brown v. Board of Education*," according to *Education Week*, May 24, 2000. According to attorney Catherine Lhamon, however, a total of 46 schools were named in the complaint and, because the case was a class action suit, "hundreds of schools were actually involved."

171, 172 "CHEMISTRY LABS WITH NO CHEMICALS," ETC.: *Sacramento Bee*, September 21, 2001.

172 TEACHERS HAD TO SPRAY STUDENTS WITH WATER: Bryant Elementary School, San Francisco. (*Education Week*, May 24, 2000.)

CHILDREN DESCRIBE RATS IN THEIR CLASSROOM: The children's writings are included in a packet of approximately 20 narratives, many illustrated by pictures of rodents and bearing the cover-title "RATS," self-published by the students of "Mr. Ibarra's 4th Grade Class," Gulf Avenue Elementary School, Los Angeles Unified School District, January 18, 2000.

DEMOGRAPHICS OF GULF AVENUE ELEMENTARY SCHOOL: Common Core of Data, National Center for Education Statistics, U.S. Department of Education, 2001–2002.

75TH STREET ELEMENTARY SCHOOL IN LOS ANGELES: I visited the school in April 2003.

LEAD PAINT AND EXPOSED ASBESTOS: Rebecca Constantino, a writer and former teacher who is also the founder and director of Access Books, described these conditions to me during our visit to the school.

TEACHERS ADVISE PARENTS TO TEST CHILDREN FOR LEAD POISON: "WARNING to 75th Street School Parents: Your child may be at risk for cancer, brain damage, and other serious health problems due to contamination or infection at this school site. . . . You may take your child to be tested for LEAD POISONING at the Hubert Humphrey Medical Center, 5850 South Main Street. . . . Call for an appointment today." (Distributed to children and parents by the 75th Street School Health and Safety Committee, which consisted primarily of teachers, June 2002.)

173 STUDENT DEMOGRAPHICS: School Profile of 75th Street Elementary School, Los Angeles Unified School District, 2002–2003.

TEACHERS WORKING ON EMERGENCY CREDENTIALS: In the year before my visit, 22 of the school's 86 teachers were teaching on "Emergency Credential," 45 on "Full Credential." (School Accountability Report Card for 75th Street Elementary School, California Department of Education, 2001–2002.) Two years later, despite a provision in the federal law No Child Left Behind that all children were to be given "qualified" instructors, only 54 percent of teachers at the school were on "Full Credential," compared to nearly 91 percent statewide. (School Profile for 75th Street Elementary School, Education Data Partnership, Palo Alto, California, 2003–2004.)

SUCCESS FOR ALL IN KINDERGARTEN CLASSES: More commonly in California at the time, the scripted literacy program used in elementary grades was Open Court, published by a subsidiary of McGraw-Hill. Los Angeles School Superintendent Roy Romer, according to *The New York Times* (February 2, 2002), mandated the use of Open Court for all low-performing schools in 2002; but the 75th Street School was using SFA in spring 2003.

175 "THE ETHNIC DISTINCTIONS HERE ARE VERY OBVIOUS": ACLU attorney Catherine Lhamon, interview with author, March 2004.

DESCRIPTION OF FREMONT HIGH SCHOOL AS A "NEIGHBORHOOD FORTRESS": *Los Angeles Times,* July 14, 2002. My visit to the school took place in April 2003.

FREMONT HIGH SCHOOL STUDENT READING LEVELS AND ATTRITION RATE: School Accountability Report Card for Fremont High School, California Department of Education, 2002–2003; School Enrollment by Grade for Fremont High School, Educational Demographics Unit, California Department of Education, 1999–2000 and 2002–2003. See also *Los Angeles Times,* July 14, 2002.

175, 176 TWENTY-SEVEN HOMEROOMS FOR NINTH GRADERS, NINE FOR TWELFTH GRADERS, ESTIMATES OF THE NUMBER OF CLASSES IN PORTABLES, CONVERTED CLOSETS OR SHOP ROOMS, AND LARGE

CLASS SIZE: Counselors and teachers described these problems to me at a meeting at the end of the schoolday. Sarah Knopp, the social studies teacher who invited me to participate in her class, estimated there were about two classes in converted storage closets on each floor and other classes in converted shop rooms.

176 NUMBER OF CLASSES WITH 33 TO MORE THAN 40 STUDENTS: The School Accountability Report for 2002–2003 lists 219 classes, including 66 in social studies and 52 in math, with 33 or more students. Teachers and students described several classes with more than 40. Documentation submitted in *Williams v. California* ("Plaintiffs' Liability Disclosure Statement," October 3, 2002) confirms that "course enrollments reach as high as 52 and even 60 students in core academic classes."

177 COURT PAPERS DOCUMENTING PROBLEMS WITH BATHROOMS, EXTREME HEAT IN CLASSROOMS, RATS EATING HAMBURGER BUNS, ETC.: See "Plaintiffs' Liability Disclosure Statement," cited above, and "First Amended Complaint for Injunctive and Declaratory Relief," August 14, 2000.

178, 179 COURSE REQUIREMENTS IN "TECHNICAL ARTS": According to teacher Sarah Knopp, students needed to take two classes in Technical Arts, which included "hair-dressing, shop, sewing, mechanics, and computers," among other options. "I don't think any counselors are telling girls they *have* to take two sewing or hair-dressing classes," but she said they are often programmed into them to meet requirements for graduation if the other electives are closed. She noted, for example, that there was a film-making elective, but that there was "only one film-making class, with 20 slots, for the entire school."

179 "TECHNICAL ARTS" OPTIONS AT BEVERLY HILLS HIGH SCHOOL: "Beverly Hills High School Course Descriptions," Beverly Hills High School, 2003–2004.

180 TEACHER SUBBING FOR A SUBSTITUTE: "Plaintiffs' Liability Disclosure Statement," cited above.

181 CREDIT FOR "SERVICE CLASSES," CREDIT FOR JOBS, "GREAT CUSTOMER SERVICE": See "Plaintiffs' Liability Disclosure Statement" and "First Amended Complaint for Injunctive and Declaratory Relief," cited above. The jobs program at Fremont High, for which students could receive ten credits (the equivalent of two classes), is known as the Shell program because, according to Fremont teacher Sarah Knopp, it is sponsored by the Shell Oil Company.

181, 182 LONGER SCHOOLDAYS, LESS HOMEWORK, 20 FEWER DAYS OF SCHOOL: See also "First Amended Complaint for Injunctive and Declaratory Relief," filed in *Williams v. California,* cited above.

182, 183 STUDENTS FREQUENTLY CANNOT USE LIBRARY: Teachers and librarian cited from late-afternoon meeting with faculty. "Three AP classes take place in the library this year," said the librarian, who estimated that the library was closed 25–30 percent of the time for testing, teacher meetings, or AP preparation. The reason AP prep sessions sometimes take place in the library, as teacher

Sarah Knopp later explained, is related to the year-round schedule of the school. "The AP tests take place in May, so if you're on a track that's not in session in January and February, you've lost two months of prep time for the AP tests. Some of the AP teachers therefore use the library to meet their students while they and their students are officially 'on break.' "

184 "STRICKED NEW PRINCIPLE": For a favorable portrayal of the new principal, see *Los Angeles Times,* November 14 and 15, 2002.

CALIFORNIA'S STRICT ACCOUNTABILITY AGENDA WAS BEING PUT IN PLACE WHILE FREMONT STUDENTS HAD BEEN IN ELEMENTARY SCHOOL AND MIDDLE SCHOOL: See "California Standards and Assessments," by R. James Milgram and Veronica Norriss, Department of Mathematics, Stanford University, October 21, 1999.

CHAPTER 8: FALSE PROMISES

187ff. HIGHER HORIZONS AND SIMILAR PROGRAMS, INITIAL PRAISE, ULTIMATE DISAPPOINTMENT: "Racial Isolation in the Public Schools," U.S. Commission on Civil Rights, Washington, D.C., 1967; *New York Times,* February 23 and 27 and November 17, 1961, and July 10, 1966.

190 DESEGREGATION EFFORTS IN NEW YORK CITY LIMITED AND UNSUCCESSFUL: U.S. Commission on Civil Rights, cited above.

COMPENSATORY VS. DESEGREGATION PROGRAMS: "Evaluations of programs of compensatory education conducted in schools that are isolated by race and social class suggest that these programs have not had lasting effects in improving the achievement of the students.... Negro children attending desegregated schools that do not have compensatory education programs perform better than Negro children in racially isolated schools with such programs." (U.S. Commission on Civil Rights, cited above.)

190, 191 NEW FRONTIERS PROGRAM IN ROOSEVELT: *New York Times,* December 27, 1961.

191 BOSTON'S OPERATION COUNTERPOISE: See *Death at an Early Age,* cited above.

192 "EFFECTIVE SCHOOLS": See notes on Oklahoma City in Chapter 7.

"MORE EFFECTIVE SCHOOLS": *New York Times,* May 1, June 7 and 30, and July 1, 7, and 10, 1964; December 9, 1966; May 27, June 19 and 29, 1967. Also see "Study... Finds More Effective Schools Program Has Had No 'Significant' Impact," *New York Times,* October 10, 1967.

193 FRED HECHINGER CITED: *New York Times,* November 21, 1966.

193, 194 QUALITY EDUCATION FOR MINORITIES: "Education That Works: An Action Plan for the Education of Minorities," Quality Education for Minorities Project, Massachusetts Institute of Technology, Cambridge, January 1990. "First, go for quality.... Second, reward success.... Education, like private enterprise, can improve by restructuring," attributed in this document to an earlier publication, "To Secure Our Future," National Center on Education and the Economy, 1989.

194 "WHAT WORKS": The 66-page report ("What Works: Research About Teaching and Learning"), which is introduced with a foreword by then Secretary of Education William Bennett, was released by the U.S. Department of Education in March 1986. See also *New York Times,* March 1, 1986.

194, 195 SUCCESSIVE LISTS OF THINGS "THAT WORK": *Newsweek,* May 2, 1988; *Education Life* (a Sunday supplement), *New York Times,* January 5, 1992; *BusinessWeek,* March 19, 2001. See also "Saving Our Schools," *Fortune* (special issue), Spring 1990; and *U.S. News & World Report,* October 9, 2000.

195, 196 THOMAS SOBOL CITED: Conversation with author at Teachers College, New York, December 2003.

"THE SYSTEM JUST DEVOURS THEM": "The city has had ten schools chancellors over the last 20 years, and most left the job under a cloud of political denunciations," *The New York Times* noted (August 16, 2001) when yet another highly capable chancellor, Harold Levy, began to undergo attacks from Mayor Rudolph Giuliani in 2001.

CHANCELLOR RICHARD GREEN: See *Savage Inequalities,* cited above.

196 PRAISE FOR CHANCELLOR JOSEPH FERNANDEZ ON ARRIVAL: *New York Times,* November 22, 1989; *New York Daily News,* September 21, 1989, and January 25, 1990; *Newsday,* February 20, 1990. Two years into Joseph Fernandez's tenure in New York, *The New York Times* (May 2, 1992) reported that the dropout rate had suddenly dropped to 17 percent from 46 percent only six years before. "The change may be partly due to New York's faltering economy as students stay in school because there are no jobs. A surer reason is Schools Chancellor Joseph Fernandez and his initiatives to rescue students before they disappear." In reality, the actual number had never dropped to anywhere near 17 percent. Tens of thousands of dropouts were simply not reported and instead were labeled "discharged students" by administrators. See my discussion of this practice in the 1990s in New York on p. 360 of *Ordinary Resurrections,* cited above.

197 CRITICISM OF FERNANDEZ ON DISMISSAL: *New York Times,* February 11, 1993; *Newsday,* February 28, 1993.

FERNANDEZ'S SUCCESSOR RESIGNS AFTER CONFLICT WITH NEW YORK MAYOR RUDOLPH GIULIANI: Chancellor Ramon Cortines, who was appointed in 1993, later explained, "I left in 1995, with three years more on my contract, because I did not believe that I could continue without the mayor's support. The tension was just too much of a distraction." (*New York Times,* January 4, 2000.)

197, 198 CHANCELLOR CREW'S REFLECTIONS AFTER HIS DISMISSAL FROM NEW YORK CITY SCHOOLS: Conversation with Dr. Crew, Seattle, Washington, September 2000.

198 "THE NICELY REFINED TORTURE A MAN CAN EXPERIENCE": *Notes of a Native Son,* by James Baldwin (Boston: Beacon Press, 1955).

198, 199 "WITH LIGHTNING SPEED" NEW HIGH SCHOOL PRINCIPAL BRINGS ABOUT DRAMATIC TURNAROUND: See, for example, "State Praises Turnaround. . . . New leadership is cited in success of L.A.'s Fremont High," *Los Angeles Times,* November 14, 2002; and "A Failing School Perks Up," *Los Angeles Times* (editorial), November 15, 2002. "John C. Fremont High School had nowhere to go but further down," said the editorial. "Then along came a real leader and genuine help from the district. . . . The rate of change has state and local officials breathless . . . , amazed by its fledgling turnaround. . . . Early reports are dazzling."

199, 200 PATERSON, NEW JERSEY, PRINCIPAL JOE CLARK: *Time,* February 1, 1988. Also see *Savage Inequalities,* cited above.

201 PRESIDENT GEORGE H. BUSH, AMERICA 2000: *New York Times,* April 18 and 19 and November 13, 1991.

A COMMITMENT TO SCHOOL READINESS FOR ALL CHILDREN: "By the year 2000, all children in America will start school ready to learn": White House Briefing by President George H. Bush, Federal News Service, June 13, 1991. See also *New York Times,* February 1 and 26, 1990; State of the Union address, January 31, 1990; and White House Proclamation 6339, September 23, 1991 ("One of the first aims of America 2000, our comprehensive strategy for achieving excellence in education, is ensuring that every child in the nation starts school ready to learn"), *Federal Register,* September 25, 1991.

"EDUCATION AND EXPECTATION GO HAND IN HAND": *New York Times,* September 4, 1991.

"NO RENAISSANCE WITHOUT REVOLUTION": *New York Times,* April 19, 1991.

FEW NEW FUNDS PROVIDED: *New York Times,* April 19, 1991.

202 NEW SCHOOLS THAT WOULD "BREAK THE MOULD": See, for example, *New York Times,* July 21, 1991.

FRED HECHINGER CITED: *New York Times,* March 16, 1990.

NO CHILD LEFT BEHIND: Passed by Congress December 18, 2001, signed into law by President George W. Bush January 8, 2002.

203 PROBLEMS CONCERNING "TRANSFERS": In New York, according to *The New York Times* (May 13, 2003), "most of the children eligible for the transfers live in neighborhoods without any high-performing schools" and, in 2002, "just 1,500 of the 6,400 students who applied for transfers received them." By 2003, 8,000 New York City children had been allowed to transfer (*New York Times,* October 1, 2003), but one third of these students "have been moved from one school labeled failing to another failing school." In Washington, D.C., according to *Education Week* (September 1, 2004), "roughly 33,000 children," who represented more than half the 64,000 students in the district, were eligible to transfer but, by late August 2004, "only 106 students had applied. . . ." Numbers provided in the text for transfers in the 2003–2004 school year were made available by Michael

Casserly, executive director of the Council of Great City Schools. (Correspondence, February 2005.)

NATIONWIDE, ONLY ONE PERCENT OF ELIGIBLE CHILDREN WERE ABLE TO MAKE TRANSFERS IN 2003–2004: *Education Week,* March 16, 2005.

203, 204 TRANSFERS BETWEEN URBAN AND SUBURBAN DISTRICTS: In an enlightening commentary, Michael Winerip (*New York Times,* September 10, 2003) described the dilemma of a parent in the North Bronx who, in order to "take advantage of the . . . transfer provision," was sending her child on a 90-minute ride by public transportation to attend a school "in far southern Manhattan." Noting that the family lived near the border of affluent Westchester County, Winerip wrote, "It would seem to make more sense to give a child at a poor, failing Bronx school the opportunity to transfer to nearby Westchester, which has some of the richest schools and smallest class sizes in the nation. But the federal officials who drafted No Child Left Behind did not have the stomach to mandate that rich districts help out poor ones." Michael Casserly, cited above, notes that there is language in No Child Left Behind that permits cross-district transfers but that the White House has not required suburbs to accept children from the city nor encouraged them to do so. "There is nothing in the law to compel the surrounding suburbs to accept these kids," says Casserly. "Not one suburban school district I know of takes transfer students under No Child Left Behind."

204 SCHOOL INFRASTRUCTURE COSTS OF $100 BILLION TO $200 BILLION: *New York Times,* January 24, 2001, and May 16, 2003.

205 "NOW IS THE TIME": President George W. Bush at the Republican convention in July 2000, cited in *Education Week,* October 13, 2004.

EXCLUSION OF CHILDREN ELIGIBLE FOR HEAD START HAS INCREASED: Marian Wright Edelman, conversation with author, February 2005. See also notes for Chapter 2.

206 "HOUSTON . . . PILLAR OF SO-CALLED TEXAS MIRACLE IN EDUCATION": *New York Times,* July 11, 2003.

IMPLAUSIBLE TEST-SCORE FLUCTUATIONS IN HOUSTON SCHOOLS: *Education Week,* January 19, 2005.

WIDESPREAD CHEATING ON ELEMENTARY SCHOOL EXAMINATIONS, APPARENTLY ENCOURAGED BY ADMINISTRATORS IN HOUSTON AND OTHER TEXAS DISTRICTS: *Dallas Morning News,* December 19 and 31, 2004, and January 11, February 17, 21, and 22, 2005; *Houston Chronicle,* February 17, 2005; *FairTest Examiner,* Winter 2005. The school in which teachers had been instructed how to cheat, and which had gained national acclaim for raising test scores under then Superintendent Rod Paige, was Wesley Elementary.

WESLEY ELEMENTARY SUSPECTED OF CHEATING IN 1998 AND REACTION OF PRINCIPAL: *Education Week,* June 10, 1988. Enrollment at the school was 99.4 percent black and Hispanic. There were four white children in a student body of 837. (Common Core of Data, National Center for Education Statistics, U.S. Department of Education, 1999–2000.)

207 TEACHER AT WESLEY ELEMENTARY EXPLAINS THE WAY TEACHERS WERE INSTRUCTED TO CHEAT: *Dallas Morning News,* December 31, 2004.

FALSIFIED DROPOUT FIGURES IN HOUSTON SCHOOLS: *New York Times,* July 11, and August 13 and 28, 2003, and June 26, 2004. See also *Houston Chronicle,* February 14, April 1, May 21, and July 10, 2003. "In a state that loses a lot of its public school students, the Houston Independent School District is among the worst offenders," the *Chronicle* observed (May 21, 2003). "And yet [the district's] reported number of students who drop out has been incredibly low"—" 'incredibly' as in unbelievably," the paper said. In December 2002, said the *Chronicle* (July 10, 2003), the district paid "more than $7 million in . . . bonuses" to school employees, ranging from $200 for teachers aides "to $25,000 for Superintendent Kaye Stripling." The district was now trying "to clean up misleading and sometimes false performance records" in order to "deny bonuses . . . to administrators for filing inaccurate data."

208 $75,000 IN BONUSES: *New York Times,* August 13, 2004.

INACCURATE DROPOUT FIGURES IN NEW YORK CITY: "Pushing Out At-Risk Students: An Analysis of High School Discharge Figures," Advocates for Children and the Public Advocate for the City of New York, November 21, 2002. See also *New York Times,* August 1, 2003, and May 15, 2004, and *New York Daily News* (op-ed by Elisa Hyman, deputy director of Advocates for Children), August 7, 2003. "As students are being spurred to new levels of academic achievement and required to pass stringent Regents exams to get their high school diplomas, many schools are trying to get rid of those who may tarnish a school's statistics by failing to graduate on time." (*New York Times,* July 31, 2003.)

MORE THAN 1,000 STUDENTS DISCHARGED FROM A SINGLE BRONX SCHOOL: An analysis of discharge numbers at Taft High School is included in the report by Advocates for Children, cited above.

208, 209 INACCURATE DROPOUT FIGURES IN CHICAGO: Some Illinois districts "assume that students who leave school have transferred" to another school or district, "even if they have not received any documents suggesting this has happened," notes the *Chicago Tribune,* February 26, 2004. The paper cites a report from the Harvard Civil Rights Project (*Losing Our Future,* see notes for Chapter 11) which indicates "a graduation rate of only 49 percent" for students in Chicago, in contrast with the "70 percent the system reports to the state." In the 2001–2002 school year, according to the *Chicago Sun-Times,* January 9, 2004, the Chicago Public Schools publicized a dropout rate of only 13 percent while "an analysis of state data by the Greater West Township Community Development Project found that nearly 18 percent, a total of 17,400 students, had left school prior to graduation" and "those percentages don't include

27 alternative schools." In reality, even the corrected figures provided by the *Sun-Times* do not come anywhere near the actual dropout figures for Chicago's schools, because they tell us only the percentage of twelfth grade students who graduate rather than the percentage of entering ninth grade students who stay in school long enough to enter twelfth grade and then graduate with their class.

209 "ENRON ACCOUNTING" IN HOUSTON: *New York Times,* July 11, 2003.

210, 211 CITATIONS FROM ELWOOD CUBBERLEY, WILLIAM BAGLEY, LEONARD AYRES, AND SPEAKER AT NATIONAL EDUCATION ASSOCIATION CONVENTION (1910): *Education and the Cult of Efficiency,* by Raymond Callahan (Chicago: University of Chicago Press, 1962).

211, 212 "AS FAR AS INTELLIGENCE IS CONCERNED, THE TESTS HAVE TOLD THE TRUTH": Citations from Lewis Ternan and Edward Thorndike, and biographical data on both, are drawn from "Echoes of a Forgotten Past: Eugenics, Testing, and Education Reform," by Alan Stoskopf, director of Education for Democracy at Facing History and Ourselves, Brookline, Massachusetts, published in *The Educational Forum* (Winter 2002).

212 "THEORETICALLY, ALL THE CHILDREN OF THE STATE ARE EQUALLY IMPORTANT": Elwood Cubberley is cited from *Elusive Quest,* by Edwin Margolis and Stanley Moses (New York: Apex Press, 1992).

CHAPTER 9: INVITATIONS TO RESISTANCE

215 FREMONT HIGH SCHOOL TEACHERS: See notes for Chapter 7.

216, 217 JACK WHITE: The veteran columnist is cited from *Time,* April 29, 1996.

217 P.S. 30 TEACHER LOUIS BEDROCK: See notes for Chapter 12.

218, 219 DAVID ENGLE'S RESIGNATION FROM SEATTLE'S BALLARD HIGH SCHOOL: *Seattle Times,* April 26 and May 16, 2002, interviews and correspondence with Engle, December 2004 and January 2005. "It was the Ninth Circuit Court's decision to overturn a lower court's ruling that had supported Seattle's racial tie-breaker . . . that precipitated my resignation," says Engle. "Three Ninth Circuit Court judges made that ruling in April of 2002. . . . My resignation followed within a week." Engle provided me with the text of his talk to the students at Ballard High and the letter of support from other principals. The racial tie-breaker had been "introduced in the 1970s" (Associated Press, December 16, 2003) and gave minorities "a better chance of getting into predominantly white schools. . . ."

DECLINE IN BLACK ENROLLMENT AT BALLARD HIGH FOLLOWING CANCELLATION OF "TIE-BREAKER": *Seattle Post-Intelligencer,* May 16, 2002, and June 27, 2003; interviews with, and documentation provided by, David Engle. In 2004–2005, according to Engle, the white enrollment at Ballard High was 65 percent. The school district, he notes, has not given up its legal efforts to reinstate the racial tie-breaker. In February 2005, the Ninth Circuit Court of Appeals "voted to accept the district's request for an eleven-judge panel" to reexamine the question. (*Seattle Times,* February 2, 2005.) The panel was scheduled to begin hearing arguments in the summer of 2005.

MINORITY ENROLLMENT IN KINDERGARTEN DROPS FROM 37 PERCENT TO 11 PERCENT AT SEATTLE ELEMENTARY SCHOOL: *Seattle Times,* May 16, 2002.

219 STATEMENT RELEASED BY OTHER SEATTLE PRINCIPALS IN SUPPORT OF DAVID ENGLE: *Seattle Times,* May 16, 2002.

SEATTLE SUPERINTENDENT PREDICTS INCREASED SEGREGATION: *Seattle Post-Intelligencer,* May 16, 2002; *Seattle Times,* May 16, 2002.

220, 221 INDIANAPOLIS SUPERINTENDENT DUNCAN PRITCHETT: Conversation in Indianapolis, August 2004; follow-up interview, January 2005.

221ff. GARY ORFIELD CITED: Interview in Cambridge, June 2003; follow-up interviews and correspondence, 2003, 2004, 2005. See also *Dismantling Desegregation* and reports from the Harvard Civil Rights Project, cited in notes for Chapter 1.

223, 224 "GAUTREAUX REMEDY": See "Racial Inequality and the Black Ghetto," by Alexander Polikoff, in *Poverty and Race,* November/December 2004, a periodical published by the Poverty and Race Research Action Council.

225, 226 CHARTER SCHOOLS MORE SEGREGATED THAN THE AVERAGE PUBLIC SCHOOL: "Seventy percent of black students in charter schools" in 2002–2003 were in "institutions where more than 90 percent of the students were minorities," while "only 34 percent of black students go to traditional public schools" with that degree of hypersegregation, according to the Harvard Civil Rights Project's January 2003 study (see notes for Chapter 1), as summarized in *The New York Times,* July 20, 2003.

226, 227 MILWAUKEE AREA INTERDISTRICT PROGRAM: See "Choosing Integration: Chapter 220 in the Shadow of Open Enrollment," by Anneliese Dickman, Sarah Kurhajetz, and Emily Van Dunk, the Public Policy Forum, February 2003; and "Interdistrict Opportunities, Chapter 220 Suburban School Opportunities," Milwaukee Public Schools, 2004.

227 FORMER SHOREWOOD SUPERINTENDENT JACK LINEHAN CITED: Linehan, who coordinated a report on the interdistrict integration program for Wisconsin Governor Jim Doyle ("Chapter 220 Report to Governor," December 2004, released by the Suburban Schools Legislative Committee, which represents 19 of the 22 districts included in the program), tells me that 95 percent of the children who travel to the suburbs are black or Hispanic. In the Shorewood district, where 11 percent of students attend school under the 220 program, there is also a residential population of minority children. In all, 25 percent of the enrollment is minority, Linehan reports. (Interviews with Linehan, July 2004 and January

2005.) See also *The School Administrator,* November 2000, which cites Linehan in terms that he updated in our conversations.

NUMBERS OF STUDENTS ENROLLED AND NUMBER OF PARTICIPATING DISTRICTS IN ST. LOUIS AREA INTERDISTRICT PROGRAM: *St. Louis Post-Dispatch,* August 26 and December 16, 2004.

THE SCHOOL-AGE POPULATION OF BLACK CHILDREN IN ST. LOUIS: According to the U.S. Census Bureau, 2000 Census, there are approximately 44,000 black children ages six to 18 in St. Louis. Of these, according to "An Annual Report to the Community," St. Louis Public Schools, 2003–2004, about 32,000 are enrolled in public school in St. Louis.

RECENT CUTBACKS IN FUNDING AND THEIR EFFECT ON THE INTERDISTRICT PROGRAM: See notes for p. 232.

227, 228 SCHOOL INTEGRATION IN JEFFERSON COUNTY, KENTUCKY: Of the district's 92,700 students, a little less than two thirds are white, one third are black, and approximately 5,000 are Asian or Hispanic. ("Current Enrollment by Race and Sex," Accountability, Research, and Planning Department, Jefferson County Public Schools, 2003–2004.)

REACTION TO PROPOSAL TO CUT BACK INTEGRATION PROGRAM AND SURVEY REFLECTING BLACK PARENTS' PREFERENCES: *Dismantling Desegregation* and interviews with Gary Orfield, both cited above. See also *Time,* April 29, 1996.

228 PRINCE EDWARD COUNTY, VIRGINIA: See Timothy Phelps's five-part series, *"Brown v. Board of Education* 40 Years Later," *Newsday,* May 15–19, 1994; *Simple Justice,* by Richard Kluger (New York: Vintage, 1997); and "Education at the Crossroads," *Education Week,* March 24, 1999, a retrospective on the transformation of Prince Edward County's system from a bastion of resistance to *Brown v. Board of Education* to one of the most integrated systems in the nation. Prince Edward County Superintendent Margaret Blackman provided me with recent enrollment and racial demographic numbers in September 2004. According to Blackman, between 91 and 93 percent of children living in Prince Edward County attend the public system in most recent years.

229, 230 RICHARD ROTHSTEIN CITED: "When Tried, Real Integration Proves Worthwhile," *New York Times,* January 30, 2002. The illuminating book by Susan Eaton to which Rothstein refers is *The Other Boston Busing Story* (New Haven: Yale University Press, 2001).

230 SUCCESS OF STUDENTS IN, AND WAITING LIST FOR, BOSTON'S METCO PROGRAM: "With Full Funding, Metco Could Shine," *Boston Globe,* April 28, 2004; "Facts About the Success of the Metco Program," Spring 2002, and "Post-Graduation Plans of 2002 Metco Graduates," Summer 2002, Metco Inc., Roxbury, Massachusetts; interviews with Metco Director Jean McGuire, staff social worker Edward Williams, and Metco board member Thelma Burns, 2002–2005.

NUMBER OF BLACK AND HISPANIC STUDENTS IN BOSTON PUBLIC SCHOOLS: In 2003–2004, there were 28,315 black students and 18,421 Hispanic students in the city's schools. ("About the Boston Public Schools: Facts and Figures," Boston Public Schools, October 29, 2003.)

LIMITED SHARE OF COSTS FOR METCO PROVIDED BY STATE, LARGE SUMS CONTRIBUTED BY PARTICIPATING SUBURBS: *Boston Globe,* April 28, 2004; "Facts About the Success of the Metco Program," cited above.

"I WISH WE COULD TAKE IN FAR MORE METCO CHILDREN": John Dempsey, principal of the Edward Devotion School, Brookline, Massachusetts. (Conversation with author in the course of a visit to the school in spring 2004.)

231 LEGISLATION INTRODUCED TO REDUCE OR ELIMINATE MILWAUKEE INTEGRATION PROGRAM: The legislative attempts took place in 1999, 2001, and 2003. It is expected that there will be another attempt in 2005. According to former Shorewood Superintendent Jack Linehan, the peak enrollment in what is called the Chapter 220 program was in 1993, when nearly 6,000 students benefited from the interdistrict program, including nearly 800 suburban students who chose to go to schools within the city. One reason for the decline in backing for the program, Linehan notes, is financial; but another factor, in his belief, is "a more conservative approach to education" that questions the efficiency of integration programs. ("Is it efficient to bus kids 'all over the place'?" as he paraphrases the familiar question.) Others in Milwaukee make the point that the politically driven promotion of "the neighborhood school" has taken much of the steam out of the integration movement in Milwaukee and its suburbs. " 'Neighborhood schools,' " according to Barbara Miner of *Rethinking Schools,* a journal for teachers published in Milwaukee, has once again become "a rationalization for segregated schools" and "a message to middle-class whites, as well as some middle-class minorities, that we can provide you with a 'protected education' where 'you won't have to go to school with low-achievers.' " (Correspondence with author, January 2004.)

ACADEMIC OUTCOMES FOR STUDENTS IN THE MILWAUKEE TRANSFER PROGRAM: "The four-year graduation rate of inner-city minority students who have been attending school in the suburban districts as part of the Chapter 220 voluntary integration program is typically 95 percent or higher, while the graduation rate for minority students in the Milwaukee Public Schools averages below 60 percent, according to the most recent data available from the Wisconsin Department of Public Instruction," according to Jack Linehan (memo to author, February 2005). The suburban minority data is contained in the December 2004 report to Governor Jim Doyle, cited above, in which, says Linehan, "we use the more rigorous four-year graduation rate that accounts for students who drop out."

232 THREATENED PHASE-OUT OF ST. LOUIS INTEGRATION PROGRAM: Under the terms of the 1999 settlement in St. Louis, the state agreed to continue funding, although at lower levels, for an additional ten years while the districts agreed to continue participating for three years, after which they could annually decide whether to withdraw from the program. (*St. Louis Post-Dispatch,* December 16, 2004, and interview with Gary Orfield, March 2005.) A series of Supreme Court precedents, according to Theodore Shaw, represent the background for the phase-out in St. Louis. One of these precedents was a Kansas City case, *Missouri v. Jenkins,* 1995, which was litigated by Shaw, who is now director-counsel of the NAACP Legal Defense and Educational Fund. The trial judge in that case wanted to see integration programs continue until there is evidence that black children are making up for the academic damage of previous segregation; but the U.S. Supreme Court ruled, in effect, that such remedial actions must be temporary, which, in turn, limited the duration of court orders that require funding by the state to facilitate a desegregation order. According to Shaw, *Jenkins* was one of three decisive cases—the others were *Freeman v. Pitts* (Atlanta area) and *Oklahoma v. Dowell*—which "in fairly rapid succession gave the message that the federal court was getting out of the business of monitoring school desegregation." The role of the suburbs did not play a part in *Jenkins,* as it did in the St. Louis case, says Shaw, but the decisions in *Jenkins, Pitts,* and *Dowell* "cast a pall" on the St. Louis case. "Even entirely voluntary programs have now come under attack because, it is charged, they 'take race into account,' and this is now alleged to be discriminatory. It seems Orwellian, but that's where we are." (Interview with Theodore Shaw, January 2005.)

DECISION OF CLAYTON SCHOOL BOARD, REACTION OF STUDENTS, AND STATEMENT OF PRINCIPAL OF CLAYTON HIGH SCHOOL: *St. Louis Post-Dispatch,* December 16, 2004. "Because of reductions in state funding, Clayton gets $6,850 for each transfer student this year, down from the $13,222 the district received for each student last year," the paper notes. According to the Voluntary Interdistrict Choice Corporation and the St. Louis Public Schools, says the *Post-Dispatch,* "the transfer program has been underpaid by $19 million since 2001."

OVERALL REDUCTIONS IN THE INTEGRATION PROGRAM: The *St. Louis Post-Dispatch* (August 26, 2004) noted that, with the reduction in state funding, the number of participating students was expected to decline in 2004–2005 by approximately 72 percent from the number who participated six years before, even while parents' applications to the program were increasing and there were four or five applicants for every space available. "Educators, politicians and civic leaders," said the *Post-Dispatch* in an editorial (September 9, 2004), "should be working toward the day when there no longer will be a need for the interdistrict school desegregation program. But that day is far over the horizon. The need for the city-county desegregation program will disappear when housing in the suburbs is integrated and the schools in the city of St. Louis are excellent. We're not there yet by a long shot. . . . Even though the legal obligations on the suburban districts have eased, the moral obligation to provide quality, integrated education for the children of St. Louis has not. Long bus rides aren't the best way to fulfill this obligation. But they are the only way until we make greater progress integrating our neighborhoods and improving city schools."

232, 233 ACADEMIC OUTCOMES FOR STUDENTS IN ST. LOUIS INTERDISTRICT PROGRAM, INCREASE IN APPLICANTS: *St. Louis Today,* March 17, 2004; *St. Louis Post-Dispatch,* August 26, 2004; interviews with Gary Orfield, cited above. The most complete study of the program is found in *Stepping Over the Color Line,* by Amy Stuart Wells and Robert L. Crain (New Haven: Yale University Press, 1997). Wells and Crain recognize the multitude of problems that the program faced, the resistance posed by some suburban residents, and racially misguided preconceptions sometimes on the part of teachers and administrators. In the end, however, they conclude, "After examining the St. Louis . . . plan—the history of the color line that made it necessary and the specifics of the implementation of the court order—we respectfully disagree with those who would just as soon see the plan go away." The "borders between city and suburbs are artificial and malleable, constructs of antiquated laws and regulations," and "the solutions will call for people on both sides of the dividing line to join together. The St. Louis interdistrict desegregation plan is one example of how this might be done. It is in this way a model for the nation, and the African-American students who transfer to the suburbs are the border crossers that more of us must become."

233 AMERICANS VOICE FAVORABLE VIEWS OF SCHOOL DESEGREGATION: Harvard Civil Rights Project, January 2003 report, and author's conversations with Gary Orfield, cited above.

CHAPTER 10: A NATIONAL HORROR HIDDEN IN PLAIN VIEW: WHY NOT A NATIONAL RESPONSE?

237ff. ROGER WILKINS: Interview, July 2003; follow-up discussion, January 2005. Wilkins's position in the administration of President Lyndon Johnson was director of the U.S. Community Relations Service in the Department of Justice and carried the rank of assistant attorney general.

240 NO CHILD LEFT BEHIND: The Bush administration, by preparing lists of what it has termed "research-based" curriculum materials, has in effect given national authorization to instructional techniques it favors while explicitly discrediting others. Similarly, the administration has given national authorization to certain kinds of standardized exams while rejecting the authenticity of others.

Most standardized tests used in the United States, in any case, are published by the same few corporations and are, for all practical purposes, national examinations.

241ff. U.S. SUPREME COURT DECISION IN *RODRIGUEZ*: *San Antonio Independent School District v. Rodriguez,* 1973. The summation of the case presented in this chapter is excerpted from *Savage Inequalities,* cited above.

DEMOGRAPHICS OF ALAMO HEIGHTS: The present enrollment in the public schools of Alamo Heights is 29 percent Hispanic, 1.7 percent black, and 68 percent white. In San Antonio's Edgewood district, Hispanic and black children make up 98.1 percent of school enrollment. (Standard Financial, Student, Staff and Geographic Reports, Information Analysis Division, Texas Education Agency, 2004–2005.)

244, 245 VICTORIES AND DISAPPOINTMENTS IN SCHOOL FINANCE CASES: "Finance Litigation Surrounding K–12 Education," ACCESS (Advocacy Center for Children's Educational Success with Standards), Campaign for Fiscal Equity, New York, October 12, 2003. The director of the ACCESS Project, Molly Hunter, who is also director of legal research for the Campaign for Fiscal Equity, assisted my colleague Elizabeth Gish in a painstaking and updated assessment of the progress achieved, or not achieved, in the 27 cases in which courtroom victories were won. Ms. Hunter emphasized the incremental and ongoing nature of these litigation efforts and noted that several states in which progress had been made in previous years have now reverted to practices in which neither equity nor adequacy is provided. By my own analysis of the cases summarized in the 2003 ACCESS report, and of Ms. Hunter's assessment of their present status, it appears that between 10 and, at most, 13 states where legal actions were successful have complied with court decisions or court-supervised settlements on a persistent basis.

245ff. TOP 25 PERCENT OF DISTRICTS IN TERMS OF CHILD POVERTY RECEIVE LESS FUNDING THAN BOTTOM 25 PERCENT: "The Funding Gap," by Kevin Carey, the Education Trust, Fall 2003. Carey's concluding words cited on p. 247 are from the same report.

ALL OTHER CITATIONS FROM THE EDUCATION TRUST: "The Funding Gap 2004," by Kevin Carey, the Education Trust, Fall 2004.

247, 248 MICHAEL REBELL, EXECUTIVE DIRECTOR AND COUNSEL OF THE CAMPAIGN FOR FISCAL EQUITY: Mr. Rebell spoke with me in New York City in April 2003.

248 MR. REBELL'S WORDS ON "ADEQUACY" VS. "EQUITY": *New York Times,* June 6, 2004. See also Mr. Rebell's opinion piece in *Education Week,* April 24, 2002.

"TRYING TO MOVE SOCIETY AN INCH . . . WHEN IT NEEDS TO BE MOVED A MILE": Attorney Joseph Wayland, co-counsel with Michael Rebell in the New York case. (See note for p. 259.)

249 SUPREME COURT JUSTICES APPOINTED BY PRESIDENT RICHARD NIXON: The decision in *Rodriguez,* notes Richard Kluger, "came 20

years and 69 days after *Brown I*—and just a month before Nixon was shamed out of office. It was, in a way, his final gesture of neglect for black America, for the Court's five-man majority . . . included all four Nixon appointees." (*Simple Justice,* by Richard Kluger, cited above.)

249, 250 BILL INTRODUCED BY U.S. REPRESENTATIVE CHAKA FATTAH: "Students Bill of Rights," HR 236, introduced in January 2001. My interview with Mr. Fattah took place in July 2003.

251 AMENDMENT INTRODUCED BY U.S. SENATOR CHRISTOPHER DODD: Senate Amendment 459, proposed June 6, 2001, defeated by a vote of 58–42, June 12, 2001. See also *New York Times,* June 13, 2001, and *Philadelphia Daily News,* June 18, 2001.

251ff. CONSTITUTIONAL AMENDMENT PROPOSED BY U.S. REPRESENTATIVE JESSE JACKSON JR.: HJ Resolution 29, "Proposing an amendment to the Constitution of the United States regarding the right of all citizens of the United States to a public education of equal high quality," introduced in March 2003.

CONGRESSMAN JACKSON CITED: Interview with Mr. Jackson, July 2003; follow-up conversations and correspondence, 2003 and 2004. See also *A More Perfect Union: Advancing New American Rights,* by Jesse Jackson, Jr., with Frank Watkins (New York: Welcome Rain Publishers, 2000).

252 "A PROMISSORY NOTE . . . INSUFFICIENT FUNDS": Congressman Jackson was citing Dr. Martin Luther King Jr. from his speech "I Have a Dream," delivered in Washington, D.C., on August 28, 1965.

252, 253 U.S. SUPREME COURT'S RULING IN *MILLIKEN:* For a discussion of the effects of *Milliken v. Bradley,* 1974, see *Simple Justice,* by Richard Kluger, cited above. The decision in *Milliken,* Orfield observes, did not prohibit the participation of the suburbs in desegregation orders but made it far more difficult for courts to order their participation because, under *Milliken,* attorneys must prove "suburban and/or state complicity" in furthering the segregation of an urban district in order to compel the suburbs to participate in a solution. The latter argument was successfully made in Wilmington, Delaware, and in Indianapolis, he notes. In Milwaukee and St. Louis, the suburbs had reason to believe that they would not prevail in court, and these cases therefore ended in consent agreements.

253 ATTORNEY WILLIAM TAYLOR CITED: Interview, July 2003. Mr. Taylor, who is currently chairman of the Citizens' Commission on Civil Rights, was the staff director of the U.S. Civil Rights Commission in 1965 at the time the commission released its landmark report "Racial Isolation in the Public Schools." (See notes for Chapter 8.) See also *The Passion of My Times,* by William Taylor (New York: Carroll and Graf, 2004).

253, 254 ATTORNEY THEODORE SHAW CITED: Interview, April 2003.

254 SCHOOL FINANCE LITIGATION IN NEW JERSEY: For examples of victories achieved in the New Jersey case, *Abbott v. Burke,* see notes for p. 261.

SCHOOL FINANCE LITIGATION IN OHIO: *DeRolph v. State,* which challenged the constitutionality of Ohio's school funding system, was filed in 1991. "The Ohio Supreme Court declared Ohio's funding system unconstitutional on March 24, 1997, May 11, 2000, September 6, 2001, and December 11, 2002," according to William Phillis, director of the Columbus-based Ohio Coalition for Equity and Adequacy (correspondence with author, August 2004). "The state has provided some additional financial resources, particularly to the lower-wealth districts, but this has not overhauled the system as ordered by the Court. . . . The quality of education in Ohio is still a function of property wealth per pupil within school districts."

254, 255 LITIGATION IN NEW YORK: The trial court decision in *Campaign for Fiscal Equity v. State of New York,* which had been filed in 1993, was handed down by Justice Leland DeGrasse in January 2001. An intermediate-level appeals court overturned the DeGrasse decision in June 2002, but a year later the state's highest court overturned this ruling and returned the case to Justice DeGrasse. The state was then given until July 30, 2004, to implement the terms of the DeGrasse decision. When the state failed to meet this deadline, Justice DeGrasse appointed two former judges and a former dean of Fordham University Law School to serve as judicial referees in establishing a funding level that the state must meet in order to enable New York City to provide its children with a constitutionally adequate education. In late November 2004, the panel recommended $9 billion for capital needs such as school infrastructure, beginning in 2005, and a series of increases in annual spending, rising to the level of an additional $5.6 billion in 2008–2009. (Report and Recommendations of the Judicial Referees, State Supreme Court of New York, *Campaign for Fiscal Equity v. State of New York,* November 30, 2004. See also *New York Times,* November 30 and December 1 and 2, 2004; *Newsday,* December 1 and 2, 2004; *New York Daily News,* November 30 and December 1, 2004.) These recommendations were embodied in a new court order from Justice DeGrasse that took effect in March 2005, requiring compliance within 90 days. New York Governor George Pataki has since appealed this ruling and obtained a "stay" from the court order. The next court hearing will take place in fall 2005, with the likelihood that there will be no outcome for at least an additional year. (ACCESS report, Campaign for Fiscal Equity, 2003; "Summary of the Decision by the Court of Appeals," released by Campaign for Fiscal Equity, June 26, 2003; *Education Week,* November 10, 2004; *New York Times,* October 2, 2002, June 4, December 1 and 2, 2004, and February 15 and March 19, 2005; Campaign for Fiscal Equity, press releases, April 19 and May 2 and 3, 2005.

255, 256 SETTLEMENT OF LEGAL ACTION IN CALIFORNIA: The agreement ending litigation in *Williams v. California* (see notes for Chapter 7) was announced by Governor Arnold Schwarzenegger on August 13, 2004. According to ACLU attorney Catherine Lhamon (interview, January 2005), who was one of the three lead attorneys in the case, the initial $188 million and subsequent $800 million committed by the state are to be targeted on low-performing schools that serve about two million children. The state has also agreed, according to Lhamon, to "an actual definition" of what is meant by "sufficient textbooks" ("one book for every child to use at school without sharing and to be able to bring home") and to "good repair of school facilities" ("unlock the bathrooms," "a classroom seat for every child"). When I asked Lhamon what effect $800 million for emergency repairs would have upon the massive overcrowding of the California schools (the cost of building only ten new high schools in a single district might approach $2 billion), she explained that money for construction of new schools was not included in the settlement and that construction funds were expected to come from customary sources of revenue. Los Angeles, she says, has already opened four new schools, with nearly 30 more schools projected to be built between 2005 and 2012. Lhamon concedes that the fulfillment of such commitments in Los Angeles and elsewhere might be derailed by any number of political and legislative factors, as has been the case in other states. Then, too, despite the "180 days of education" promised by the year 2012, "some schools will remain on year-round calendars," says Lhamon, because of shortages of space; and there is no prohibition against continuing or expanding the use of portables, nor is there provision for reducing class size. "You always get less in a legal action than you hoped for . . . ," Lhamon says. "I couldn't believe at first we were fighting so hard and so long to win so little. But we felt these students are so far behind that we needed to get everybody to a floor beneath which no school can fall, and then begin to have another conversation on what children actually *need.*"

256 MICHAEL KIRST CITED: *Education Week,* September 1, 2004.

256, 257 AVERAGE PER-PUPIL FUNDING IN MISSISSIPPI AND CONNECTICUT: "Current Expenditures for Public K–12 Schools per Student . . . 2002–2003, Rankings and Estimates of the States 2003," National Education Association, 2004.

257, 258 ATTORNEY THEODORE SHAW CITED: Interview, December 2003.

259 ATTORNEY JOSEPH WAYLAND CITED: Interview with author, April 2003. Mr. Wayland, the distinguished attorney from the well-known firm of Simpson, Thacher & Bartlett, has provided his services pro bono during the many years of litigation.

259, 260 CITATIONS FROM MR. WAYLAND'S OPENING STATEMENT TO THE COURT: Proceedings of Morning Session, October 12, 1999, before Justice Leland DeGrasse, New York State Supreme Court, *Campaign for Fiscal Equity v. State of New York.* See also *Newsday,* October 11, 1999.

260 CITATION FROM *BROWN V. BOARD OF EDUCATION OF TOPEKA:* See *Simple Justice,* by Richard Kluger, cited in Chapter 1.

261 IMPORTANT BENEFITS TO CHILDREN ACHIEVED IN THE NEW JERSEY CASE: The program of full-day kindergarten and two years of full-day preschool for children in the 31 low-income "Abbott districts" (so-named because of the longstanding lawsuit *Abbott v. Burke,* which has resulted in these and many other victories for New Jersey's children) was described to me by Assistant Commissioner Judith Weiss, New Jersey Department of Education, in correspondence and telephone conversation, March 2005, and by Commissioner William Librera in a meeting in May 2005. The original trial court decision in *Abbott v. Burke,* which was filed in 1981, was handed down in 1985 (for a description of the trial court's ruling, see *Savage Inequalities,* cited above). There has been a long series of subsequent *Abbott* rulings in suits brought by the Education Law Center of New Jersey in the two decades since. As of 1997, according to the Education Law Center's executive director, David Sciarra (correspondence with author, April 2005), "New Jersey became the first and only state where funding for children in high-poverty districts was equalized at the level spent in successful, more affluent school districts." The state, moreover, "has sustained funding parity every year since" and, because of the supplemental funds provided for children at risk, the funding for high-poverty districts now exceeds what is spent per pupil in the wealthier districts.

A THIRD OF A CENTURY OF LITIGATION IN NEW JERSEY: *Abbott v. Burke* was successor to an earlier case, *Robinson v. Cahill,* in which the New Jersey Supreme Court (1973) found the state's school funding system unconstitutional. (ACCESS study, Campaign for Fiscal Equity, cited above.)

PERSISTENT INEQUALITIES IN ILLINOIS, OHIO, PENNSYLVANIA, ETC.: "The Funding Gap," reports issued in 2003 and 2004, the Education Trust, cited above.

REVERSAL OF GAINS PREVIOUSLY WON IN KENTUCKY: The original court victory in a widely celebrated adequacy case, *Rose v. Council for Better Education,* in 1989, led to major reforms in school funding and to a specific definition of what constituted adequate education. In 2003, a coalition of 150 public schools was forced to return to court in a suit charging that the state had "not lived up to its constitutional mandate" and had not provided sufficient funds to give children an adequate education. (*New York Times,* December 6, 2004; *Education Week,* December 8, 2004; ACCESS report, Campaign for Fiscal Equity, cited above.)

REVERSAL OF GAINS IN TEXAS: On September 15, 2004, Travis County Chief Judge John Dietz found the state's school finance system unconstitutional—"financially inefficient, inadequate, and unsuitable," with too large a gap between "the haves and the have-nots"—and threatened to order that all state funding for public education cease by fall 2005 if the legislature has not acted by that time. (*Boston Globe,* September 16, 2004; *Education Week,* December 8, 2004.) This comes as a disappointing postscript to 11 years of litigation led by veteran civil rights attorney Al Kauffman, who was counsel to the plaintiffs in the landmark case *Edgewood v. Kirby,* filed initially in 1984 and revisited three times *(Edgewood II, Edgewood III, Edgewood IV)* up to 1995, when a more equitable funding system, finally implemented by the legislature, was at last deemed constitutional. "By the time we won," says Kauffman, "the youngest grandchild of Demetrio Rodriguez," plaintiff in the original federal case rejected by the Supreme Court in 1973, "was nearly done with high school." According to Kauffman, now a senior associate at Harvard's Civil Rights Project, the four *Edgewood* cases did achieve important gains for Texas children. ("Texas no longer has gross inequities as in New York," he notes.) Still, given the political disposition of the present Texas governor and legislature, it appears that major battles lie ahead. (Interview with Kauffman, July 2003. See also *New York Times,* April 21, 2004; *Houston Chronicle,* January 9, 10, and 13 and February 8 and 10, 2005; *Dallas Morning News,* January 9, 10, and 13 and February 7, 2005.)

261, 262 REVERSAL OF GAINS IN KANSAS: In May 2004, Shawnee County District Judge Terry Bullock in Topeka, Kansas, found the state's educational funding system "inadequate and inequitable," and therefore unconstitutional, after the legislature adjourned without taking action on a ruling he had initially made in 1999. Judge Bullock ordered that all Kansas schools be closed until the legislature acted. The state appealed Judge Bullock's ruling, and the Kansas Supreme Court stayed his order, pending its hearing on the appeal. In January 2005, the Supreme Court affirmed Judge Bullock's conclusion that the state's school finance system was unconstitutional and gave the state until April 2005 to act in compliance with this ruling. In April, the state legislature passed a modest funding increase for the public schools without identifying any longterm source of revenue to pay for it. The court will soon review the legislature's plan and decide on further action. (*Boston Globe,* May 12, 2004; *Catalyst Cleveland,* June 2004; *Kansas City Star,* December 3, 5, 13, and 16, 2003, May 12, 14, 16, and October 10, 2004, and January 1, 3, and 4, 2005; Associated Press, April 11 and 15, 2005.)

262, 263 EDWIN MARGOLIS AND STANLEY MOSES: See *Elusive Quest,* cited in note for p. 212.

CHAPTER 11: DEADLY LIES

265 "SOFT BIGOTRY": President Bush has made this accusation repeatedly from 2000 to 2004. See, for example, *Los Angeles Times,* July 11 and October 17, 2000, and August 24, 2002; *Washington*

Post, August 4, 2000, and July 29, 2003; press release, the White House, January 8, 2004.

"RACIST NONSENSE": "Williamson M. Evers, a member of President Bush's committee to oversee federal education research," according to Richard Rothstein (*New York Times,* April 10, 2002), said that a list of so-called high-flying schools—schools with significant numbers of minority and low-income children who tested high on standardized exams—"had proved that it was 'racist nonsense' to deny that accountability alone could generate equal outcomes for poor and middle-class students."

"A TERRORIST ORGANIZATION": *Chicago Sun-Times,* February 24, 2004.

266 HEAD START BUDGET: See notes for Chapters 2 and 8.

267 EFFORTS TO REDUCE CLASS SIZE OR OBSERVE DESEGREGATION ORDERS TO BE SUBORDINATED TO THE STIPULATIONS OF NO CHILD LEFT BEHIND: *New York Times,* November 27, 2002.

SUMMATION OF POLICY POSITIONS PRESENTED TO GRADUATE STUDENTS IN A COURSE ON STANDARDS-BASED REFORM: My colleague and research associate Rachel Becker was a student in this class in 2003.

268 "A VESTED INTEREST IN UNDERSTANDING": *The Affluent Society,* by John Kenneth Galbraith (Boston: Houghton Mifflin, 1958).

269, 270 EXCESSES OF "OPEN EDUCATION" MOVEMENT: See my book *Free Schools* (Boston: Houghton Mifflin, 1972).

274 "THE CHILDREN OF DISAPPOINTMENT": *The Souls of Black Folk,* by W. E. B. DuBois (New York: Vintage, 1990), published initially in 1903. DuBois's reference to "the ghost of an untrue dream" appears in a discussion of the loss of faith incurred by the people of Atlanta in the aftermath of the War Between the States.

274, 275 THEODORE SHAW CITED: Interview, December 2003.

275 DEBORAH MEIER'S VISION OF A GOOD SMALL SCHOOL: *The Power of Their Ideas,* by Deborah Meier (Boston: Beacon Press, 1995); *In Schools We Trust,* by Deborah Meier (Boston: Beacon Press, 2002). My visits to the Mission Hill School and conversations with Mrs. Meier took place in 2002 and 2003. Mrs. Meier resigned as principal of Mission Hill in 2004.

276 EMERGENCE OF SMALL MILITARY SCHOOLS TARGETING MINORITY STUDENTS: *New York Times,* April 6, 2005. The military presence, as *The Times* also notes (June 3, 2005), is increasingly intruding upon mainstream public schools as well, because the federal law No Child Left Behind "mandates that school districts can receive federal funds only if they grant military recruiters 'the same access to secondary school students' as is provided to colleges and employers." Under the legislation, schools are required to give "students' home phone numbers and addresses" to recruiters from the military branches.

276, 277 SURVEY OF 145 SMALL HIGH SCHOOLS IN NEW YORK CITY: The survey, conducted under the direction of Clara Hemphill, is available online at Insideschools.com, a project of Advocates for Children, cited earlier. Hemphill, who is also the author of several guidebooks to the best schools in the New York City system (see notes for Chapter 6), has emerged as one of the most hard-hitting and effective advocates for poor and minority children who are the least likely to obtain admission to many of the schools highlighted in those guidebooks. Insideschools.com has become an invaluable resource for those trying to obtain an accurate snapshot of specific New York City schools and often provides more helpful information than do the schools' official report cards.

277 THE MONROE ACADEMY FOR BUSINESS AND LAW: Insideschools .com (see above). Demographic and dropout data for this academy is found in its Annual School Report, New York City Public Schools, 2002–2003. In all but one of the six small schools created out of the former Monroe High School, which range in size between 375 and 490 students each, not more than 45 students reach twelfth grade. Many of the new small schools, as Insideschools observes, have compiled better records. But even if all 200 small schools that have been established or proposed in New York City were to be successful, as *New York Times* education writer Samuel Freedman observes (December 22, 2004), "a vast majority of New York's high school pupils will still attend large, traditional schools."

277ff. SEATTLE'S CENTER SCHOOL AND AFRICAN-AMERICAN ACADEMY: Interviews and correspondence with former Ballard High School principal David Engle (see notes for Chapter 9); interviews and correspondence (2002–2005) with John Morefield, senior associate at the Center for Educational Leadership, University of Washington.

WHITE FAMILIES WHO WERE ACTIVE IN PRESSING FOR CREATION OF CENTER SCHOOL HAD ALSO BEEN LEADERS IN THE LEGAL ACTION TO OVERTHROW THE RACIAL TIE-BREAKER: "The Center School was perceived (accurately, in my belief) as a way of giving something that they wanted to white parents, primarily in the Queen Anne and Magnolia neighborhoods, whose children could not always get into Ballard High School under the tie-breaker," says Engle. "Ultimately, they got both." The *Seattle Times* (June 27, 2003) described "a Magnolia resident whose daughter was turned away from Ballard and two other high schools" as a result of the tie-breaker and who supported the legal action that ended the tie-breaker because "the racial tie-breaker is discrimination." According to John Morefield, Seattle had desegregated voluntarily, without court order, many years before. "I was a part of that when I was young," he said. "To see it all unravel now is hard. There had always been some numbers of disgruntled parents in the white community who were resistant to desegregation. Now, with the tie-breaker no longer in effect, these parents feel emboldened."

ACADEMIC AND CULTURAL OFFERINGS OF CENTER SCHOOL: Annual Report for the Center School, Seattle Public Schools, 2002–2003.

278 RACIAL DEMOGRAPHICS OF CENTER SCHOOL: Washington State Report Cards for the Center School, 2001–2002, 2002–2003, 2003–2004. The percentage of white students at the school declined somewhat after the initial academic year, while a larger number of Asian and Hispanic students were admitted; but the black enrollment remained frozen at less than six percent. (In October 2003, there were 231 white children but only 17 black children at the Center School.) By October 2004, according to Morefield, white enrollment at the Center School had climbed again, to 81 percent, while black enrollment had dropped to 5 percent. The principal, says Morefield, "is chagrined by the difficulty he now faces" in trying to convince black students to apply.

278, 279 DEMOGRAPHICS OF AFRICAN-AMERICAN ACADEMY: In October 2003, 93 percent of students at the school were black, 4 percent were Hispanic, Asian, or Native American, and 3 percent were white. (Annual Report for African-American Academy, Seattle Public Schools, 2002–2003, providing demographics for fall 2003.)

279 OBSERVATIONS ON AFRICAN-AMERICAN ACADEMY: John Morefield notes that the school is located, not in a black community, but in a predominantly white and Asian neighborhood. Ninety percent of the students are bused to the school from other sections of the city. The hypersegregation of the school, therefore, is unrelated to residential patterns but is a consequence of the niche effect associated with small schools that target narrow sectors of a population.

280 NUMBER OF STANDARDIZED EXAMS HAS MORE THAN DOUBLED SINCE ENACTMENT OF NO CHILD LEFT BEHIND, PROJECTIONS FOR FUTURE YEARS: Interviews and correspondence with Michael Casserly, executive director, the Council of Great City Schools, cited in notes for Chapter 8. See also *USA Today,* October 12, 2004.

ACHIEVEMENT GAP BETWEEN BLACK AND WHITE STUDENTS: "While National Assessment of Educational Progress (NAEP) results have shown that, over time, black and Hispanic students have made great strides in narrowing the breach that separates them from their white peers, that progress seems to have come to a halt since the mid-1980s. For example, in 2003, while 39 percent of white students scored at the proficient level or higher on the fourth grade reading exam portion [of the NAEP], only 12 percent of black students and 14 percent of Hispanic students did so," according to an online compilation of data posted and updated by the Education Week Research Center on October 7, 2004, citing the U.S. Department of Education, 2003. "There was a tremendous amount of gap-narrowing in the '70s and '80s," but "somewhere around 1990, that gap-narrowing stopped," according to Craig Jerald of the Education Trust. (*Education Week,* January 21, 2004.) After years of progress from the 1960s through the 1980s, the "learning gap seemed to become chronic—and sometimes grew larger—in the 1990s," notes *Education Week,* October 6, 2004.

280, 281 PERIODIC UPTICKS IN MINORITY TEST SCORES CELEBRATED BY

MEDIA: For recent examples of this recurring phenomenon, see *New York Post,* June 2, 2005; *New York Daily News,* June 2, 2005; *New York Times,* June 2 and July 15, 2005.

281 READING AND MATH PROFICIENCIES OF BLACK AND HISPANIC TWELFTH GRADE STUDENTS ARE BELOW THOSE OF WHITE SEVENTH GRADERS: Kati Haycock, director of the Education Trust, cited in *Education Week,* November 3, 2004. While Ms. Haycock noted that "some districts and some states are figuring out how to keep the progress going," she nonetheless conceded that "on our watch," the achievement gaps between white and minority students have "widened."

282 HIGH SCHOOL ATTRITION RATES OF BLACK AND HISPANIC STUDENTS NATIONWIDE: *Losing Our Future,* by Gary Orfield, Daniel Losen, Johanna Wald, and Christopher Swanson, a joint publication by the Civil Rights Project at Harvard, Advocates for Children in New York, the Urban Institute, and the Civil Society Institute (Cambridge: The Civil Rights Project, 2004); "High School Graduation Rates: Alternative Methods and Implications," by Walter Haney and Jing Mao, the Center for the Study of Testing, Boston College, published in *Educational Policy Analysis Archives,* October 15, 2004; "Locating the Dropout Crisis," by Robert Balfanz and Nettie Letgers, Center for Social Organization of Schools, Johns Hopkins University, June 2004. According to Haney at the Center for the Study of Testing (correspondence with author, April 2005), in at least three states he has examined, Texas, New York, and Florida, "it's clear that the racial gap in graduation rates has widened.... In New York State, which has the worst graduation rate for blacks and Hispanics, the numbers declined dramatically from approximately 1995 to 2001, and there is no reason to believe this trend has changed in the years since." The largest growth in national dropout rates, says Haney, parallels the period when high-stakes tests and nonpromotion practices were instituted. See also "Rapid Rise Found in Tenth Grade Dropout Rates," *Boston Globe,* January 18, 2004, which, citing an earlier study released by the Center for the Study of Testing, notes that "the rate at which ninth grade students do not reach tenth grade has tripled" since the early 1970s.

NEW YORK CITY AND CHICAGO FAIL TO GRADUATE MORE THAN 70 PERCENT OF BLACK MALE STUDENTS WITH THEIR ENTERING CLASSMATES: *Education Week,* December 1, 2004, citing "Public Education and Black Students," a national survey released by the Schott Foundation for Public Education, Cambridge, Massachusetts, 2004.

DROPOUT RATES IN PREDOMINANTLY WHITE AND PREDOMINANTLY MINORITY DISTRICTS IN NEW YORK STATE: *Losing Our Future,* by Orfield et al., cited above. According to the report, the graduation rate in New York State, which is the seventh lowest in the nation, is "particularly low for black and Hispanic males," with less than 30 percent graduating from high school, in contrast with 71 percent of white males. "The growing segregation of our public schools will like contribute further to low graduation rates among minorities."

PERCENTAGE OF NINTH GRADE STUDENTS NOT PROMOTED TO TENTH GRADE IN TYPICAL LARGE HIGH SCHOOLS IN THE BRONX: "Rethinking High School: an introduction to New York City's experience," by Tracy Huebner, released by the Bill and Melinda Gates Foundation, 2005.

282, 283 RACIAL GAP IN SAT SCORES, DECLINE IN BLACK ADMISSIONS TO PREMIER STATE UNIVERSITIES: "Ranks of Black Freshmen Shrink at State Universities," *Washington Post,* November 28, 2004. Also see *Washington Post,* November 22, 2004; *New York Times,* October 14, 2004.

284 "IT'S WORKING. IT'S MAKING A DIFFERENCE": The president's claim that his school reform policies have been successful for minority children and his reiterated attack upon "the soft bigotry of low expectations" were included in a speech delivered in King of Prussia, Pennsylvania, September 22, 2004. (*New York Times,* September 23, 2004; *Education Week,* October 13, 2004.)

CHAPTER 12: TREASURED PLACES

287ff. P.S. 30: My portrayal of this school is based on visits between 1995 and 2005. Descriptions of the first grade teacher and of Mr. Bedrock's class are from 2001 and 2002.

296 "TEACHERS—THE LOWLIEST OF BUREAUCRATS": John Chubb and Terry Moe are cited from their book *Politics, Markets, and America's Schools* (Washington, D.C.: The Brookings Institute, 1990). The authors argue that only in the market setting of competitive private education are educators able to escape these bureaucratic roles.

298, 299 CLASSROOM IN DURHAM, NORTH CAROLINA: I visited Robin Franklin's second grade class at the E. K. Powe Elementary School in October 2003 and spoke with her again in January 2005.

EPILOGUE

301 CHANGES AT P.S. 30: Aida Rosa retired as principal in July 2002. I revisited the school and talked with the new principal, Roxann Marks, and her colleagues in December 2003, May 2004, and May 2005.

302, 303 VISITS TO CLASSES AT ARTS AND TECHNOLOGY HIGH SCHOOL AT MARTIN LUTHER KING SCHOOL: November 2002, December and April 2003, June 2005. Also see Insideschools, March 2003.

"IF I'M TEACHING IN A SCHOOL NAMED MARTIN LUTHER KING": Arts and Technology teacher Nina de Fels, April 2003.

"I WANT YOU TO MEET ONE OF MY SIX WHITE STUDENTS": The principal of Arts and Technology High School is Anne Geiger.

304ff. VISITS TO P.S. 65 SINCE APPOINTMENT OF NEW PRINCIPAL: December 2003, May 2004, May 2005. Insideschools (April 2004) characterized the school in a mixed report that indicated there was more disorder than in previous years. This does not accord with my own impression in my visit to the school in May of the same year and in my most recent visit in 2005.

307 NEW YORK CITY SCHOOLS CHANCELLOR'S DECISION TO ALTER LITERACY APPROACH: "The approach we are implementing today," said Chancellor Joel Klein (*New York Times,* January 22, 2003), "is not scripted reading, it's not a cookie-cutter approach. . . . Teachers who are cookie-cutters are not what we need. We need teachers who are creative and empowered."

MODIFIED PHONICS PROGRAM "TOTALLY DISREGARDS THE SCIENTIFIC EVIDENCE": *New York Post,* October 20, 2003.

CHANCELLOR HAS STOOD HIS GROUND: See "Schools Chancellor Stands by His Choice of Reading Program," *New York Times,* February 26, 2003. In order to avoid the loss of federal funds under the No Child Left Behind legislation, however, the chancellor has introduced a somewhat scripted program called Read 180, published by Scholastic, which is used in several dozen schools.

307, 308 SCRIPTED METHODS CONTINUE TO BE WIDELY USED IN LOW-INCOME DISTRICTS: In February 2005, the president of the Success For All Foundation advised me that SFA is used in 1,300 schools. According to School Profiles, Columbus Public Schools, 2003–2004, 22 Columbus Elementary Schools use SFA. According to the Success For All Foundation, 10 Chicago schools were using SFA in 2003–2004, with 7 other Chicago schools implementing portions of the program. According to New Jersey State Education Commissioner William Librera (meeting with author, May 2005), as many as 31 low-income districts in New Jersey have been using SFA in recent years—a practice, however, he has started to reverse. According to *Education Week* (June 10, 1998), more than 70 Houston schools were making use of SFA in 1998; but it is unclear how many of these Houston schools still use it. All but a few elementary schools in Hartford, Connecticut, and Lawrence, Massachusetts, have been using SFA for several years and continue to do so. Another scripted literacy program, known as Open Court, is used in thousands of other elementary schools, especially in major inner-city districts such as Los Angeles, where it is mandated for low-performing schools. (See notes for p. 173.)

308 PRINCIPALS SOMETIMES HESITATE TO RISK A PRELIMINARY DROP IN SCORES BY ABANDONING A SCRIPTED SYSTEM: In discussing a decline in test scores after the abandonment of SFA at P.S. 65, the principal told me (August 2004) that the transition from the scripted environment was "extremely challenging" for many of her teachers. They were "literally forced to learn how to teach reading and writing . . . , comprehension and decoding skills . . . , by use of literary works." Many didn't know "how to do it when they started in September," and "only a handful caught on by

midyear." Although she had anticipated the decline in scores when we had discussed this likelihood eight months earlier, she nonetheless said it "made me physically sick when I read it in the newspapers." Still, she told me she has refused to return to the school's former practice of drilling students for their tests for many months preceding the exams, as well as incorporating test-prep materials into daily lessons. "I've put in only four weeks of helping them with test-taking strategies before the English Language Arts exam," she said. "If we don't make it, we're going to go down in the right way."

SEVERE CUTBACKS IN FUNDING: "The National Education Association said in an August [2003] newsletter that the nation's school districts were grappling with 'the worst budget shortfalls since World War Two.' " (*New York Times,* August 31, 2003.)

EFFECTS OF FISCAL CUTBACKS: In Winthrop, Massachusetts, school libraries have been padlocked and a fee of $1,000 has been instituted for full-day kindergarten. ("Good Schools," District Profile of Winthrop Public Schools, Massachusetts Teachers Association, 2004.) "We originally offered full-day kindergarten to everyone," Winthrop Superintendent Thomas Giancristiano informed me. "This year, only those who can afford it can have full-day kindergarten. Along with user fees, we are creating an unfair division between the 'haves' and 'have-nots.' " (Letter to author from Dr. Giancristiano, September 2003.) After being compelled to eliminate 22 positions, including "librarians, foreign language teachers, teachers in grades kindergarten through four, a program for the gifted," as well as remedial reading programs for kids at risk, secretaries, nurses, and even crossing guards (*Boston Globe,* February 19, 2004), Dr. Giancristiano announced his retirement. See also *Boston Globe,* September 2, 2003, and January 18, 2004.

PARENTS ARE OBLIGED TO PAY FOR FULL DAY KINDERGARTEN IN SCHOOLS IN SEVERAL STATES: *Education Week,* February 20, 2002.

THE PRESIDENT SAYS THE MONEY IS "IN PLACE" FOR TESTING: *New York Times,* September 9, 2003.

308, 309 A VIRTUALLY NEW PROFESSION OF "TEST-CHECKING" PERSONNEL: See, for example, *Dallas Morning News,* February 22, 2005.

309 "RATHER THAN FIGHT SCHOOL SEGREGATION, THE BUSH ADMINISTRATION HAS BEEN HAPPY TO EXPLOIT IT": *New York Times* (editorial), January 27, 2003.

RELIGIOUS GROUPS TEND TO BE DRAWN TO SERVICE PROGRAMS: National leaders of several denominations, most notably the United Church of Christ, have taken strong positions on questions of inequity in funding; but very few have openly protested the return to segregated schooling. At parish levels, virtually all emphasis tends to be on charitable actions.

310 INTERNAL DISSONANCE WITHIN PROGRESSIVE MEDIA: Two of the great exceptions to this pattern are *Newsday* (see notes for Chapter 6) and the *St. Louis Post-Dispatch,* which has published powerful editorials in favor of school integration in its own immediate com-

munity. (See, for example, *St. Louis Post-Dispatch,* September 9, 2004.)

310ff. CONVERSATION WITH CONGRESSMAN JOHN LEWIS: Washington, D.C., September 2003.

312, 313 HIGH SCHOOL IN ATLANTA DESCRIBED BY CONGRESSMAN LEWIS: The school he refers to is Booker T. Washington High School. In September 2000, the school enrolled 571 ninth grade students in the class of 2004. Only 288 of these students were enrolled in twelfth grade in spring 2004. (Annual Report Cards for Washington High School, Governor's Office of Student Achievement, State of Georgia, 2002–2003 and 2003–2004, providing enrollment numbers for 2000–2004.) According to the King Center in Atlanta, Dr. Martin Luther King, Jr., attended the school in tenth and eleventh grades, from 1942 to 1944, then entered Morehouse College on early admission.

VISIT OF PRESIDENT GEORGE W. BUSH TO BOOKER T. WASHINGTON HIGH SCHOOL: *Atlanta Journal-Constitution,* January 31, 2002.

313 MEMOIRS OF CONGRESSMAN LEWIS CITED: *Walking with the Wind,* by John Lewis with Michael D'Orso (New York: Harcourt Brace, 1998).

INDEX

INDEX